A Brief Introduction to the Philosophy of Mind

A Brief Introduction to the Philosophy of Mind

Jack S. Crumley II

ROWMAN & LITTLEFIELD PUBLISHERS, INC.
Lanham • Boulder • New York • Toronto • Oxford

ROWMAN & LITTLEFIELD PUBLISHERS, INC.

Published in the United States of America
by Rowman & Littlefield Publishers, Inc.
A wholly owned subsidiary of The Rowman & Littlefield Publishing Group, Inc.
4501 Forbes Boulevard, Suite 200, Lanham, Maryland 20706
www.rowmanlittlefield.com

PO Box 317
Oxford
OX2 9RU, UK

British Library Cataloguing in Publication Information Available

Library of Congress Cataloging-in-Publication Data

Crumley, Jack S.
    A brief introduction to the philosophy of mind / Jack S. Crumley II.
        p. cm.
    Includes bibliographical references and index.
    ISBN-13: 978-0-7425-4495-6 (cloth : alk. paper)
    ISBN-10: 0-7425-4495-8 (cloth : alk. paper)
    ISBN-13: 978-0-7425-4496-3 (pbk. : alk. paper)
    ISBN-10: 0-7425-4496-6 (pbk. : alk. paper)
    1. Philosophy of mind. I. Title.
    BD418.3.C77 2006
    128'.2—dc22   2005027271

Printed in the United States of America

♾️™ The paper used in this publication meets the minimum requirements of American
National Standard for Information Sciences—Permanence of Paper for Printed Library
Materials, ANSI/NISO Z39.48-1992.

For Mom and Danny

Contents

Preface

The second time you get kicked in the head by a mule, it's not a learning experience.

—Ebb Dozier Jr.'s Dad

This has taken somewhat longer coming to fruition than I originally anticipated. In the process, I've had a chance to think a little more about what a brief introduction to philosophy of mind ought to look like. This book is intended for students with little or no background in philosophy and for readers interested in learning something about the current landscape in philosophy of mind.

The point of departure is roughly what practitioners in the field know as commonsense psychology, that view of the mind that is most familiar to us. Of course, there are standard topics for philosophy of mind. But included are some issues and topics that I hope might prove interesting, such as the chapter on concepts and images.

Striking a balance between accessibility and rigorous analysis of the issues is not always easy. If the balance here leans at all, it probably leans toward accessibility. At least I hope it does. Toward this end—and at the request of some readers—I left out issues that might easily have been included, such as Kripke's argument against identity theory and the distinction between causal relevance and causal efficacy. I also hope that the text reveals that the debates are ongoing, are far from resolved, and very often have good arguments on both sides of an issue.

A running subtheme is the interdisciplinary character of many of the issues, and at various places, I hope to have provided something of the context in which these issues are now treated.

My mentors in philosophy of mind—Radu Bogdan and the late Norton Nelkin—led me to see how exciting a field it is. If the text excites someone else about the field, then that will be my way of thanking those two individuals.

I am grateful to Ken King for the original opportunity and especially to Jon-David Hague for helping the project to find a new home. I'm also indebted to the readers from Mayfield/McGraw-Hill and Rowman & Littlefield.

Special thanks go to a former student, Julia Engelstad, who read several of the chapters in draft form. Her comments and questions helped to clarify the approach to and explanation of various topics. I also owe a debt of gratitude to Ken Keith, a colleague in the psychology department at the University of San Diego who helped me to avoid mistakes in the chapter on behaviorism.

Two minor notes: I know sometime long ago I came across the arithmetical example in chapter 5, but I don't remember who originated it or where. The occasional references to slightly odd laws in various municipalities regarding the treatment of various animals are from an article in the *San Diego Union*; I have been unable to find the source.

I also owe a very special debt to Tyler Hower, whose patient and thoughtful comments on three of the chapters were especially helpful.

There is simply no doubt that this project would never have seen the light of day were it not for the assistance of the department's executive assistant, Leeanna Cummings. Where should I begin? Her advice, support, and work are invaluable. Work on this project was also supported by various Faculty Research Grants from the University of San Diego.

And, of course, my thanks to my family for their patience and support—Bobbie, Danny, Karen, Thatcher, Clement, and Billy.

Beginning Matters

Beginning with Common Sense

No doubt part of the excitement of philosophy of mind arises from so many disciplines having something to say about the nature of the mind. As a book on *philosophy* of mind, of course, philosophical theories of the mind occupy center stage here. However, philosophy of mind has "grown," especially in the last stages of the twentieth century. Researchers from fields as diverse as linguistics, computer science, cognitive neuroscience, cognitive psychology, developmental psychology, and immunology have joined the debate about the nature of the mental.

In such company, you might be surprised to find that the layman's commonsense conception of the mind is, often enough, the starting point for philosophers' questions and the touchstone for their investigations. The commonsense view of the mind figures so prominently in fact that philosophers have given it a name—folk psychology.

"Folk psychology" is variously described, but two of its features are of special interest. First, folk psychology holds that people have various mental states, including emotions, moods, sensations such as pain or the visual detection of something red, and propositional attitudes such as beliefs, desires, fears, and hopes. The latter category is especially important for philosophy of mind. Beliefs, desires, hopes, and the like are mental states comprising the content of one's thought and his or her attitude toward that content. For example, "Danny believes that it is illegal in Miami to imitate animals" tells us

Danny's attitude—belief—and the content or *what* he believes—the illegality of imitating animals in a certain municipality in South Florida. Similarly, "Deirdre hopes that it is illegal in California to hunt whales from your car" tells us Deirdre's attitude—hope—and *what* she hopes. In general, the proposition or clause following the verb gives the content of the thought, and the verb (believe, hope, fear) indicates the type of attitude the person has toward that content.

The second aspect of folk psychology is perhaps more familiar and important. Common sense typically regards propositional attitudes as the framework for explaining and predicting behavior; intentional states are thought of as the *causes* of our behavior. Danny reaches for the plum because he believes that plums are nutritious and he desires something nutritious to eat. We explain Sam's attendance at the party in terms of his hope of seeing Sara and his belief that she will be there. Propositional attitudes thus play a *causal role* in our explanations and predictions of behavior. Folk psychology is thus *realist* about mental states, such as beliefs and desires, counting them as existent states having various properties.

Contemporary theories of mind go beyond and at times against our commonsense view of the mind. We may be tempted to think that someone who challenges our commonsense convictions lacks just that—common sense. But on such occasions, we might remind ourselves of the ways in which common sense has been a little or a lot off the mark. Galileo, Darwin, Pasteur, Einstein—these are just a few of the persons who forced common sense to a new understanding of the world. While philosophy of mind often begins with the folk wisdom, with common sense, we should not expect that we will always end up back where we started—with the same commonsense picture we began with.

In this book, we will in part be tracing the ways in which theory moves beyond our common and familiar folk psychology.

Four Issues

Contemporary philosophy of mind began in earnest in the late 1950s; however, many of its currently central debates first took shape in the 1970s. That these debates are but a few decades old should not mislead, for some of the issues are of perennial interest in philosophy. Indeed, perhaps the most storied controversy in the philosophy of mind is the mind–body debate, that is, the relation of the mind (the mental) to the body (the physical).

Very informally, the aims of philosophy of mind are to identify the *nature* of the mind (or the mental) and its properties and to explain the relationship between the mental and the physical. Characterizing philosophy of mind in this way sees it as part of metaphysics, the attempt to understand the nature and structure of the most general features of our world. We describe the nature of something—the mind or the mental, in this case—by describing its essential properties or the kind of thing it is (a *kind* or a *type* is a class of things in that each has a common property definitive of the classification). Some philosophers, for example, insist that minds are essentially different from the physical; they are a different *kind* of thing. Sometimes philosophers talk about the *ontological status* of minds and their properties, but this is only another way of asking about the nature of the mind (*ontology* is a part of metaphysics that attempts to identify the kinds of things that exist).

The first and larger part of this book focuses on this fundamental question about whether the mental and the physical are of the same or different kinds. These initial chapters examine six theories about the relation between the mental and the physical. Some of these theories suggest the interdisciplinary character of contemporary philosophy of mind: Behaviorism, for example, begins as a theory in psychology. Type identity theory and eliminative materialism take part of their inspiration from the results and promise of the neurosciences. And functionalism finds inspiration in both an analogy between minds and computers and the relatively new discipline of cognitive psychology.

The business of minds—what do minds do?—occupies the second part. Among their many properties, minds *represent* the world. It is the function of at least some mental states to carry information about or represent aspects of the world around us. The nature of mental representation—these information-bearing or representational mental states—looms large in recent philosophy of mind and is reflected in two chapters, on images and concepts and theories of mental content. The chapter on images and concepts again illustrates the various disciplines that are taking part in the philosophical debate. Cognitive psychology, developmental psychology, neuroscience, and theoretical computer science all make their distinctive contributions to theories of mental images and theories of concepts. Chapter 8 surveys three theories of mental content—explanations of how mental states or mental representations come to have their particular structure.

The third chapter in part 2 surveys past attempts to explain the sense, if any, in which the mental plays a causal role in our behavior. As already noted, our commonsense view counts mental states among the causes of our behavior: Danny leaves his comfortable spot and journeys to the kitchen *because* he desires something to eat and he believes that cookies lie thereabouts. Although our folk psychology accords this causal status to the mental, it proves a difficult task to explain how the mental serves to bring about, to cause, our behavior.

Almost ignored for decades, the nature of consciousness is among the most active and contested debates in the philosophy of mind. From the mental life of bats to zombies, from "neural Darwinism" to suggestions that we radically revise our understanding of consciousness, books and articles have burst on the scene in the last twenty years. Theories of consciousness are truly interdisciplinary. Of course our interest is philosophical, but results from so many different fields collide when we turn to theories of consciousness. In chapter 10, we can survey but a few of the theories of consciousness, examining three important arguments about the nature of consciousness and our understanding of it.

These four issues—the mind–body relation, mental representation or mental content, mental causation, and the nature of consciousness—are not the only issues in the philosophy of mind. But they form the core of philosophy of mind.

Debates in the philosophy of mind continue; the theories examined in this book are very much alive, vigorously defended, and still the subject of controversy. Matters in mind may be clearer, but they are far from settled. We can explain a theory, examine the motivation or reasons for it, analyze its supporting arguments, and evaluate objections. (In this sense, at least, the present approach is "analytic.") Although the final story of the mind is not yet written, you are encouraged to sympathize with what you see as a plausible approach or to argue for a particular theory that makes sense to you.

Some Initial Terms

Like most disciplines, debates in philosophy of mind rely on a somewhat technical vocabulary. Some of these terms are specific to the issues examined in subsequent chapters, but are some drawn from a general philosophical vocabulary.

Almost uncontroversially, the dominant outlook in current philosophy of mind is *physicalism*. In some respects, the physicalist outlook is congenial to our commonsense view; yet some aspects or consequences of physicalism in philosophy of mind seem inhospitable to some.

Monism holds that there is only one kind (or type or category) of thing—that everything in existence is either an instance of that kind of thing or some modification of that type. As a version of monism, physicalism claims that only physical things and their properties exist. (There is, of course, the opposite theory—a "mental monism" or *idealism*—which holds that everything that exists is either a mind or a property of a mind.) Even those who reject or are suspicious of physicalism typically do not deny the existence of physical things; they simply hold that there is something other than the merely physical. But we will return to this after we explore the notion of physicalism a little more fully.

At least two claims are constitutive of physicalism. The first is a distinctly ontological claim that everything that exists is either an entity or a property recognized by physical sciences, or is composed of such entities (a *property* is a characteristic or feature of some object or substance). We take a rather broad view of the physical sciences here; they include physics, chemistry, biology, hybrid fields such as physical chemistry and molecular biology, and perhaps most importantly for our purposes, neuroscience. Some people hold it is not such a simple matter to say what physicalism is. Some physicalists claim that the mental is reducible to the physical, while others argue that it is not. Very briefly, to claim that the mental is reducible to the physical is to state that mental concepts may be replaced by physical concepts without losing any of our ability to explain mental phenomena. For the moment, we will be content with this broader notion of physicalism: All that exists is physical, and to be physical is to be something or some property that is recognized by one of the natural (or physical) sciences.

The second integral claim of physicalism is that all causal processes are ultimately physical processes. Any time some change occurs—a change in properties, for example—that change is ultimately explained by appealing to or identifying some physical process; there is no supernatural or extraphysical causation. As we will see in the mental causation chapter, however, the idea that all causal processes are physical processes might conflict with our commonsense view, our folk psychological view, that mental states are causally effective—that they can bring about physical changes (causing the raising of one's arm, for example) or mental changes (one thought bringing about another thought).

Two more "isms" are closely related to physicalism: materialism and naturalism. The philosophical doctrine of *materialism* holds that everything that exists is ultimately material. At various points in the history of philosophy, the existence and nature of matter, the underlying "substrate" of particular physical objects, has been vigorously contested. The terms "materialism" and "physicalism" are now often used interchangeably, the special historical debate about matter having dropped from view in recent philosophy of mind. *Naturalism*, like physicalism, also holds that anything that exists is physical, but to this ontological doctrine, naturalists sometimes add a methodological doctrine. According to this methodological doctrine, the only acceptable methods of inquiry are the methods of the natural sciences. More specifically, the only acceptable methods of inquiry are *empirical* methods. Perhaps predictably, it turns out that there is some debate about whether this methodological feature is indeed a necessary feature of naturalism. Also predictably, this methodological claim attracts more attention in *epistemology*—the philosophical discipline that explores the conditions and sources of our knowledge and justified beliefs—than in philosophy of mind. For our purposes, the common and significant feature of physicalism, materialism, and naturalism is the acceptance of the ontological tenet.

Philosophy of mind is not immune to methodological questions—questions about the appropriate methods for studying the nature of the mental. The *a priori* method, distinctive of much of the history of philosophy, holds that philosophy of mind investigates by analyzing distinctively mental concepts. A particular mental concept is analyzed by identifying its connections to other concepts; for example, logical behaviorism, as we will see, ties mental concepts to behavioral concepts.

Two other pairs of notions are closely related. We might know or have reason to believe that a sentence or proposition is either a priori or *a posteriori*. We know something a priori if our reason for believing (our justification) is independent of any empirical investigation; a posteriori knowledge results from experience or empirical investigations—some sort of interaction with the world (for further explanation, see chapter 8 of Jack Crumley, *Introduction to Epistemology* [Mountain View, CA: Mayfield, 1999]).

The second pair of notions is necessary and sufficient conditions. *Necessary conditions* are like minimum requirements: A is a necessary condition of B if B can't exist or happen without A. A necessary condition of being president of the United States is being 35 years of age. *Sufficient conditions* identify those conditions that are enough: if you have A, that's enough to bring about B. If you receive a majority of Electoral College votes and Congress certifies those votes, that's enough for you to be president of the United States. In a sense, "conceptual analysis" provides the necessary and sufficient conditions for the application of a term or concept.

Although chapter 7 discusses the nature of concepts, we can note one aspect of the relationship between concepts and objects or properties. Concepts—loosely, ideas—are about or refer to a kind or type of object having certain properties. The concept of a "tangerine" refers to or picks out those things having a specific cluster of properties—orangish, a little smaller than a tennis ball, a fruit, and so on. The concept "gold" is about things having the properties of being shiny, metallic, malleable, and of the atomic number 79.

Perhaps once the preferred method in philosophy of mind, the relation between philosophy of mind and the sciences is now more nuanced. Indeed, philosophers of mind still make use of a priori arguments, often in the form of "thought experiments" (hypothetical experiments designed to tease out certain intuitions or conclusions). But many philosophers see the results of empirical research as at the very least placing a kind of constraint on theories of mind. An adequate theory should, at the very least, be able to account for empirical findings, whether from neuroscience, cognitive psychology, or some other empirical discipline.

It is possible, of course, to take a still more empirical approach in philosophy of mind. Thus, one might think that an adequate theory of mind is but a continuation of empirical theorizing. Empirical theories provide more than constraints; they provide the data and the concepts for an adequate theory of the mental. In one form or another, we will encounter each of these three methodological approaches in the following chapters.

Returning to metaphysics, we alluded to the idea that physicalism is not everyone's preferred outlook. We find hints of the principal alternative to physicalism as far back as Plato and Aristotle, but most trace the explicit expression of this alternative to René Descartes. This alternative, as you might know, is *dualism*. This is the subject of chapter 1.

P A R T   1

THE NATURE OF THE MENTAL AND THE PHYSICAL

1

Dualism

We're no angels. We are not just spirits in the material world. Or so common sense seems to tell us. Our commonsense view tells us that we are body *and* mind, mental *and* physical.

During the course of our daily affairs, we are naturally inclined to distinguish between the mental and the physical. My belief that my glass is empty or Sara's desire to talk to Sam about the upcoming meeting do not seem to have the properties we normally associate with the physical. Whether we consider the belief or the desire, neither appears to have shape, size, or weight; nor do they appear to have velocity or momentum. We would be more than a bit puzzled if Sara claimed that her desire was rectangular or that it was traveling much too fast for her to keep up. Propositional attitudes (beliefs, desires, wishes, etc.) seem different from the physical.

Similarly, feelings, emotions and sensations are not obviously physical. My being sad or angry does not appear to have a size or shape. Nor does the sensation I have when tasting Jamoca® Almond Fudge ice cream seem to have a weight. Despite the fact that feelings, emotions, and sensations very often have concomitant physical manifestations, these manifestations do not seem necessary. I can be angry that someone used the sports page to protect the table while painting, and yet there might be no physical evidence that I am angry.

We sometimes are tempted by a further distinction. Properties—or characteristics or qualities—are possessed by some *thing* or *object*. Thus, for example, we distinguish between the property of "not fitting with the décor" and the chair that has that property. A knife may be dull or sharp, a pencil may be lost or of #2 hardness. Each of these properties—not fitting with the décor of a room, being dull or sharp, being lost, or being a #2 pencil—*belong to* or are *possessed by* some object. Likewise, we ascribe mental properties to some things. Typically we ascribe mental properties to creatures with minds. More simply, we say that minds are the type of thing that possesses mental properties, and that physical objects are the type of object possessing physical properties.

Nonetheless, our commonsense view is doubtless affected by the progress of the sciences. We are now more easily tempted by the idea that minds and mental properties are in some way physical, or at the very least, closely connected to the physical. Over the last three centuries, and especially during recent decades, the sciences have provided ample reason to think that there is a physical explanation for any object and its properties. (Actually, as early as the fifth century B.C., Hippocrates claimed that the brain and the heart were the loci of the intellect and the emotions, respectively.) Indeed, we are familiar with at least the broad outlines of an evolutionary story that tells us how the human species came to be. This story reminds us that even mental features are the products of a long and complicated evolutionary process. We are reminded daily, by television reports, magazines, and newspapers, of some new drug that relieves depression or anxiety, or of some new discovery that a particular area of the brain is tied to a specific mental function. Many consider it the task of sciences, such as neuroscience, to explain that mental properties are only complicated physical properties.

Seemingly, then, we are drawn in two different directions. One inclines us toward thinking of the mental as something quite different from the physical; the other pushes us toward thinking that understanding the nature of the mental requires simply that we understand more about the physical. If you were to conclude—after due reflection—that the mental is something *essentially* different from the physical, that the mental is simply too *unlike* the physical for the sciences to tell us the whole story of the mental, then you would be leaning toward the view known as dualism.

Dualism is the view that certain things—minds, in particular, or mental properties such as the contents of our thoughts, sensations, or consciousness—are not physical in nature. The dualist holds that a complete physical inventory of the world would leave something out—the mental. The nature of the mental, the *essence* of the mental, cannot be explained by appealing only to physical entities and their properties, no matter how physically complex those entities and properties might be.

Here the distinction between minds and mental properties is crucial. **Substance dualism** is the view that minds are a unique category of thing or substance (historically, the notion of *substance* referred to an entity that can exist by itself), distinct from the category of physical substance. Substance dualists, of whom René Descartes (1596–1650) is the classic example, admit the existence and functioning of brains, but also hold that we have non-physical minds. According to the dualist, advances in neuroscience may reveal the inner secrets of the brain, but they will not reveal the nature of minds. Similarly, no scientific investigation will reveal the nature of distinctively mental properties, such as thinking or feeling.

René Descartes: The Father of Modern Philosophy

René Descartes (1596–1650) was one of the most influential thinkers in Western civilization. He is a leading figure in what has been called the "Century of Genius," the 17th century. Known primarily for his work in philosophy, Descartes was active in mathematics and physics as well. Descartes spent much of his adult life outside of France, much of it in Holland (from 1628 to 1649). A Catholic all his life, Descartes is sometimes viewed as cautious. After hearing of the difficulty Galileo encountered espousing revolutionary ideas, Descartes stopped publication of his own work on features of the world (it was not published until two decades after his death), and he began his *Meditations* with a long letter addressed to the learned men (including clergy) of his day, explaining the "appropriate" view they should take of the work.

Despite this prudential approach, there can be little doubt that Descartes thought his metaphysical and scientific views superior to Aristotelianism, which was then the dominant outlook. Nor can there be much doubt that Descartes played a significant role in ushering Aristotelianism from center stage. The brief but seminal *Meditations on First Philosophy* was published in 1641. It was accompanied by a set of six objections from leading thinkers of Descartes' day, together with Descartes' replies. Most of the standard objections to Descartes are first voiced in the objections.

The *Meditations* contains several of the most famous arguments in philosophy. The most famous and most foundational is the cogito: "I think, therefore I am" (*cogito ergo sum*). Of more concern here is that Descartes places dualism squarely in the forefront of modern philosophy. Arguments in both the 2nd and 6th meditations are designed to show the metaphysical distinctness of mind and body (a version of one of these arguments is in the text).

Property dualism, unlike substance dualism, accepts that there is only one type of substance—physical substance—but claims that there are distinctively mental properties that are not physical in nature. No purely physical account reveals the nature of these mental properties.

Common to both substance and property dualism is the claim that we should not rest content with a purely physical story of the world, for that story is necessarily incomplete. This chapter explores the motivations for both substance and property dualism. Is there good reason for thinking that the mental is something decidedly different from the physical? Before proceeding, it might be worth our while to try to find some general characterization of the mental, some mark of the mental.

The Mark of the Mental

Dualism claims to have identified something—whether a substance, a property, or both—that is distinctively mental. Thus far, we have been content with examples: beliefs, desires, sensations, moods, and the like. But is there some general criterion that would enable us to distinguish the mental from the physical? Is there some characteristic by virtue of which an item can be classified as mental? Typically two distinct criteria emerge.

Propositional attitudes—beliefs, desires, hopes, fears—have a salient feature. They have content; they are *about* something. Sara believes that Sam is waiting for her by the door. Sara's belief is about a particular state of affairs—that Sam waits in a particular location. Meanwhile, Sam desires something to eat. Again, Sam's desire has a particular content—the food that he does not have. This feature of propositional attitudes suggests one possible criterion for the mental: its *intentionality*, its "aboutness" or content. Franz Brentano (1838–1917) first suggested that the distinctive property of consciousness is its intentionality, that experiences always refer to or are about something. This is summarized in the slogan "Intentionality is the mark of the mental." More simply, the mental is essentially *about* something while the physical is not. This table is not about anything; it doesn't refer to anything. But my thought about the lucky bums out on the golf course has content.

For some, the intentionality criterion seems too narrow. Yes, beliefs and desires have content, but is it obvious that the same can be said about sensations? My arm itches, but is that itch about anything? You have a sensation of sweet and cold; does that sensation have content? My friend may be feeling a bit blue, but it is not obvious that her feeling is about anything. Thus, the intentionality criterion apparently fails to characterize some mental states (Dretske [1997] has a contrary view).

Mental states such as sensations or feelings can instead be characterized by the fact that we are personally aware of them. When you have an itch or a headache, you have direct access to that fact. You do not need to ask your sister or your friend if your head hurts. You are aware of your sensations and feelings; you can tell that you have them. How do you do this? The technical term is "introspection." You introspect that you are sad or that your foot is tingling. You simply *look inside*.

Typically we recognize these states by their distinctive *feel* or quality to them. An itch feels one way, a tickle another. Anger feels different from sadness. (Philosophers sometimes call these "raw feels" or the "experiential aspect" of mental states.) These qualitative properties are called *phenomenal properties*.

Is it possible to extend this second criterion of the mental—things of which we are introspectively aware—to include the propositional attitudes? Unfortunately, it appears not. We are not aware of all our beliefs or desires. Some of our beliefs and desires are unconscious or dispositional (states of which we are not currently aware, but could be). We may act on unconscious beliefs and desires without being aware of them. Conversely, behavioral evidence may lead us to see that we do not have beliefs or desires we thought we had. Sam may tell Sara he doesn't care which candidate wins the election, yet as election night drags on, his behavior may indicate that he had a decided preference after all. Sam can learn, through his behavior, that in fact he wanted a particular candidate to win. Thus, the introspective access criterion also seems too narrow.

We have then two apparently overly narrow criteria for discerning the mental, one focusing on intentionality, the other on introspective access. Although we cannot settle the issue here, it is worth noting that dualists seem to have a clear preference for the introspective access criterion. Dualists hold that introspective access provides our best evidence of the existence of a distinctly mental realm. This is true not only of Descartes but of contemporary dualists as well (Descartes 1641; Swinburne 1986, chap. 8; Foster 1991, chap. 7). Provisional adoption of either criterion should not distract us from the dualists' central point: The mental is something different from the physical.

What's Going On: Mental Events

Events happen. As a matter of fact, they happen a lot. But what does it mean to say that there are "mental events"?

Objects frequently undergo changes in the properties they possess. For example, we might talk about Sam becoming hungry or Sara no longer having the pain in her arm. Such changes in properties are typically considered *events*. The election of a new president, a going-out-of-business sale, or going for a drive are examples of the kinds of things we ordinarily think of as events. Even these more familiar events comprise changes of some sort. A nation chooses a new leader; a particular building is soon to be vacant; a group of people change their location. Here we are extending the notion of an event to include changes in mental properties.

My coming to believe that there is no orange juice in my glass is a change in the properties I have, and hence, an event. Admittedly, it is not a very momentous event. It is, however, a *mental* event, a change in my mental properties. Similarly, there are brain events, such as the activation of a particular neural structure. Of course, brain events are also physical events. For convenience, we use the terms "process" and "event" interchangeably. "Brain process" or "brain event" simply note a change in brain properties. Similarly, we can speak indifferently of mental processes and mental events. Note that we now have a further characterization of the central dualist claim: Mental events are not physical events. Mental events fall outside the scope of an exhaustive description of all the physical events in the world.

This new terminology also distinguishes substance dualism from property dualism. Property dualism claims that there are only physical objects, but that there are two different types of events, mental and physical. Sam, for example, has a physical body that sometimes changes its purely physical properties. But his body—specifically, his brain—sometimes changes its mental properties, such as when Sam acquires a new belief. Substance dualists, however, hold that mental events are always changes in a nonphysical *mental subject*. Mental properties belong not to brains but to minds, since the mind is a substance distinct from the brain. According to the substance dualist, then, if you change your mental properties, you've changed your mind. Now, that's an event! And the biography of a mental subject, of a mind, is the history of all its mental events. Whether there is good reason to think that there are distinctively mental subjects is the topic of the next section.

Minds without Bodies:
Four Arguments for Substance Dualism

The key feature of substance dualism is that there are two distinct types of substance, two kinds of things in the world: physical things and mental things—minds. As *nonphysical* objects, minds do not have physical properties. They have neither size nor shape, color nor weight; minds are not spatial objects. Descartes described this feature of minds as their lack of *exten-*

sion. Physical things are extended; they take up space. (Dualists differ over whether we should think of minds as located someplace.)

If minds lack physical properties entirely, can we say anything positive about them? Descartes provides us with the following answer: The essential feature of minds is *what they do.* And what do minds do? They think! Descartes construed "thinking" quite broadly as including not only reasoning and having beliefs or opinions, wishes or desires, but also having sensations or emotions, feeling giddy or morose, and deciding to do something. Thinking includes knowing, having insight, dreaming, and daydreaming.

Perhaps the most interesting feature of substance dualism is that minds do not need bodies. No body? No matter! You still have your mind! Less informally, in principle, minds are separate and distinct substances. Since minds possess no physical properties, a mind would not lose anything if it lost its body, and thus there appears to be no logical barrier to the existence of a mind without a body. As we will see presently, some find this an especially attractive feature of dualism.

Although a mind might exist without a body, many substance dualists think there is an intimate, causal connection between a mind and some physical body. Minds are "attached" to physical bodies. In particular, bodies influence minds, and minds influence the behavior of bodies. Hitting your thumb with a hammer causes a feeling of pain. Sara's belief that Sam will again be late causes her to stop by a friend's apartment. Sam's desire to see the end of the game causes his body to remain on the couch. Now, this is not a necessary feature of substance dualism. Some deny that minds and bodies causally interact, but most substance dualists subscribe to the commonsense view that minds causally influence bodies. And it turns out that this adherence to common sense creates a serious problem for substance dualism.

Common sense aside, is there is any good reason for adopting substance dualism? There are at least four arguments supporting substance dualism as the best way to understand the relation between the mental and the physical. The rest of this section surveys these arguments.

Surviving the Body's Demise: The Argument from Survival after Death
Some are drawn to substance dualism because it appears that only substance dualism is compatible with the *person's* survival after death. Descartes, for example, saw this as a commendable consequence of substance dualism. If one accepts that a person continues to exist after the biological death of one's body, then it would seem that the person must be something other than the body. That is, the person must be something *nonphysical.* This something, the repository of one's personal identity or essence, is the mind or soul. Invoking

the concept of a soul has distinctly religious connotations, although this is not a necessary feature of survival after death. We might term this the *argument from survival after death.*

Suppose that people do in fact survive their deaths. Upon your death, you cast off your mortal coil; your body ceases to function—but you continue to exist. Since you continue after death, you must be something other than the physical body. The physicalist alternative to substance dualism cannot account for this possibility; hence, substance dualism is the best explanation of survival after death.

At least two reasons undermine this argument, however. First, one will find this argument less than plausible if one doubts the plausibility of survival after death. Second, and more important, it is not obvious that survival after death *requires* substance dualism. Substance dualism is not a necessary condition for survival after death. Ray Kurzweil, a popular futurist author, for example, suggests that survival after death might and will come about by placing the appropriate computer program in an artificial body (Kurzweil 2002). Despite its science fiction feel, if this type of survival is possible—and the argument does nothing to rule out this possibility—then substance dualism is not the only explanation of survival after death. If we could somehow

Other Minds

A rather startling implication of dualism is that we do not know that other human beings have minds! Since minds lack physical properties and are unobservable, and since we cannot introspect another's mind, it would seem that we cannot tell whether our fellow humans have minds at all.

The two most common responses to the *problem of other minds* are the argument from analogy and the inference to the best explanation. The first claims that, since in my own case I know that behavior is connected to a mind, by analogy I can infer that others' behavior is connected to minds. Analogies based on a single case, however, leave something to be desired. Many consider the second response stronger: The best explanation of the complex system of behavior of other creatures is that they are minded. Continuing and novel occurrences of seemingly intelligent behavior are best explained by a mind directing the behavior (see Graham 1993).

develop a computer program for a person's mind and run this program on a "computer brain" located in an artificial body, we would have a physicalist account of survival after death.

Looking Inside: The Argument from Introspection

Perhaps our most familiar and best evidence for the existence of mental substance is access to our own minds. Introspection reveals a range of states and properties—beliefs, desires, feelings, sensations—that appear distinctly nonphysical. The *argument from introspection* begins with the claim that we introspect nonphysical states and properties and concludes that substance dualism offers the best explanation of the results of introspection. When we look inside, when we introspect, we find mental states and properties—the desire for a glass of iced tea, the belief that a project is due tomorrow, the sensation of a red apple. Such states appear nonphysical; they seem not to take up space or have size, color, or weight. Introspection reveals a distinctly nonphysical realm—a mental realm.

Some doubt this conclusion, however. That introspection reveals a nonphysical mind would seem to depend on whether introspection reveals the *real* nature of the mental. My awareness that I am feeling a bit blue at the moment may reveal no obvious physical properties. Yet my blue feeling may ultimately turn out to be physical. As an analogy, imagine that I hear the final notes of Beethoven's Ninth Symphony. The auditory sense, hearing, enables me to detect sounds but does not tell me that such sounds are actually complicated patterns of air waves. Similarly, the critic of the introspection argument contends that introspection may be attuned only to "surface properties" and may not be designed to tell us that introspected states are ultimately physical properties. Thus, we have yet to prove the existence of a nonphysical property or substance.

It is worth noting that as an argument for *substance* dualism, the argument from introspection assumes that states and properties must belong to some substance. Descartes undoubtedly made this assumption, which drew the attention of his earliest critics. A century later, David Hume (1711–1776) argued that introspection reveals mental properties but no substantial self. Some contemporary substance dualists recognize the need to argue against the Humean conception and for the Cartesian conception of mental substance (e.g., Foster 1991). Now, it is plausible to suppose that properties require a substance. Properties are not free-floating; they belong to some substance. Without further shoring up, however, it may be that the argument from introspection supports at most property dualism.

Reasoning and Communicating: The Poverty Argument
The *poverty argument* claims that no physical explanation could account for two mental properties: the ability to communicate and the ability to reason. Language enables us to communicate to others thoughts about a virtually un-limited number of topics. Minds have a further property, as well: the ability to reason—to analyze, to hypothesize, to draw inferences. The poverty argu-ment maintains that no *purely* physical arrangement could account for either of these abilities.

Descartes deployed this argument in his *Discourse on Method* (1637), claiming that the organs of some animals are very similar to ours. If reason-ing, for example, depended only on physical structure, then animals—having a sufficiently similar physical structure—should be able to reason. Given this similarity, and given their evident lack of linguistic or reasoning abilities, he concludes that these properties could not be possessed by anything other than a nonphysical mind. Descartes also thought that no machine, no mat-ter how cleverly constructed, could ever possess such capacities.

What are we to make of this argument? The central claim of the argument is, of course, the contention that no physical system could produce certain kinds of mental properties. Let a physical system be as similar to our own bodies as you please, that system would not and *could not* possess the relevant cognitive capacities. *Arrange physical matters in any way you want, you won't get a mind.* Descartes drew support for this claim from his views about ani-mals, views which were unfortunately misguided. He held, for example, that animals are *automata*, complex machines incapable of feeling pain.

But consider computers. Computers generate complicated proofs in logic, solve sophisticated mathematical problems, and in the case of expert systems, undertake a "decision procedure," determining what steps ought to be taken next. Indeed, computerized robots have, almost entirely on their own, de-signed and built other robots (*Sacramento Bee* 2000). Computers might also come to have the ability to communicate; as many of us have found out, they seem especially fond of telling us that they are unable to perform a desired task. We might also note that some computer programs have the ability to learn, or at least to adapt to the unique cadences and pronunciation of the owner's spoken commands. Some very sophisticated computers have a com-mand of fragments of natural language. Within restricted contexts, such computers appear to communicate and understand. Descartes could scarcely have been expected to anticipate such technological developments, and it is hard to know what he would make of them.

These considerations do *not* show that we have succeeded in constructing "thinking machines" (a contentious point considered in a subsequent chapter). Rather, Descartes' pessimism over physical systems seems premature and by no means necessary. If, as critics contend, we have taken the first steps toward mechanizing—"physicalizing"—these allegedly nonphysical capacities, then we do not as yet have a clear signal of a nonphysical mind. Minds may turn out to be matter, after all.

In one sense, then, the poverty argument brings us to an impasse. The physicalist claims that the mental is, in the end, physical: *No matter, no minds*. The dualist claims that the essence of the mental exceeds the physical: *Minds don't need matter*. Thus, we come to the most significant argument for substance dualism.

The Argument from Conceivability

A more formal version of this argument appears soon, but let's begin with an intuitive consideration. Reflect for a moment on the concept of mind (or the mental). Analyze it carefully. Now here is something you will not find: the concept of a body. Think about thoughts; think about feelings and moods. Notice what you are *not* thinking about—you are not thinking about bodies or brains. The concept of the mental does not seem to involve the concept of the physical. That is, the physical is not *necessary* for the mental. The suggested conclusion of these informal considerations is that minds are in principle separable from bodies: *Minds don't need bodies*.

The formulation of the *argument from conceivability* requires a special concept: logical possibility. We are familiar with physical possibility—an event or state of affairs is physically possible if it conforms to the laws of nature; otherwise, it is physically impossible. Given our current understanding, it is physically impossible to go faster than the speed of light. Nature imposes this limitation: no speeding (and speeding counts as anything faster than 186,000 miles per second). Nature won't let us, as my father once suggested, get something going that fast and then give it a little push.

Yet Nature might have been different. There is, after all, no contradiction in supposing that a different set of rules might apply in some other time or place. This is the heart of logical possibility: A proposition (sentence) is *logically possible* if and only if it is not self-contradictory. There is no contradiction in supposing that an object might travel at twice the speed of light; it is logically (but not physically) possible. But now think of a four-sided triangle. Can't do it? You cannot because the concept of a four-sided triangle is logically self-contradictory: If it's a triangle, then it has three sides, not four; if it has four sides, then it is not a triangle.

The argument from conceivability, especially prized by dualists, claims that we can conceive of mind existing wholly separately from body. Since this state of affairs is conceivable, it must be logically possible that mind and body are separable—there is nothing self-contradictory about this notion. Carrying this a step further, if it is logically possible that mind and body exist separately, then there is no logically necessary connection between mind and body. Thus, there is no contradiction in supposing that minds exist apart from bodies. Minds do not *require* body, or anything physical. This implies that mind is a distinct substance (since a substance does not depend on any other thing for its existence).

It is sometimes tempting to think that too much of this argument is carried by the notion of logical possibility. How does one draw the conclusion that there are two types of distinct substance in the world from the starting point "It is logically possible that . . ."? But the dualist's aim is simply to undermine the suggestion that minds are ultimately physical. The dualist wants to show that the physical is not *necessary* for the mental.

A common thread runs through various criticisms of the conceivability argument (e.g., Levine 2001), namely, that the substance dualist is premature in making judgment about the absence of a connection between our concepts of the mental and the physical. We may think that there is no contradiction in supposing that mind could exist independently, but that may simply reflect our ignorance. Science often reveals connections between concepts that we might have previously thought unimaginable. At one time, reflection on our concept of "water" would never have revealed the concepts "hydrogen" and "oxygen"; contemplation of "copper" would not have led to the concept of "electrical conductivity." Similarly, we once thought it inconceivable to treat certain mental conditions as complicated physical conditions, but we now recognize a connection between certain mental and physical states. As neuroscience progresses, we may come to a similar conclusion regarding the connection between mental and physical concepts. We may recognize connections between mental and physical concepts that we previously *could not conceive*. Thus, the dualist premise—because it's *conceivable* that minds and bodies are separable, it's *logically possible* that they are—is, according to critics, an indication of our limited conception of the nature of the mind, and not an indication of nonphysical mental properties. In this sense, the dualist premise might well turn out false. Viewing matters in this way blocks the conclusion that minds and bodies are independent substances.

Of course, the dualist retorts that the burden of proof lies with the physicalist. The physicalist needs to show us how it is logically contradictory to suppose that a mind could exist independently of the body. The physicalist needs to show us the larger explanatory framework in which we find the necessary connection between our concepts of the physical and the mental.

The conceivability argument is central to the substance dualist position, yet it remains controversial. While it may be a good argument, the considerations so far suggest that we are not obligated to accept the substance dualist conclusion.

Property Dualism

Property dualists, remember, reject the existence of a mental substance. Instead, they hold that when physical entities are arranged in a suitably complex manner, a uniquely mental property arises. The vast number of neural processes in the brain produce not only neural or brain properties but also mental properties. Having a thought about a canyon or a desire for orange juice, having an ache or a sensation of sweetness, or simply having an awareness of one's surroundings are all instances of mental properties, properties that come about as a result of the complex functioning of our bodies and our brains in particular.

Although mental properties are properties of brains, they are not physical in nature, say the property dualists. No amount of physical theory will capture or explain the essence of mental properties. Appeals to neural processes inevitably leave out some essential feature of mental properties. The property dualist concedes the distinctive contribution of the brain to the occurrence of mental properties, yet retains the idea that there is, after all, something special—something nonphysical—about the mental. We are, according to property dualism, one substance comprising two types of properties.

Property dualists, while agreed that brain properties cause mental properties, divide over whether mental properties causally influence the physical. There are thus two types of property dualism: interactionist property dualism and epiphenomenalism.

Epiphenomenalism denies that mental properties have any causal powers; physical events cause mental properties, but mental properties have no causal powers. This is a startling claim! It conflicts with our commonsense intuition that mental states bring about physical states—that my wanting an apple leads to my reaching for an apple. Epiphenomenalism also rejects a second important type of causation—mental states bringing about other mental states. Again, common sense counts this kind of mental causation as one of the fundamental aspects of the mental. My thoughts, for example, that all women are mortal and that Xanthippe is a woman lead to a further thought: Xanthippe is mortal. Epiphenomenalism claims that we are simply misguided about the real causes in these apparent cases of mental causation. The real causes are entirely physical.

Consider a simple analogy (adapted from Wesley Salmon). Suppose we line up a number of flashlights, facing a wall. We then shine the first flashlight on

Nomological Danglers

The term *nomological* occurs frequently in contemporary philosophy of mind; it derives from the Greek word *nomos*, meaning "law." The sciences discover and articulate the laws of nature, such as Boyle's Law or Newton's familiar $F = ma$. Laws connect one type of object or property with another; for example, Boyle's Law connects pressure with increases or decreases in volume. Notice that scientific laws connect physical properties with other physical properties. In this sense, science reveals a world that is a closed system.

Herbert Feigl claims that epiphenomenalism commits us to "nomological danglers." According to Feigl, the property dualist holds that brain processes cause or bring about mental properties. It is the task of some branch of science, perhaps neuropsychology, to articulate the laws governing the connection between brains and mental properties. However, this would seem to introduce a very different kind of scientific law. While we normally expect scientific laws to connect different physical properties, these special laws would connect physical properties with properties that "dangle" outside the rest of the physical world. Property dualism thus gives us nomological danglers (Feigl 1960).

the wall for a moment, followed by shining the second flashlight briefly, and continuing down the line. Each of these shinings produces an illuminated spot on the wall. Were we uninformed about these illuminated spots, we might think that the first spot had caused the second, which in turn caused the third, and so on. Of course, we would be mistaken. The cause of an illuminated spot was simply the shining of an individual flashlight, nothing more. Epiphenomenalism claims that mental properties are like the illuminated spots on the wall: They are real, and they are caused in ways we can understand, but they don't *do* anything.

Epiphenomenalism has a checkered history. Often rejected because it conflicts with our deeply entrenched folk psychological view, epiphenomenalist worries resurface about mental causation and consciousness. Some now argue that epiphenomenalism is the best way to understand the *qualitative feel* of some mental states, such as pain, or that it is the best way to understand consciousness. Epiphenomenalism is also a charge leveled against some physicalist theories of mental causation. (Both points are considered in later chapters.)

Not all property dualists are epiphenomenalists. Some believe that the mental and physical obviously interact; hence, their name—interactionist property dualists (Jacquette 1994). **Interactionist property dualism** claims that mental properties do have causal powers. One thought may cause another, or a mental state may bring about physical changes.

In property dualism, mental properties are *emergent properties*. They *emerge* from complex arrangements of purely physical objects. We can see what the property dualist has in mind through a brief consideration of an example.

In biology, we encounter an important emergent property—being alive. Living organisms depend on four types of organic compounds (nucleic acids such as DNA and RNA, proteins composed of amino acids, carbohydrates, and lipids—basically fats). Taken singly, none of the four compounds is "alive." Combined, however, in the appropriate way, they are constituents, the basic building blocks, of cells. One-celled organisms are *living* organisms. These one-celled structures exhibit a property not found in any less complex arrangement of physical-chemical constituents, the property of being alive. *Being alive* emerges from the distinctive, extremely complex arrangement of these constituents. Being alive is thus an emergent property.

The property dualist suggests that we continue this story a little longer. A long evolutionary process culminates in the human species and the development of the extremely complicated human brain. Among their many properties, brains have a special type of emergent property, the *mental*.

Property dualism insists that a purely physicalist explanatory framework leaves out the nature of mental properties. The property of being alive, while an emergent property, is part of our physical understanding of the world. Once we tell the physical-chemical-biological story of *being alive*, we have said everything we need to say. Tracing the mechanisms of replication, growth, development, and heredity (among others) provides a complete story of living organisms. Yet mental properties, which arise from the physical, are not *reducible* to the physical—mental properties cannot be completely explained by our physical concepts. What a bee sting feels like and what it is to have a thought about the tuna salad in the refrigerator are mental properties that are not fully explained by our ever-increasing neuroscientific understanding of the brain.

The virtue of property dualism—maintaining the key intuitions of both physicalism and dualism—is also, for some, its chief vice. The worry arises from property dualism counting mental properties as a fundamentally different kind of property. Physicalism acknowledges emergent properties. Yet, in every other case of an emergent property—whether it is something as basic as the valence of an ion, as complex as the self-replicating ability of DNA, or as significant as the appearance of living organisms—we still count such properties as physical. The physicalist finds puzzling the property dualist's claim of an emergent *nonphysical* property. Property dualism insists that this one case, the nature and functioning of brains, produces a type of property that falls *outside* the physicalist understanding of the world. But why—*in this one case*—do we get a *non*physical property? asks the physicalist. Why reject the idea that physical science will eventually explain the feeling of a sensation or the aboutness of a thought?

In response, property dualism insists first that the notion of an emergent property is the notion of the emergence of a *different type* of property, a new kind of property. Study brains as long as we wish—their constituent parts, properties, and behavior—and we will still not be able to explain the nature of the mental property simply by talking about physical objects and their properties (Jacquette 1994, 19–28).

This is the central dispute between physicalists and property dualists: whether the physical constituents and their properties are sufficient for explaining the existence and nature of mental properties. Physicalists agree, for example, that special combinations of objects produce properties that we have not seen before. *Watery stuff* emerges from combinations of many hydrogen and oxygen atoms; *living stuff* emerges from complexes of proteins. But they deny that there is something special about the mental properties that precludes a physical explanation of their nature.

We cannot trace here the various arguments given on behalf of emergence (Jacquette 1994; Hasker 1999), but this dispute resurfaces in part in later chapters. However, if physicalism is successful in explaining mental properties, the case for property dualism (and dualism in general) will be seriously undermined.

Does the Mind Move Us? Dualism and Mental Causation

In a letter to Descartes in 1643, Princess Elisabeth of Bohemia articulated the most celebrated hurdle facing dualism: How can two wholly distinct substances causally interact? Interaction lies at the heart of our commonsense view of the mind. Doubtless we would be far less interested in the mental if we did not think that the mental played a causal role in our daily lives. We think, for example, that it is *because* Sam wants a cheese sandwich and believes that cheese is in the kitchen that he walks into the kitchen. And we believe that thoughts cause other thoughts; mental causation includes mental states causing other mental states. Sara believes that a certain candidate deserves election *because* she believes that this candidate supports reform and that only supporters of reform deserve election. Lastly, of course, we are at times painfully aware that physical events cause mental events: Catching your finger in the car door causes pain. These three types of mental causation—the physical causing mental changes, the mental causing other mental changes, and the mental causing physical changes—seem indispensable to our commonsense view. Explaining this latter kind of mental causation has attracted the most attention.

The physicalist suspects that the dualist is at a distinct disadvantage when it comes to explaining mental causation. Dualism seems faced with three equally unattractive options: (1) mental causation must be abandoned, as in epiphenomenalism; (2) some suspect metaphysical claim must be invoked (as we will see when we consider two variants of dualism); or (3) dualism simply fails to give us an adequate account of mental causation. But why does the physicalist think that mental causation proves so intractable for the dualist?

Our notion of causation involves the idea of one thing changing another. Explanations of causal influence, according to one prominent philosopher of mind, involve the notion of a causal mechanism. Explaining the causal mechanism involves describing the series of intermediate steps or stages that transform one state into another state. And our best understanding of causal mechanisms are physical mechanisms (Fodor 1989). When we ask about the means that brings about some state, we are asking about the series of steps that occurs to bring about the new state. Why does placing the pot of water on a burner cause the water to boil? Because heat transfers from burner to pot, exciting the water molecules into a near frenzy. Why do I see the green book on the table? Because light of a certain wavelength deflects from the book, strikes my retinas, initiating a complicated chain of electrochemical impulses, which result in my visual experience of a green book. If the mental brings about changes in the physical, then we want to know what mechanism is at work; how does it happen?

Notice the apparent difficulty for the dualist in explaining the mechanism or transformation process, for example, in my *desire* to have an apple, which sets in motion the set of neural impulses that eventually bring about the raising of my arm. Mental properties are not physical properties. In what sense, then, can mental properties "exert a force" necessary to get the physical ball rolling? In what sense does the mind move us? Mental properties appear to be the wrong type of property to stimulate neurons in the brain. Electrical properties stimulate neurons, but the mind—since it is nonphysical—is simply not electrifying.

Descartes suggests that the pineal gland is the locus of interaction between mind and brain, but this tells us nothing of the nature of interaction.

Changes in physical objects come about as the result of various forces acting on the objects. Our commonsense explanations of routine events frequently invoke such forces: A glass tips over when inadvertently bumped by someone's elbow; a match lights because of the friction between match head and match cover. In the same vein, the physicalist wonders, how does the mental exert forces that cause changes in the physical? What conceivable mechanism is there? It is these sorts of considerations that are sometimes summed up in the question, "How can two things [or properties] that are completely unlike one another causally interact?" The physicalist suspects that dualism is simply unable to provide the answer to this question.

Variations on a Theme: Occasionalism and Parallelism

Two variants of substance dualism, occasionalism and parallelism, were born of the interaction problem. **Occasionalism** concedes the absence of interaction between mental and physical substance. Apparent cases of interaction are really *occasions* for God to intervene and bring about the appropriate event. Imagine, for example, that you accidentally touch a hot pan on the stove. Contrary to our intuition, the activation of your nerve endings does not produce the pain. Rather, God intervenes and produces the appropriate mental state, a burning sensation. Similarly, imagine that you decide to put an ice cube against your burned fingers. Again, contrary to our intuition, this mental state of yours—deciding—does not cause your arm to move toward an ice cube. God intervenes and produces the appropriate change in your body, which results in your arm moving toward the ice cube. Thus, every instance of apparent interaction is simply an occasion for God's intervention. However, though God is doubtless beneficent, the skeptic might wonder *why* he should intervene in the manner suggested.

Parallelism is similarly tied to a metaphysical outlook not widely held today. Parallelism holds that mental and physical substances do not interact but are coordinated in such a way so as to give the *appearance* of interaction. Within our universe, we find two parallel "subuniverses," the mental and the physical. According to parallelism, these subuniverses are distinct, noninteracting series of events that are nevertheless temporally coordinated. This coordination produces the appearance of interaction, but it is appearance only. Parallelism perhaps raises more questions than it answers. For example, what explains the happy coordination of mental and physical? G. W. Leibniz (1646–1716) claimed that the coordination is a harmony preestablished by God (Leibniz 1965), but, again, one might be suspicious of such a fortuitous harmony.

The merits of occasionalism and parallelism perhaps depend on the evaluation of the underlying metaphysical outlook, which we cannot undertake here. To reject the metaphysics that underlies these two views is not to say that they are wrong. But it does suggest that some aspects of seventeenth-century metaphysics are no longer the preferred outlook, and many believe there is a simpler approach. (See, for example, Copleston 1960 for further discussion of these views.)

Can Property Dualism Explain Interaction?

Property dualism might seem to escape the interaction problem, since the property dualist acknowledges only physical substance. Nonetheless, the *interactionist* property dualist may still face a dilemma due to the mental causation problem. Consider the first part of the dilemma. Suppose the property dualist grants that causal processes are always physical. This means that any changes in a given object are always brought about by some physical mechanism. If I move my hand to scratch my knee, this is a wholly *physical* process. But then mental properties would not play the causal role common sense typically attributes to them; hence, the interactionist view collapses into epiphenomenalism.

Now, consider the second half of the dilemma. Suppose that the property dualist insists on interaction. Then we are owed an explanation of the causal role of *nonphysical, mental* properties. And here we seem to be back to our original question: What series of steps makes mental causation possible?

Basic Attraction: Proximate Causation and Substance Dualism

It is worth noting that some dualists think the interaction problem is over-rated. Daniel Garber (2001) suggests that part of the reason Descartes was not more vexed by Princess Elisabeth's worry is that he thought that *intentional causation* is our best understanding of the causal relationship. And contemporary dualists suspect that physicalism is asking for more than is required (Foster 1991; Hasker 1999). After all, physicalism is no better at explaining certain basic causal interactions.

C. J. Ducasse, a twentieth-century philosopher, exploits this notion of basic causal interaction. Ducasse (1960) argues that the request for the means of causation—the intermediate steps—is only appropriate in cases of *remote causation*; in cases of *proximate causation*, we should not expect to find intermediate stages or steps, because proximate causation is basic and thus inexplicable. To ask the "how" of proximate causation is to commit a kind of "category mistake"; it is to ask a question that doesn't apply in this type of case, to this category.

Consider a mundane example of remote causation: bringing water to a boil. Heat from the burner heats the pot, which in turn agitates the water molecules. Now consider a case of proximate causation: what causes the gravitational attraction between two bodies? Here we are at a loss; there seems to be no further explanation of this type of causation. This is just what gravity is—this *basic* attraction between bodies.

Ducasse urges that mental causation is like gravity—it is basic (proximate). There is no further explanation of the "how" of mental causation. Asking for the intermediate steps is a category mistake, brought about by overlooking the differences between remote and proximal causation. How does the mental bring about changes in the physical? Simply—it just does it. If you are a basic cause, you don't need a mechanism.

Ducasse is surely right that the causal properties of some objects seem basic, while the causal properties of others admit of further explanation. The question, however, is whether we should accept that mental causation is a basic—and inexplicable—causal force in the world.

The attractive force of gravity, while perhaps basic, is not an isolated or an indescribable feature of the physical world. We know, for example, that gravitational force decreases as the distance increases between two bodies. Moreover, our notion of gravity is explained through a system of laws governing various properties and objects. Thus, while gravitational force is a basic causal property of matter, our ability to locate gravity in a complex system of objects and causal properties increases our understanding of gravity. Similarly, suppose that the charge of an electron is a basic causal property. Taken by itself, this causal property may seem mysterious. Our understanding of electrons, however, increases as we are able to relate electrons and their properties to other objects and properties.

Hence, the physicalist's worry blossoms. Unlike cases of basic causation in the physical world, we can place the causality of the mental in no larger set of objects and properties. We are unable to connect the causal efficacy of the mental to any of the typical properties we find in the case of physical causation. Gravitational attraction, for example, varies with mass and distance, but with mental causation, there is no size or mass, no location, no charge or transfer of energy. The causal process that links the mental to the physical appears unique and isolated from all other properties and objects.

The interactionist dualist may object that matters are not that bad. We can connect the basic causal properties of the mental to at least one other kind of property—brain properties. My desire for a glass of tea brings about certain changes in my brain, which—as we are well aware—brings about still other changes in my central nervous system that culminate in some action. So, the dualist claims, the basic causal properties of the mental *can* be located in a larger set of objects and properties when we connect mental causation with changes in the brain.

No Room for the Mental? Causal Closure

We will close this discussion with one line of response to this defense of mental causation. The various sciences, including neuroscience, assume a certain principle, *causal closure of the physical world*. Very simply, causal closure claims that the cause of any physical event is always another physical event. Trace back along the causal chain, there are no causal gaps, only physical events. Consider then any particular change in the brain, say, the activation of a single neuron. What brings about the activation? Following the causal chain to antecedent events, we discover other neighboring, activated neurons that had released neurotransmitters. The activation of the neighboring neurons had in turn been caused by still other activated neurons. We find no gap in this physical causal chain. Consequently, it is difficult to identify the point in this causal chain at which the mental makes its presence felt.

More to the point, there is *no room* in this causal chain for the mental to make its presence felt. There is nowhere in our inquiry into various brain events at which we can say, "Aha! There is a gap here; we see the causes of event A, and we see the causes of event C. But there aren't any physical (neurological) causes of event B. Maybe, it's here, with B-type events, that the mental intervenes." Such cases are jarring and difficult to imagine and reflect the centrality of causal closure to our understanding of the physical realm. The principle of causal closure means that we will not encounter this sort of situation. If, however, mental causation operates in the manner suggested by the dualist, we should expect to find these kinds of cases at some point.

Accepting dualist interaction requires giving up causal closure. Perhaps we should. We may wish, however, for some clearer outline of the alternative.

A Conclusion?

Most contemporary philosophers of mind are physicalists of one sort or another. But dualism has not disappeared. Dualism resurfaces at various points in philosophy of mind, especially with the notions of mental causation and consciousness. It remains an attractive viewpoint for some. But for many others, it seems to require giving up too much of the conceptual framework by which we understand the world, especially as reflected in our notions of interaction and causal closure. We may understand what brings a bird to poke its beak into the ground and retrieve a worm; we may understand what makes the bee fly in a certain direction. But we will not understand how it is that you raise a fork or ask for a raise. We may know how the birds and the bees do it, but the worry is that dualism will prevent us from knowing how we do it.

Key Concepts

Dualism
Epiphenomenalism
Interactionist property dualism
Occasionalism
Parallelism
Property dualism
Substance dualism

Reading Questions

1. What are the essential features of substance dualism? How does it differ from property dualism?

2. Describe the introspection argument. Why might someone disagree with this argument?

3. The poverty argument claims that our linguistic and reasoning abilities are evidence for existence of nonphysical minds. Explain why.

4. What is logical possibility? What is its role in the conceivability argument?

5. What is the difference between epiphenomenalism and interactionist property dualism?

6. What is the difference between remote and proximate causation? How does Ducasse use these concepts to defend dualism? How might someone respond to Ducasse?

7. What is the principle of the causal closure of the world? How does the physicalist use this principle to respond to the dualist?

References

Copleston, Frederick Charles. 1960. *A history of philosophy*, vol. 4, *Descartes to Leibniz*. Rev. ed. London: Burns, Oates, & Washbourne.

Descartes, René. 1637. Discourse on method. Reprinted in *The philosophical works of Descartes*, vol. 1, trans. Elizabeth Haldane and G. R. T. Ross, 79–130. Cambridge: Cambridge University Press, 1968.

———. 1641. *Meditations on first philosophy*. Reprinted in *The philosophical works of Descartes*, vol. 1, trans. Elizabeth Haldane and G. R. T. Ross, 131–99. Cambridge: Cambridge University Press, 1968.

Dretske, Fred. 1997. *Naturalizing the mind*. Cambridge, MA: MIT Press.

Ducasse, C. J. 1960. In defense of dualism. In *Dimensions of mind*, ed. Sidney Hook, 85–90. New York: New York University Press.

Feigl, Herbert. 1960. Mind–body, not a pseudoproblem. In *Dimensions of mind*, ed. Sidney Hook, 33–44. New York: New York University Press.

Fodor, Jerry A. 1989. Making mind matter more. *Philosophical Topics* 17, no. 1: 59–79. Reprinted in *Problems in mind: Readings in contemporary philosophy of mind*, ed. Jack S. Crumley II (Mountain View, CA: Mayfield, 2000), 474–88.

Foster, John. 1991. *The immaterial self: A defence of the Cartesian dualist conception of the mind*. London: Routledge.

Garber, Daniel. 2001. Understanding interaction: What Descartes should have told Elisabeth. In *Descartes embodied: Reading Cartesian philosophy through Cartesian science*, 168–88. Cambridge: Cambridge University Press.

Graham, George. 1993. *Philosophy of mind*. Oxford: Blackwell.

Hasker, William. 1999. *The emergent self*. Ithaca, NY: Cornell University Press.

Jacquette, Dale. 1994. *Philosophy of mind*. Englewood Cliffs, NJ: Prentice-Hall.

Kurzweil, Ray. 2002. *Are we spiritual machines?* Seattle: Discovery Institute Press.

Leibniz, G. W. 1965. *"Monadology" and other philosophical essays*. Englewood Cliffs, NJ: Prentice-Hall.

Levine, Joseph. 2001. *Purple haze: The puzzle of consciousness*. Oxford: Oxford University Press.

Sacramento Bee. 2000. Let there be (machine) life: Robots re-create themselves. August 31.

Swinburne, Richard. 1986. *The evolution of the soul*. Oxford: Clarendon Press.

Additional Readings

Campbell, Keith. *Body and Mind*. Garden City, NY: Anchor, 1970. Reprint. Notre Dame, IN: University of Notre Dame Press, 1984.

Cornman, James, and Keith Lehrer. *Philosophical Problems and Arguments*, 237–79. 2nd ed. New York: Macmillan, 1974.

Crane, Tim. "Intentionality and the Mark of the Mental." In *Current Issues in Philosophy of Mind*, ed. Anthony O'Hear. Cambridge: Cambridge University Press, 1998.

———. "Physicalism (2): Against Physicalism." In *A Companion to the Philosophy of Mind*, ed. Samuel Guttenplan, 479–84. Oxford: Blackwell, 1994.

Gillet, Carl, and Barry Loewer, eds. *Physicalism and Its Discontents*. Cambridge: Cambridge University Press, 2001.

Warner, Richard, and Tadeusz Szubka, eds. *The Mind–Body Problem: A Guide to the Current Debate*. Oxford: Blackwell, 1994.

2

Only Skin Deep: Behaviorism

At the end of the nineteenth century and the beginning of the twentieth, psychologists faced a choice. Some thought the best way to understand the mind, to understand consciousness, was to ask subjects what they had in mind. This approach is characteristic of the introspectionist school. Unhappy with the results of the introspectionist program, various psychologists urged a new task and a new goal for psychology—the study of behavior. This new paradigm for psychology is known as *behaviorism* and was the dominant theory in America into the 1960s; many philosophers also found the view congenial. It is now widely rejected, and this chapter examines the reasons for its adoption and later rejection. But a little history first.

The Path to the Mind: Introspectionism

In the last quarter of the nineteenth century, experimental psychologists, led by the introspectionist school, attempted to secure psychology's place as a natural science. The introspectionists viewed their central task as the study of the mind, or more specifically, consciousness.

Consciousness manifests itself in myriad ways. Think, for a moment, of an apple. We can be conscious or aware of the redness of the apple, of its scent, of its taste, of its texture, or of the cool feel of the exterior of apple on the skin. Each is a distinct sensation or state of awareness: the scent differs from the taste, which differs from texture. The way to understand consciousness, according to the introspectionists, begins with the identification of its distinct states. This in itself is a formidable task, but the introspectionists faced an even greater challenge: *how* to identify the distinct states of mind.

As you might guess, the preferred method was introspection. Subjects would be asked to introspect—to look inside and report the results of this "looking inside." Compiling these introspective reports was the first step in identifying the essential characteristics of each distinct state of mind. Introspecting does not seem a very difficult task. But finding *reliable* "introspecters" was one of the more difficult challenges for the introspectionist school. Introspective subjects needed to be taught what to notice and what to ignore. This difficulty perhaps manifests itself in the results of the introspectionists' studies: The two most prominent introspectionist institutes differed by a few *thousand* on the number of distinct mental states! Imagine for a moment scientists in the United States disagreeing with European scientists about the number of elements that should appear in the periodic table by a few dozen. One or two perhaps, but a few dozen? Now, imagine them disagreeing by a few *thousand* on the number of basic elements. In essence, this is the problem the introspectionists faced (Viney 1993). Their only method (introspection) led to significant disagreement about the basic elements of mind. Perhaps worse, the introspectionists had no clear way to resolve their differences. Not exactly an auspicious beginning for an experimental science!

Three Types of Behaviorism

Although we recognize and rely on the connection, it certainly seems to us that we can distinguish between a mental state, such as anger or a desire, and the consequent behavior. Indeed, our intuition tells us that someone might be angry but not show it, or that someone might want the last piece of cake without giving any indication of that desire. A mental state might exist, we suppose, independently of any correlative behavior; behavior is an *indication* of a mental state, not the *essence* of that state.

Behaviorism sees a much closer connection between behavior and the mental. As we will see, different accounts of the connection give rise to various types of behaviorism. But we can identify two common themes. First, our best hope of understanding the mental is in terms of behavior. If we want to know what it is to be angry or sad, to desire cake, or to believe that an appointment is at 10:00, we can look to the behavioral characteristics of individuals. We *should* look at behavioral characteristics, according to behaviorism, precisely because there is a *necessary* connection between mental states and behavior. This is a stronger connection than that envisioned by our more ordinary view.

Other Minds II

Behaviorism provides an easy solution to the problem of other minds, since it counts minds as neither internal nor private. Understanding mental concepts as referring to complex behavioral dispositions means that we need look no further than behavior to "see" another's "mind." Behaviorism thus implies, somewhat counterintuitively, that we are in no better position to know our own thoughts than those of any other person. An old behaviorist joke highlights this feature: One behaviorist meets another and says, "You're fine; how am I?"

Second, the behaviorist thinks that *the search for inner mental causes is a lost cause*. You might think that your sister slams the door *because* she is angry, or that your brother takes his umbrella *because* he thinks it will rain and wants to stay dry. We tend to think of such states—anger, desires, beliefs—as inner mental states that are the *causes* of our behavior. But the behaviorist dissents, dismissing inner mental causes as remnants of a dualistic outlook that requires supplanting by a thoroughgoing scientific outlook. If we want to identify the *real* causes of behavior, the behaviorist claims, we should instead look to our genetic endowment, the environment, and the history of our interactions with the environment.

Methodological behaviorism holds that as a matter of scientific practice we should focus on the *observable* characteristics of an individual. Since inner mental states are not observable, psychology should restrict its attention to environmental stimuli and behavioral responses. Interpreted in this way, methodological behaviorism is agnostic about the existence and nature of inner mental states.

Logical behaviorism (sometimes called *philosophical behaviorism*) is a theory about the *meaning* of mental or psychological terms. According to logical behaviorism, any sentence containing mental or psychological terms can be "translated into" or reduced to a sentence containing only behavioral terms. "I wish I had a peach" can be translated into a sentence where my wish is replaced by terms referring only to its behavioral equivalents. As we will see, this new sentence is doubtless long and rather complicated. Since logical behaviorism focuses on the meaning of mental terms, it is thought of as philosophical theory rather than an empirical theory in psychology. Indeed, philosophers gave some of the earliest and clearest articulations of this view as a means of "legitimizing" our ordinary, routine references to mental states. Mental state terms are shorthand descriptions for more complicated—and more accurate—descriptions of behavior. According to logical behaviorism, mental state terms are abbreviations.

A more radical view, **ontological behaviorism**, rejects the existence of inner mental states. The mental is nothing more than complicated behavioral and physical characteristics. As we will see, this definition is less straightforward than it seems. For now it is enough to note that, according to ontological behaviorists, mental states don't exist.

These three types of behaviorism are independent of one another. Quite clearly, one could adopt methodological behaviorism without adopting, for example, ontological behaviorism. Ignoring mental states does not require denying their existence. Similarly, one could adopt ontological behaviorism without also committing to the view that mental terms are reducible to behavioral terms. Although there is no necessary connection between these views, two prominent twentieth-century behaviorist psychologists have adopted features of each. We will use John B. Watson's views to highlight the central features of methodological behaviorism.

Methodological Behaviorism

Led by John Watson (1878–1958), behaviorists identified the problem besetting introspectionism as *methodological* and determined to avoid it. Introspected mental states are *unobservable*. Watson (1930) notes that the behaviorist psychologist has never seen, smelled, or tasted consciousness; nor, presumably, has anyone else. The behaviorist thus rejects the claim that psychology is the study of the mind or consciousness as *inner mental states*.

What is the aim of psychology then? Psychology is the science of *behavior*, and its aim is the prediction and control of behavior. The aim of other natural sciences, Watson points out, is the prediction and control of various natural phenomena: chemistry aims at prediction and control of chemical phenomena, biology at biological phenomena, and so forth. Furthermore, the success of the natural sciences is directly tied to a methodology that relies only on publicly observable phenomena. Since the essence of the human phenomenon is behavior, Watson argues, psychology as a science should aim at the prediction and control of human *behavior*, and its success will come with adoption of a similar method.

Thus, we have the core of methodological behaviorism: Mental states are ignored while behaviorism focuses on the observable. The official doctrine then is to avoid commitment on the question of the ontological status—on the nature and existence—of mental states. Notions such as consciousness and attention are shunned: "Behaviorism claims that 'consciousness' is neither a definable nor a usable concept" (Watson 1930, 1).

It is method, not ontology, that concerns the behaviorist. The data for the science of behaviorism are observables, not introspected states of mind. But what is it that is observed? According to the early methodological behaviorists, the observable data comprise environmental *stimuli* and behavioral *responses*. When we know which stimuli are correlated with which responses, we can then predict and control behavior.

Very simple models of stimulus and response are not hard to find. Prey flees at the sight of a predator; the green banana is passed over and the yellow one selected; touching hot metal is followed by the almost instantaneous withdrawal of one's hand; the bee sting is followed by wincing. As human beings confront their environment, they, like the rest of the animal world, respond almost automatically to a variety of stimuli. In cases like the touching of a hot stove, the stimulus and the response are easy to identify.

My mother once inadvertently caught our puppy's rather bushy tail in the power roller brush of a vacuum cleaner as he slept peacefully beneath my bed. After much mutual weeping, the puppy forgave my mother, but he never forgot the vacuum cleaner that once awoke him from his canine slumber. The mere appearance of the vacuum would send him in search of protection. The stimulus—the somewhat painful, certainly terrifying vacuum—is as easy to identify as the consequent response: avoidance behavior.

Human behavior, however, far exceeds simple, automatic response. What does the behaviorist offer us as an explanation of these more complicated behaviors? What stimuli, for example, are to be connected with someone taking a vacuum cleaner out of the closet and spending the next 45 minutes pushing and pulling it across a house? According to Watson, careful, repeated, detailed observation of human behavior enables us to identify the responses that are correlated with particular stimuli. Watson describes at length how we might acquire the initial raw data from which to construct the behaviorist account of human behavior. Painstakingly careful and minute observation *from infancy* would enable us to identify those features that are stimuli and their consequent responses. Such observation, together with additional laboratory data, would enable us, for each stimulus, to predict the response, and for each response, to predict (or retrodict) the stimulus.

The methodological behaviorist sees the connection between stimulus and response as governed by natural law—behavioral laws, but natural laws nonetheless. Our ability to predict and control other natural phenomena depends on our ability to ferret out the appropriate natural law. Because of our understanding of various laws, we can predict how fast a body will be traveling at impact when dropped from a ten-story building or use quartz crystals to keep accurate clocks. Behaviorism, viewed as a *science*, is no different. The prediction and control of human behavior depend on the behaviorist's ability to identify the stimulus-response laws that govern human action. Since mental concepts, which refer to unobservable states, cannot appear in natural laws, such concepts are unnecessary. They only serve to distract us from the real data that underlie the genuine science of human behavior. Mental concepts are unfortunate remnants of dualistic thinking.

The discovery of stimulus-response laws governing human behavior is a daunting task. Yet early behaviorists like Watson were nonetheless optimistic; Watson once claimed that given any twelve healthy infants, in the appropriately designed environment, he could turn them into doctors, lawyers, artists, beggars, thieves, whatever he chose (82)!

Methodological behaviorists thus argue something like the following: Mental concepts refer to unobservable states or characteristics. But genuine science is based on observation, on what we can see, touch, and hear. Thus, there is no room in science for mental concepts—concepts that pick out unobservable states. And mental concepts cannot figure in the laws of a genuine natural science.

The methodological behaviorist is willing to take a certain gamble. If the laws connecting stimuli and subsequent behavioral responses are successfully identified, then leaving out references to mental states will not matter, even if such states exist. The methodological behaviorist simply bypasses reference to anything "inner" as unnecessary: *The mental doesn't matter.*

Within barely a decade of Watson's view first appearing in 1913 in *Psychology Review*, behaviorism replaced introspectionism as the dominant approach in American psychology, and it remained so for another four decades. Behaviorism seemed to free psychology from nineteenth-century struggles with the mind–body problem, while delivering results. It promised to install psychology as a genuine science, one capable of delivering observable and reliable results (Baars 1986, chaps. 1 and 2).

While the emphasis on method and observation may seem to deliver psychology from the clutches of dualism, it is not so clear that observation alone is the hallmark of science. The success of modern science depends crucially on the employment of theoretical—nonobservational—concepts. It is not hard to see that the progress of science depends on just this leap into the theoretical. Concepts, such as "gene" or "electron," are introduced to explain various natural phenomena long before they are in any sense observable. The merit of introducing such theoretical terms is judged by several factors, including subsequent experiment, the ability of such terms to explain and predict novel phenomena, and the subsequent connections established between previously separate fields of inquiry. A science that only collects facts, but never explains, is science that moves but slowly, if at all. The engine of scientific progress is a theoretical engine.

How do these remarks bear on methodological behaviorism? Even if we grant that a mental state cannot be observed in the same way that we observe someone raising a hand or a pigeon pecking a lever, it does not follow that mental concepts have no place in a scientific psychology. In fairness to behaviorism, many sought to dispense with nonobservational concepts. Ernst Mach (1838–1916) claimed that scientific laws are but summaries of observations. Theories are only instruments, not descriptions of an unobserved reality (Jones 1969, 2:202–6; Alexander 1967). The suggestion, however, is that a "science of mind" can be scientific despite its reliance on mental concepts. A "mentalist" psychology will be judged in the same way as any other science, including methodological behaviorism: on the continued success of its explanations.

Ontological Behaviorism

Disavowing the use of mental concepts is one thing; denying the existence of mental states is another. Ontological behaviorism rejects the existence of inner mental states, and this definition seems straightforward. It can be construed as a rejection of dualism. When looked at in this way, ontological behaviorism is in the company of other physicalist theories of mind. Very few physicalists incline toward ontological behaviorism, however. So, just what is it about ontological behaviorism that leads physicalists to look elsewhere? Let's examine the theory more closely.

Although there is some controversy regarding his position, we will use B. F. Skinner (1904–1990) as an example of an ontological behaviorist. There is no controversy about Skinner's adoption of a position he called "radical behaviorism." Like the methodological behaviorist, Skinner claimed that psychology is the science of behavior, which has as its ultimate aim the prediction and control of human behavior. In a foreword to *Walden Two* (1948), the fictional account of a community guided by behaviorist ideals, Skinner suggests that behaviorism affords us the opportunity to substantially improve society. An understanding of behavioral laws is within our grasp, and these laws could permit us to shape human behavior and social structures beneficially.

B. F. Skinner

Born in Pennsylvania in 1904, Burrhus Frederic Skinner hoped to become a writer. Later he explained that he failed as a writer because he had nothing interesting to say, which stemmed from his not understanding human behavior (Richelle 1993). Reading Bertrand Russell (among others) as an undergraduate influenced Skinner's move toward behaviorism, with his serious study and research beginning in graduate school at Harvard. He developed the essentials of operant conditioning between 1930 and 1935. Skinner believed that behaviorism—and operant conditioning in particular—provides the scientific approach to human society. His *Walden Two* (1948) is sometimes characterized as a utopian novel, but Skinner clearly holds that it provides the model for a radically new—and better—approach to social institutions and communities.

Perhaps one reason for the initial popular success of behaviorism is its promise, and occasional deliverance, of results in some programs of "behavior modification," whether this involves a pigeon playing the piano or child learning not to suck his thumb. Pictures of a "Skinner box" are widely circulated: a small chamber containing a lever or similar device that an animal presses under appropriate conditions to receive a pellet of food. Project Pigeon in World War II is perhaps one of Skinner's more interesting applications of his behaviorism, training or "shaping" pigeons to pilot an armed glider. The practical application of Skinner's ideas did not stop there; for example, variants of behavior modification strategies were introduced into some prisons.

Less popularly accepted is Skinner's "reinterpretation" of concepts such as free will. Skinner claimed that it is only our ignorance that gives rise to the illusion that we are free to act or to refrain from acting. Once we are aware of the behavior effects of our environmental history, he wrote, we will better be able to avoid those actions that produce unwanted consequences.

Skinner spent the last several years of his life defending behaviorism, particularly against cognitive psychology. He died in 1990 just after finishing the paper "Can Psychology Be a Science of the Mind?"

This understanding is within our grasp, however, only if we identify the *real causes* of human behavior; Skinner wanted to understand *why* we behave as we do. But these causes are not always what we think they are. Unlike the methodological behaviorist, Skinner saw no harm in looking "inside the skin." Our internal structure, especially our genetic makeup, is important for understanding human behavior. But let us take matters more slowly.

Do You Want That Pickle? Common Sense and the Mental

Think for a moment about why our commonsense view counts mental states or properties as real. Two reasons seem obvious. The first is the role of mental states in the causation of behavior. Take as an example: You and I are sitting in a diner. My dinner finished, I still *feel* hungry. I spy a delectable but untouched pickle on your plate. I *want* or *desire* that pickle. I *believe* that if I ask—politely, of course—I just might be the proud consumer of that pickle. Finally, at an appropriate moment, I ask, "Do you want that pickle?" These mental states have *caused* my behavior. If I did not *want* the pickle, if I did not *believe* that asking would be an effective means of obtaining it, I would not have asked.

To say that the mental has causal powers or plays a causal role is just to say that the mental brings about certain behaviors; the mental *does things*. Of course, the causal powers of mental states are not restricted to retrieving pickles. Mental causes are a pervasive feature of our daily lives. Moreover, we might note that one need not be a dualist in order to attribute causal roles to mental states. It is easy enough to imagine that causally effective mental states are in some way brain states. In the next two chapters, we will look at such views in greater detail. For now, you are simply asked to count as plausible the claim that a physicalist might think that mental states are sometimes among the causes of behavior.

Our folk psychological view also recognizes the reality of sensations. Upon bumping your shin against a coffee table, you experience a sharp sensation, a pain sensation. Or, in the produce aisle at the supermarket, you reach past the green bananas for a bright yellow one. Sensations of colors, sounds, warmth or cold, and pain are genuine parts of our inner mental lives.

Sensations and intentional states are unmistakable features of our mental life, in our commonsense view. Their existence appears as real to us as a pickle, the blameworthy coffee table, or the yellow banana. Why then does the ontological behaviorist reject the existence of such states?

All Roads Lead Out: Skinner's View of the Real Causes of Behavior

The ontological behaviorist claims that common sense misidentifies the causes of our behavior. The real causes, she would say, are found in our environmental history and our internal, physical structure. More specifically, the ontologi-cal behaviorist holds that there are *only behavioral facts*; there are no distinc-tively mental facts. But what might be meant by such a claim? Here it is in-structive to consider Skinner's revision of the simplified stimulus–response model of behavior.

Skinner claimed that *operant conditioning* is the key notion for under-standing why we act the way that we do. He acknowledged that we contin-ually encounter stimuli from our environment. Some of these stimuli pro-duce a response; some do not. Skinner extended this simple model by claiming that our behaviors *operate* on our environment, thus modifying cer-tain of its features. When this happens, depending on circumstances, such behaviors are either positively or negatively reinforced. Our behaviors are thus *conditioned*, depending on the positive or negative reinforcement.

A person's entire environmental history—the cumulative effects of prior conditioning—determines which behaviors a person is likely to undertake. Deirdre listens to Brahms, not because she innately *likes* Brahms—not be-cause of some internal mental state—but because of the effects of her past conditioning (for example, her initial encounters with Brahms were in pleas-ant circumstances). The real cause of her behavior—reaching for Brahms rather than Nirvana—is to be found in her environmental history. Skinner claimed that we count mental states as causes because we are ignorant of the real causes; we invent fictional causes because we do not fully grasp our en-vironmental history or this past conditioning (1974, chaps. 1 and 9).

Skinner counted our internal structure as relevant only as far as it em-bodies our genetic makeup. He believed that our genetic makeup—a product of natural selection—"biases" us toward certain types of conditioning. Now, you might be tempted to make the following response to Skinner. Since in-ternal structure makes a difference to our behavior, isn't it reasonable to sup-pose that our *brains* make a difference in our behavior? And if our brains make a difference, then perhaps we can "locate" mental states in our brain. After all, the (simplified) neuroscientific story of Deirdre reaching for a CD of Brahms is that her brain has sent an electrochemical signal through her nervous system, which resulted in her hand grasping the Brahms. And why not, while we are telling this (simplified) neuroscientific story, "locate" Deirdre's liking of Brahms—a mental state—somewhere in her brain? Wouldn't this explanation, one which neuroscientists could elaborate in much greater detail, save the notion of mental states and mental causes?

Skinner was fairly explicit about this neuroscientific attempt to save men-tal causes. He claimed that understanding the real causes of behavior "clari-fies the assignment of the neurosciences, *saving the time that would otherwise be wasted in searching for the neurological counterparts of sensations, stored memories, and thought processes"* (1987, 76; emphasis added). Skinner's opposition to the mental cannot be construed as merely an opposition to dualism; he also rejected any attempt to save the mental by turning to physicalism.

Just as he portrayed mental states as fictions, revealing nothing about genuine behavioral causes, so Skinner adopted a similarly dismissive attitude toward sensations: We identify sensations as internal mental states only because we are ignorant of the complex set of stimuli, both internal and external, that affect our current condition (1974, chaps. 4–5).

Central to ontological behaviorism is the rejection of inner mental states and properties, whether these are the familiar beliefs and desires, or feelings or sensations. The motive for this rejection is not rooted solely in the opposition to dualism. The ontological behaviorist holds that the mental is at best a metaphorical and at worst a fictional account of behavior, rooted in our ignorance of the real causes, which are to be found in the behavioral history of a person. We should not search for mental facts to explain human behavior, for that is a fool's errand. The only facts are behavioral.

Have We Found the Real Causes of Behavior?

Questions arise, however, about whether we ought to accept a view that dismisses the mental in favor of environmental, genetic, and behavioral facts. Three issues concern us here: that the causes of behavior are environmental causes, the explanatory value of mental states, and the connection between behavior and the mental.

We are mistaken, according to ontological behaviorism, if we think that, for example, the cause of Danny's going to the movie is his desire to see the new *Star Wars* movie. It is also a mistake to think that the cause might be some complicated brain state. We must still explain the cause of such inner physiological states. And this leads inevitably, the ontological behaviorist insists, to environmental causes (Skinner 1953, 23–25). Explaining why Danny has this particular brain state (the movie-going brain state) requires looking to the history of Danny's interaction with the environment. We will know the *real* cause of Danny's going to the movie when we "know what has happened when he has gone to the theater in the past, what he heard or read . . . what other things in his past or present environments might have induced him to go" (Skinner 1972, 13).

No one denies the influence of past experience on current behavior. My present behavior—using a sophisticated word-processing program—is undoubtedly influenced by past history, including my father's insistence many years ago that I take a typing class. It does not follow, however, that the existence of antecedent causes of my desire to finish this chapter undermines the causal role of the desire. There are antecedent causes of my striking a match to light a candle—my walking to the kitchen to get matches, for example. Should we claim, then, striking a match is not a cause because I walked to the kitchen? More generally, the claim that environmental history causally influences present behavior does not imply that inner mental states are not also causes.

The deeper worry for the ontological behaviorist, however, is whether the appeal to mental states is genuinely explanatory (Skinner 1953, 23–25). Citing a mental state or a sensation as a cause of behavior only forestalls the real explanation. Of course, we need to know in what sense appealing to the mental fails to give the real explanation.

Consider two ways that mentalist explanations might fail. First, we might fail to give the real explanation by citing a fictional cause. If I claim that my gladiolas are not blooming this year because I have been cursed by a witch who lives down the street, I have failed to give the real explanation. A second way in which we might fail to provide the real explanation is by appealing to the very thing we are to explain. The classic illustration is from the French playwright Molière: The powder makes one fall asleep because it has a "sleeping power," a power to make one fall asleep. This "explanation" merely invites us to ask the question again.

Skinner, as we have seen, claimed that mentalist explanations rely on fictional states. But he also worried that intentional explanations presuppose the concepts to be explained. If we want to explain intelligent behavior, appealing to beliefs and desires seems to presuppose that a person is rational—which seems to return us to the notion of intelligent behavior, the concept we wanted to explain.

Should we accept the claim that mental states are but fictional states and turn rather to examination of environmental history? We might have reason to do so if either (1) our mentalist explanations frequently lead us astray or (2) behaviorists can provide alternative, more compelling explanations. Neither of these conditions is clearly satisfied, however. Although our commonsense explanations are fallible, they provide reliable predictive guides to the actions of human beings. If Danny sees Deirdre accidentally drop a five-dollar bill, he can reasonably expect that she will want it back and act in such a way so as to retrieve the bill. On the other hand, we seem to lack the detailed environmental histories envisioned by the behaviorist. At best, we have incomplete and inconclusive behavioral histories. While it is true that we sometimes cite aspects of individuals' behavioral histories to explain their behavior, we tend to view these as supplements to our typical folk psychological explanations, not as competitors. Consequently, we need not accept the claim that folk psychological explanations are faulty because they rely on fictional causes. If we are to reject the idea that the mental causes behavior, we must find some more compelling reason.

The Problem of Novel Behaviors

Recall that the behaviorist worries that mentalist explanations are question-begging accounts of intelligent behavior. In other words, the behaviorist suspects that appealing to beliefs and desires is but another way of saying that the behavior is intelligent: Deirdre grabs the apple because she desires food and believes the apple will do the trick. This explanation works only if we already assume that, to put it less than delicately, Deirdre isn't dumb. That is to say, the explanation works only if we assume that Deirdre is rational—that she's intelligent.

The behaviorist, as a natural scientist, wants to break out of this circle of mental terms; otherwise, we will not understand any more than we did at the outset. We are promised, however, that the behavioral explanation will lead us to the real causes. If we follow the behaviorist path, we will know more than when we started. By now, it should not surprise you that the behaviorist path leads to a person's environmental history. But does this path really provide us with the actual causes of behavior?

Daniel Dennett (1978) argues that the appeal to environmental history does not really tell us anything important. Dennett observes that were he held up and asked for his wallet, he would hand it over, despite never before having encountered this type of situation. Dennett is no dummy; he knows the intelligent thing to do when he sees it. Handing over his wallet when it is demanded of him is, for Dennett, a *novel behavior*. This specific type of behavioral response—handing over his wallet to a mugger—cannot have been reinforced.

Nevertheless, according to the behaviorist, Dennett is giving up his wallet not because he *believes* the thief is menacing and he *desires* not to be harmed, but because this behavior has somehow been produced by Dennett's previous environmental history. Certain aspects of his environmental history are sufficiently relevant to this situation and have been reinforced in ways that now cause him to surrender his wallet. That is, although there are no stick-ups in Dennett's history, there are "stick 'em up"–relevant events that were reinforced in "stick 'em up"–relevant ways, so as to now produce the wallet-surrendering behavior. The behaviorist must infer the existence of such types of reinforcement.

So, Dennett asks, what explanation will an accosted behaviorist offer for surrendering his wallet? The reply must be, "Because I must have had in the past some experiences that reinforced wallet-handing-over behavior in circumstances like this" (Dennett 1978, 67–68). But as Dennett observes, this is not much better than the "sleeping powers" explanation. In answer to the question, "Why does Dennett turn over his wallet?" we are told that his environmental history reinforced his turning over his wallet. That it is so easy to replicate such explanations suggests that the behaviorist explanation is also question-begging: At last we know why the chicken crossed the road—because its environmental history reinforced road-crossing behavior. But do you know any more than you did before? The problem of novel behaviors suggests, at least, that the behavioral explanations are no better off than our commonsense explanations of behavior.

Ontological behaviorism urges a radical departure from our folk-psychological ways. We have not seen, however, compelling reason to reject our familiar mental life. We can reasonably doubt that mental states are mere fictions and that environmental-behavioral explanations provide the best account of our behavior. Our history of interactions with the environment may influence our current behavior, but we need not give up the idea that mental states also play a causal role.

Logical Behaviorism

Arising in the early decades of the twentieth century, logical behaviorism is a distinctly philosophical cousin of the views we have seen. It holds that any sentence containing mental terms can be translated into a sentence containing terms that refer only to behavior. "Danny wants a cupcake" is but an abbreviation of a more complicated sentence that mentions only Danny's behavior or his behavioral tendencies. One of the earliest, definitive accounts of this theory was provided by Carl Hempel (1980). In *The Concept of Mind* (1949), Gilbert Ryle (1900–1982) articulated a version of logical behaviorism (although some of his work seems at odds with behaviorism; cf. Ryle 1951). Some also interpret the later works of Ludwig Wittgenstein (1889–1951) as espousing a view at least compatible with logical behaviorism.

The conceptual motivation for logical behaviorism is best seen against the philosophical background of logical positivism and the verification theory of meaning.

Verification and Behaviorism

In the 1920s, **logical positivism** emerged as a distinct view of the nature of philosophy. It claims that the principal task of philosophy is *linguistic analysis*. Terms—whether scientific, philosophical, ethical, or religious—are legitimate only if they can be appropriately clarified or analyzed. The positivists adopted the **verification criterion of meaning**: A contingent sentence is cognitively meaningful if and only if it is verifiable or falsifiable by some set of experiences. Although we may not actually be able to verify or falsify a sentence, we can at least formulate the conditions that would serve to show that some set of experiences would verify or falsify it. Sentences that are insusceptible to verification or falsification are meaningless. For example, "There are elephants in my backyard" is meaningful because there is some set of experiences—observations of the backyard—that would show that this sentence is either true or false. On the other hand, "God exists" is meaningless, since no obvious set of experiences could show the sentence to be either true or false.

The theoretical sentences of science—those containing terms such as "electron"—also count as meaningful since, in principle, we can identify a set of procedures for determining their truth or falsity. On the other hand, a psychology that relies on mental terms—belief, sensation, image—is suspect, since it might be linked to the unverifiable claims of dualism. This psychology could be put on an equal footing with other sciences, however, if its claims could be legitimated—if any sentence containing the suspect terms could be translated or analyzed into sentences that refer only to physical states or properties. Logical behaviorism identifies the "acceptable terms" as behavioral terms, terms that refer to behavior. Mental terms are simply abbreviations or shorthand descriptions of more complicated behavioral expressions. Since the mental terms can be redescribed in purely physical terms, without loss of meaning, logical behaviorism is sometimes characterized as a *reductionistic* view. Mental terms are reduced to purely behavioral terms.

We can put this more simply. Aided by the verification criterion, psychology is a legitimate science. Translating mental terms into behavioral terms allays a perhaps dark suspicion that the use of a term such as "mind" is only a covert and *unverifiable* reference to soul, or ghostlike substance, or some other equally illegitimate nonphysical substance or characteristic. Happily, it turns out that talk of minds or mental states is all right. What we really *meant* by "Polly wants a cracker" is something about Polly's behavior.

How You Learned to Talk about the Mind:
An Argument for Logical Behaviorism

But could this be what we really meant? Why think that the sentence "Deirdre believes that Danny wants to go to the movie" is really a sentence about behavior? The logical behaviorist thinks there is a plausible answer.

A typical story is that we teach a child the meaning of certain words by pointing to examples, pointing to a red shirt or red book or red ball to teach the concept "red." Children's books commonly contain pictures along with the word: below a picture of a cow is the word "cow"; below a picture of a chicken is "chicken." Now imagine that a child wakes up crying in the middle of the night, telling us that some creature, a giant chicken, say, was chasing him. We tell the child that he was having a bad *dream*. Or imagine a child that is crying because she has accidentally fallen and scraped a knee. We tell her that this spray will make the hurt—the *pain*—go away. We notice a child, face contorted, chewing slowly, almost painfully, and we ask, "Don't you *like* broccoli?" We can imagine similar stories for teaching children various feelings or moods such as sadness or anger.

The important point of these simplified reconstructions of language learning is that the *meaning* of a mental term is tied to certain behavioral conditions. The implicit argument is the following. Learning a term depends on learning the appropriate conditions for using that term. Similarly, learning the meaning of mental terms requires learning the appropriate *behavioral* conditions for using the terms. Thus, the meaning of a mental term is given by those characteristic behavioral conditions.

Despite some intuitive appeal, this argument faces challenges. Critics argue that a child's linguistic ability can hardly be traced to a few isolated instances of "attaching" a term to some physical circumstance (Fodor 1968, chap. 2). Along similar lines, one might question whether a term's meaning is to be identified with its "use conditions," how it is used in various circumstances (Devitt and Sterelny 1999, chap. 9).

Dispositions and the Mental

"I can't talk right now because I am expecting someone for dinner." If the logical behaviorist is right, then we should expect there to be a translation of this very ordinary sentence that makes no use of the mental term "expecting." Indeed we should expect that for any sentence containing mental terms, there is an appropriate behavioral translation. Sentences as common as "Danny likes Deirdre" or "I hope we get there on time" should have their behavioral equivalents.

The logical behaviorist notices first that mental terms are connected to tendencies or *dispositions* to act in certain ways. If Deirdre *wants* an apple, she tends to reach for one; if Danny *believes* it is raining, he tends to pick up his umbrella. Skinner, who occasionally utilized a version of logical behaviorism, described belief as a "probability of action." Notice, however, that mental terms may be connected to different behaviors. If I am expecting someone, I may look at my watch or engage in a bit of housecleaning. If I am in pain, I may grimace, take a pill, or remain stoically silent. Based on a suggestion by

Ryle (1949), we might call such behavioral dispositions "multitracked" (see also Churchland 1988). A mental state term might refer to any number of dispositions to act.

Ryle thought that this dispositional account of the mental precludes us from making the category mistake of thinking that there is some inner mental state that is the cause of our actions. Consider the following example: Danny brings Deirdre flowers because he *likes* her. In the logical behaviorist view, Danny's liking Deirdre is but a complicated set of behavioral tendencies. There is no inner mental state that might be identified as the causal source of Danny's bringing Deirdre flowers. Thus, like methodological and ontological behaviorism, logical behaviorism teaches that searching for the inner mental causes of behavior is a lost cause.

There are two initial problems with this approach. First, it is conceivable that some mental state may not have any associated dispositions. A person may have a belief or desire for which there is no behavioral disposition. Hilary Putnam (1963) asks us to imagine a race of superbeings who experience pain without ever giving any behavioral clue. It is not that they *resist* the inclination to wince or moan. For them, the sensation of pain is simply not connected to any behavioral tendency.

A second problem for logical behaviorism emerges when we realize that we will need a rather long list of conditions to fill in the "conditions C" clause. For example, a good many things will have to be true in order for Danny to eat Jamoca® Almond Fudge ice cream (assuming that eating the ice cream is the characteristic behavior associated with wanting it): The ice cream will need to be available; Danny must believe that it is available; he must not want to disguise this desire for ice cream; he must not have any conflicting desires, e.g., wanting to lose weight; and so on. A little imagination could continue the list indefinitely. Now, this is not fatal to logical behaviorism, but it is at least disconcerting. We are told by the logical behaviorist that mental state terms can be translated into sentences containing only references to dispositions. Yet when we ask to see a candidate translation for a sentence as mundane as "I want Jamoca® Almond Fudge ice cream," we are told that the translation may be indefinitely long. Indeed, it is worth noting that logical behaviorism has never yet provided a single, complete translation.

But there is an even more serious worry. In spelling out the brief list of conditions, we used mental terms, such as belief and desire. But the logical behaviorist cannot comfortably allow such terms into the reducing sentence (the behavioral translation of the original sentence). Logical behaviorism promises to show us how to avoid such terms. The worry about the logical behaviorist's explanation of mental concepts solely by descriptions of dispositions to act is that such descriptions will inevitably rely on mental or intentional concepts—and every behavioral translation of those concepts will involve still more mental terms. The project of translation seems never-ending!

Matters may be still worse, however. The key notion is that of behavior or actions. But think of how we typically identify actions. We count some bodily movements as actions, but ignore others. Reflex movements (e.g., rapidly withdrawing your hand from a hot stove) or stumbling are paradigm cases of bodily movements that are not actions. Which movements we notice and which we ignore depends on the beliefs and desires we attribute to a person.

Consider again a simple example: "Danny likes Deirdre." We need a translation of the mental term "likes" into behavioral dispositions, and we know that such dispositions are multitracked—the disposition shows up in various different behaviors. Let us follow but one of the tracks; let us suppose that on occasion Danny manifests his affection by *pretending to ignore* Deirdre. Precisely which of Danny's bodily movements count as part of the pretending? The crossing of his legs, the scratching of his shoulder, the tugging at his shirt, the minute inspection of the plant next to the bench he's sitting on, or the quick, sideward glance as she walks by? We can make sense of some or all of these movements as components of a complicated behavioral disposition only against a background of mental and intentional concepts. It is *because* we attribute to Danny certain beliefs, desires, likes, and hopes that we are able to identify particular bodily movements as "pretending to ignore Deirdre." We need to make use of mental concepts in order to pick out the relevant behaviors. The mental explanation explains the "behavioral dispositions," not the other way around!

This dependence of the identification of behaviors on a background of mental attributions seems completely general. It is not only Danny-likes-Deirdre that is problematic; it would appear that this is true of *any* attempted translation of mental terms into behavioral terms. We will *always* need to use mental concepts to explain why we select particular bodily movements as the relevant behaviors. Simply, there seems to be no escape from the use of mental concepts.

The considerations in this section seem to show that logical behaviorism faces perhaps insuperable difficulty in carrying out its task. There seems little reason to expect that mental terms can be fairly translated into purely behavioral terms. Not only are such translations or reductions unwieldy, they inevitably depend on the very terms and concepts they are intended to translate.

So . . . There Are No More Behaviorists?

We have hinted that behaviorism no longer occupies the dominant position in psychology that it once did, but psychologists are still seriously engaged in the study of behavior.

Later chapters note that the rise of interest in neuroscience and artificial intelligence, along with the development of cognitive psychology—briefly, the view that mental processes are information transforming processes—signaled the retreat of behaviorism. Two conferences, in 1948 and 1956, were watershed moments in the advance of cognitive psychology as the leading theoretical approach in psychology.

A number of psychologists consider *operant psychology* to be a fruitful approach for studying human behavior. Operant psychologists look for regularities and laws that connect features of the environment with behavior, formulating hypotheses and experiments in order to identify such regularities. Many characteristic notions of behaviorism—stimulus, response, and reinforcement—are still used.

Operant psychologists differ in part from behaviorist B. F. Skinner by suggesting a division of labor. On the one hand, operant psychology looks for the laws that connect environment and behavior. On the other hand, cognitive psychology attempts to explain how these causes produce their effects, and that explanation consists of identifying the relevant mental processes. To put it simply, operant psychology says *what* happens and cognitive psychology explains *how* it happens. (It should be noted that not all operant psychologists are so conciliatory toward cognitive psychology.)

A significant number of operant psychologists no longer believe that Skinner's attempt to identify a set of "basic behaviors" is a viable project, and "schedule analysis" (Skinner's preferred method) reached its zenith in the late 1950s. In the operant psychologist's view, operant psychology and cognitive psychology are complementary disciplines. (This brief sketch was based on Smith 1994.)

While there are still behaviorists and operant psychologists, it is unlikely that behaviorism will recapture the dominance of its first fifty years.

Behaviorism, Behavior, and the Mental

Descartes once wondered whether the people he saw in the street, behaving as though they had a mental life, might be nothing more than automatons—robots. Years of science fiction movies and television shows have yet to persuade many people that a computerized robot—whether R2D2 of *Star Wars* fame or Data of *Star Trek: The Next Generation*—even one that behaves much as we would under similar conditions, is a minded creature. But if this notion that behavior could exist without a mind is coherent, then behavior alone is not enough to guarantee the existence of the mental: Behavior is not *sufficient* for the mental.

Now, consider a somewhat different situation. Imagine a mind that is wholly separate from a physical body—a mind having thoughts and feelings, pangs of desire and wishes for the future, none of which ever issue in behavior. If dualism is right, then behavior is not *necessary* for the mental. It is possible to have a mind but no behavior (Byrne 1994).

These little exercises should leave us wondering: Just what is the connection between the mental and behavior? After all, we rely on this connection all the time.

Logical behaviorism would have us believe that the connection is conceptual. For any mental event, we can always dispense with talking about it by means of a description of behavioral tendencies. But if we no longer trust the logical behaviorist to supply us with the requisite descriptions, this suggests that we must look elsewhere for the connection.

Behaviorism at times seems counterintuitive; it seems to run too much against common sense. Perhaps we can then turn to common sense for some help: What does common sense say about the connection between the mental and behavior? We don't have to look far.

Danny takes a chocolate out of the box, takes a bite, puts it back, takes another, bites it, puts it back . . . repeating this procedure—annoyingly, no doubt—until finally he takes a bite, smiles, and savors the rest of that piece, as if he were being feted at a five-star restaurant. Why did Danny act this way? Why did he *behave* this way? *Because* he *likes* it! His behavior comes about *because* he *likes* this kind of chocolate and not the others. Common sense seems to suggest that the connection is causal.

Now we can see more clearly why common sense and behaviorism appear at odds. It is the causal connection between the mental and behavior that the behaviorist—whether it is Watson, Skinner, or Ryle—most wishes to dismiss. And yet it is this same causal connection that animates so much of the commonsense view—our familiar folk-psychological view—of the mind.

Mental states are particular items that play a causal role. We would like some further explanation of how this causal connection comes about. Worries about its dismissive view of mental causes inclines us against behaviorism. There are other worries about behaviorism, certainly, but this is a central worry. But it would be interesting to explore a theory of the mind that promises an account of the causal role of the mental.

Behavior is connected to the mental. We exploit this connection all the time. But it is unlikely that there is the tight connection supposed by behaviorism. It is even less likely that the mental might be dismissed in favor of behavior.

Key Concepts

Logical behaviorism

Methodological behaviorism

Ontological behaviorism

Verification criterion of meaning

Reading Questions

1. Why does methodological behaviorism argue that psychology should ignore mental states? Should science rely only on observational terms?

2. What is the difference between methodological and ontological behaviorism?

3. Why does Skinner think that ultimately the causes of behavior are environmental?

4. What is the problem of novel behaviors?

5. What is logical behaviorism's view of mental terms?

6. Explain two criticisms of logical behaviorism.

References

Alexander, Peter. 1967. Ernst Mach. In *The encyclopedia of philosophy*, ed. Paul Edwards, 5:115–19. New York: Macmillan.

Baars, Bernard J. 1986. *The cognitive revolution in psychology*. New York: Guilford Press.

Block, Ned, ed. 1980. *Readings in the philosophy of psychology*. Vol. 1. Cambridge, MA: Harvard University Press.

Byrne, Alex. 1994. Behaviorism. In *A companion to the philosophy of mind*, ed. Samuel Guttenplan, 132–40. Oxford: Blackwell.

Churchland, Paul. 1988. *Matter and consciousness*. Rev. ed. Cambridge, MA: MIT Press.

Dennett, Daniel C. 1978. Skinner skinned. In *Brainstorms: Philosophical essays on mind and psychology*, 53–70. Montgomery, VT: Bradford Books.

Devitt, Michael, and Kim Sterelny. 1999. *Language and philosophy*. 2nd ed. Cambridge, MA: MIT Press.

Fodor, Jerry. 1968. *Psychological explanation: An introduction to the philosophy of psychology*. New York: Random House.

Hempel, Carl. 1980. The logical analysis of psychology. In Block 1980, 14–23. (First published in French, 1935.)

Jones, W. T. 1969. *A history of Western philosophy*. 4 vols. 2nd ed. New York: Harcourt, Brace and World.

Putnam, Hilary. 1963. Brains and behavior. In *Analytical Philosophy*, ed. R. J. Butler. New York: Barnes & Noble. Reprinted in Hilary Putnam, *Mind, language, and reality: Philosophical papers* (Cambridge: Cambridge University Press), 2:325–41, and in Block 1980, 24–36.

Richelle, Marc N. 1993. *B. F. Skinner: A reappraisal*. East Sussex, England: Lawrence Erlbaum.

Ryle, Gilbert. 1949. *The concept of mind*. London: Hutchinson.

———. 1951. Feelings. *Philosophical Quarterly* 1:193–205.

Skinner, B. F. 1948. *Walden two*. New York: Macmillan. Reprinted with a new introduction by the author. New York: Macmillan, 1976.

———. 1953. *Science and human behavior*. New York: Macmillan.

———. 1972. *Beyond freedom and dignity*. New York: Alfred A. Knopf.

———. 1974. *About behaviorism*. New York: Alfred A. Knopf.

———. 1987. Behaviorism, Skinner on. In *The Oxford companion to the mind*, ed. Richard L. Gregory, 74–76. Oxford: Oxford University Press.

Smith, Terry L. 1994. *Behavior and its causes: Philosophical foundations of operant psychology*. Dordrecht, The Netherlands: Kluwer Academic Publishers.

Viney, Wayne. 1993. *A history of psychology: Ideas and context*. Boston: Allyn and Bacon.

Watson, John B. 1930. *Behaviorism*. Rev. ed. Chicago: University of Chicago Press.

3

It's All in Your Brain: Type Identity Theory

Identification of the mental with the physical is not unique to the late twentieth century. Galen, a second-century physician, suspected that the brain is responsible for thought and sensation. The seventeenth-century English philosopher Thomas Hobbes (1588–1679) claimed that mental activities are complex motions in the body, especially in the circulatory and nervous systems; in light of research over the last few decades, this identification may seem to some perfectly natural. Perhaps of some historical interest, what is now known as "identity theory" has its beginnings in a series of conversations between J. J. C. Smart and U. T. Place, who were dissatisfied with the logical behaviorism of Gilbert Ryle. A trio of articles in the 1950s by Herbert Feigl, Place, and Smart brought prominence to a version of physicalism known as "type identity theory" (Feigl 1970; Place 1970; Smart 1959).

Identity theory acknowledges the reality of the mental and seeks to preserve many of our commonsense intuitions about the mental within a physicalist framework. There is nothing more to the mind, according to identity theorists, than what there is to the brain. This chapter examines type identity theory and its account of the relation of the mental to the physical.

Promises: How the Brain Does It

Is there any *empirical* reason to think that—as identity theory promises—whenever we find some mental state type, we can always find the relevant brain state type? Let's take a quick look at current neuroscience, which has as one of its tasks identifying the functions of different types of brain structure.

The brain is an amazingly complicated organ. Weighing in at about two pounds, it nonetheless performs an astounding array of functions. The basic building block of the brain is the *neuron*. Characteristic of neurons are the spiny, tentacle-like appendages extending from the cell body, the *soma*. The "receiving" end appendages are *dendrites* and the "sending" end are *axons*. It is through the dendrites and axons that individual neurons communicate with other neurons. When one neuron sends a signal to another, it releases *neurotransmitters*, such as dopamine, from its axons. The neurotransmitters travel across the *synaptic cleft*—a microscopic fluid channel—and "dock" or attach to the dendrites of the second neuron, either exciting or inhibiting it. If excited, the neuron increases its "voltage potential," in essence becoming more highly charged, causing it to send neurotransmitters to still other neurons. Most researchers estimate there are around 100 billion neurons in the brain; consequently, the number of possible connections among neurons is astoundingly large, surpassing trillions.

Neurons are roughly classified as motor neurons, sensory neurons, and neurons whose job it is to pass on signals (sometimes called "interneurons"). Groups of neurons are organized into identifiable "sheets." These sheets are in turn stacked on top of one another, forming the more familiar main areas of the brain. Perhaps the most famous of these structures is the cerebral cortex, a very thin layer of neurons extending over the front and sides of the brain. The cerebral cortex, responsible for the higher-order cognitive functions such as thought, comprises approximately 10 billion neurons. If we could lay out the cerebral cortex, it would cover an area about the size and thickness of a large table napkin.

Divided into two roughly symmetrical halves or hemispheres, different parts of the brain appear dedicated to different functions, such as the somatosensory cortex, responsible for movement and coordinating perception, and the visual (or striate) cortex, which is responsible for processing visual information.

One of the more studied operations of the brain is vision. If you look at a red book, what happens in the brain? Depending on the length and intensity of the light waves striking the eye's retina, various cells in the retina—rods and cones—are activated. The pattern of activated cells forms a "retinal map" of the book. A complicated signal, preserving the features of this map, is then sent along the optic nerve. This major nerve extends from the retina, through the lateral geniculate nucleus (LGN), a sort of processing station, to the back of the brain where the visual cortex is located. Here is where the real work is done, after the signal reaches this part of the brain.

The visual cortex is divided into areas known as V1, V2, V3, V4, and V5 (recent studies suggest there may even be more). Area V1 acts as a kind of receptionist and director, receiving signals and sending the appropriate parts of the signals to the appropriate areas of the visual cortex. For example, some of our hypothetical signal (the red book) is sent to area V4, which is dedicated to color and colored forms (in this case recognizing a red rectangular shape). A particular type of damage to V4 produces a condition in which persons see only in shades of gray (this condition differs from the more ordinary type of what we think of as "color blindness," which is generally due to abnormalities in the eye). Seeing something red activates structures in V4, and seeing a red rectangle activates different neural structures than, say, seeing a red circle.

How does this serve the type identity theorist's cause? When you and I see a red book, we have the same type of visual experience—that of a red, rectangular object. Now, you and I have the same general brain structure, that is, the same *types* of structure, such as the LGN and area V1. They accomplish the same task by functioning in the same way. Thus, when you and I see a red book, according to the identity theorist, our type of visual experience is just a type of brain state (or brain activity)—the activation of a type of neural structure in V4.

Of course, identity theory claims that just as we identify the visual experience of a red rectangle with a certain *type* of activated neural structure, neuroscience can find the relevant neural type for any mental state type. We are undeniably a long way from knowing the relevant neural type for, say, believing that John Adams was the second president of the United States. Neuroscience has, however, advanced in areas other than vision. There is reason to believe that damage to an area of the cerebral cortex known as the prefrontal cortex causes defects in working (short-term) memory. On the other hand, the hippocampus seems implicated in long-term memory—the ability to remember things for more than just a few minutes; damage to the hippocampus leaves patients in a world that is literally confined to the here and now. Neuroscience also teaches us that certain defects in the lower, back portion of the brain produce color anomia: patients can experience and match colors, but they are unable to name them correctly.

Type identity theory promises that the task of identifying the more complex neural types for beliefs or desires is in principle no different from identifying the neural type that is seeing a red book or naming a color. This quick and sketchy account of how the brain "does it" illustrates a legitimate empirical basis for type identity theory. But whether it can deliver on its larger promise is, of course, another matter. (This sketch draws from Churchland 1988, Damasio and Damasio 1993, Edelman 1992, Fischbach 1993, Flanagan 1992, and Zeki 1993.)

Outline of a Theory

Identity of Mental and Physical

According to **type identity theory** (for convenience, in this chapter, we will often refer to it simply as "identity theory"), every kind of mental phenomenon, whether a thought, feeling, mood, or sensation, is just a kind of brain process. Thus, any *kind* of mental property is identical to a *kind* of brain property. Very roughly, then, identity theory claims that we have two ways of talking about minds: We can refer to (1) beliefs and desires, sensations and moods, or, if we choose to be more precise, we can talk about (2) brain processes or the activity of neural structures.

These different vocabularies should not mislead us, however. We are not talking about two different things. We have rather two theories, one folk-psychological and the other neuroscientific, each describing the same states and processes. Of course, the identity theorist thinks that the neuroscientific theory is the more basic of the two. Understanding the operations of the brain provides us with a greater understanding of minds and their processes, thus deepening our understanding of the mind. And it does so without losing any of the important aspects of the mind. Our commonsense view reveals certain essential features of the mental, and these are retained—although in a different vocabulary—in our more rigorous neuroscientific account.

Thus, *we have two theories, but only one thing; and our neuroscientific view is the more powerful of the two.* In this view, then, we are led to the real nature of the mind—it's physical. And we know how to learn more about the mind—learn about the brain.

Types and Tokens

Type identity theory claims that *types* of mental states and properties are identical to *types* of brain states and properties. Any particular thing may be considered as an instance, or a *token*, of any number of kinds, or *types*. Consider my pencil. What *type* of thing is it; that is, what *kind* of thing is it? Well, it's a pencil, certainly; but it's also a writing instrument, a wooden object, and a "thing that belongs to me." This particular pencil, the one on the table, is an instance or a token of each of these types. So, a **type** is specified by citing a characteristic or property or a group of properties. For example, "golf course" picks out a type. A **token** of this type is any particular thing that has the specified properties. Thus, a token of "golf course" is the 40 or so acres in the canyon of manicured grass, pockets of sand, and meandering streams. Moreover, there are other tokens of this type scattered throughout Southern California, and probably there are some tokens of "golf course" near you.

Now consider, for example, a particular type of mental property: "tastes sweet." There are many different tokens of this type—the sensation I had when eating melon yesterday or the sensation I had when tasting sugar this evening. Similarly you also have undoubtedly recently experienced this type of sensation. Each of these various occurrences is a token of the type "tastes sweet." Thus, you and I have different tokens of the same mental type. Type identity theory claims that this mental property type—tastes sweet—is identical to a type of brain process. You reach for a red, crunchy apple and take a bite, and have the sensation of sweet. This sensation is a token of the type "tastes sweet."

The identity theorist insists on the following rough story. When you bite the apple, a type of complicated process occurs in your central nervous system, which culminates in a kind of brain activity. Here we come across two essential claims of the type identity theorist. First, that type of brain activity (or that type of activity of your central nervous system) *is the same as that type of sensation we call "tastes sweet."* In a very real sense, having a certain type of sensation is *nothing more than* having a certain type of brain activity. Second, it does not matter whether it is you or me, Danny or Deirdre, Sam or Sara having the sensation. If you and I have the same type of sensation, then we have the same type of brain activity. In principle, according to type identity theory, we can discover the type of brain activity that is identical to *any* type of mental property. This is a bold view, breathtaking in its simplicity.

How We Learn about the Identity

Type identity theorists claim that we learn about the relevant identities in a somewhat different manner. We learn of "conceptual identities" through an understanding of the concepts or terms, determining the identity of two putatively different things by a conceptual or an a priori investigation, not through empirical investigation. Mathematics provides us with a host of examples of this sort. For example, we determine the truth of the identity "$\sqrt{25} = 5$" simply by reflecting on the concepts or by understanding the meaning of the involved terms. What we ordinarily think of as definitions provides another example. "All brothers are male siblings" asserts an identity between brothers and male siblings. There is no need to survey a representative sample of brothers and ask if they are also male siblings. Understanding the concepts is enough to know that this assertion is true.

However, we seem to find out about the identity of mental types with neural types in a different way. Reflection on the concept of the sensation "magenta" does not obviously lead to the concept of some complex neurological property. Nor for that matter is there an obvious conceptual connection between the concepts of oscillations in the cortex and visual awareness (as has recently been suggested by two prominent scientists).

Type identity theorists claim that we learn of the identity of mental types with physical types *empirically*—through empirical investigation, not through some a priori investigation. Science provides other examples of identities discoverable *a posteriori*. We learn through empirical investigation, for example, that clouds are large collections of water droplets, that static electricity is a stream of electrons, or that water is H_2O. We do not discover the identity of clouds and water droplets by reflecting on the concept of "cloud" any more than mere reflection on the meaning of "water" reveals its unique chemical composition. Nor does simple reflection on mental concepts—for example, the concept of sensation—lead to recognition of an identity with certain neuroscientific concepts. Rather it is through experiment and scientific investigation that we learn and continue to discover the identity of mental states and properties with brain properties. Thus, we *discover* that a certain type of pain is identical with a firing of C-fibers (more accurately, a certain type of pain is identical with a neural process that begins with the firing of C-fibers).

Identity theory alerts us to the fact that we should expect to find a myriad of such empirically discoverable identities as the allied brain sciences progress. As we discover the relevant identities, we learn the "real nature" of mental states. Our scientific investigations reveal the manner in which mental states are *constituted* by brain states.

A Look at Reduction

The identification of mental state types with brain state types has a further important consequence. Suppose for a moment that we have discovered that the mental state type of the sensation "magenta" (call this type M) is identical to a particular brain state type (call it B). Thus, M = B. This identity has the status of an empirical law, a scientific law. Every occasion of finding M is also an occasion of finding B. Of course, the converse is also true: Each time we find B, we know that we have found M. This sort of law is known as a **bridge law**. In general, bridge laws connect the terms of one theory with the terms of another. The bridge laws of interest to us at the moment connect mental terms with neuroscientific terms.

If identity theory is right, then for every mental state type, there is a correlative bridge law. For each term or description that names a mental state type, there is a bridge law that connects—*identifies*—the mental term with a neuroscientific term that names a brain state type. The terms specifying mental state types are just the familiar terms of our commonsense or folk-psychological view. The correlative bridge laws thus guarantee that our folk-psychological viewpoint is *reducible* to neuroscience; we have a **reduction** of one theory to another. That is, any folk-psychological explanation can be recast as a neuroscientific explanation. (Here folk psychology is the *reduced* theory, while neuroscience is the *reducing* theory.)

We may not as yet know all the bridge laws, just as we did not know at one point that genes are segments of DNA molecules; but we can be assured that there *are* such laws, merely awaiting discovery. Once we know all the relevant bridge laws, we could, if we desired, replace our folk-psychological account of the mind with purely neuroscientific accounts. Significantly, *we would not lose any explanatory power by utilizing only the neuroscientific description.* The bridge laws guarantee that our folk-psychological understanding of our mental lives is captured by the neuroscientific understanding of the brain. In this sense, folk psychology is reducible to neuroscience.

We should consider one question that the reducibility of the mental to the neuroscientific occasionally raises. Since identity claims, by themselves, don't tell us which term is more basic, why think that neuroscientific terms are more basic than mental terms? In response, identity theorists note first that neuroscience shows us the way to integrate our understanding of the mental with other natural sciences. Second, while mental terms are reducible to neuroscientific terms, not all neural terms are reducible to mental terms. Indeed the concepts of neurons, synapses, and neurotransmitters, to name but a few, cannot be identified with any complex of folk-psychological concepts. Neuroscience is thus the more comprehensive of the two views, promising not only explanations of the mental, but *additional* explanations as well. Relying only on folk psychology, we would lose significant explanatory power. The neuroscientific account—the more basic—will allow us to say everything worth saying about the mind . . . and more.

"Sensation" Doesn't Mean "Neurons Firing"

One caveat on behalf of the identity theorist is in order. Identity theory does not imply that folk-psychological terms *have the same meaning* as neuroscientific terms. Recall for a moment the identity of water and H_2O. The everyday term "water" does not have the same meaning as the chemical term "H_2O." The latter but not the former means, roughly, that two hydrogen atoms are combined with a single oxygen atom. We should not expect that every sentence containing the word "water" would have the same meaning if "water" were merely replaced with "H_2O."

One way to express this is that the two terms have the same *reference*— they pick out or designate the same type of substance—but they do not have the same *sense*; they give us different information. You would find it uninformative and uninteresting to be told that water is water, but you learn something new when told that water is H_2O. Alternatively, the two terms have the same *denotation*, but different *connotations*. Thus, the terms of the bridge laws will have the same references, but different meanings (senses).

Ben Franklin, Genes, and Causal Role: From Correlations to Identity

Still, one might harbor some doubt as to whether the identity theorist is entitled to assert the *identity* of mental states and brain states, rather than simply a *correlation* between the two. Correlations are not sufficient for identity. Indeed, Descartes recognized that changes in the nervous system or the brain correlate with having certain sensations, such as pain. But while accepting the correlation, the dualist rejected the essential contention of the identity theorist that mental states are brain states. It is not the correlation that is problematic, but the *identity*. We might wonder: Has the identity theorist mistaken mere correlation for identity?

Correlations of one type of thing to another type are abundant in nature (Richard Brandt and Jaegwon Kim [1967] first drew attention to correlation/identity). The presence of a virus correlates with fever; the presence of sunlight correlates with the greenness of plant leaves. Very often, these correlations are *lawful* correlations. Some laws of nature correlate one type of thing with another. But lawful correlation does not entail identity. The virus, although correlated, is not *identical* to the fever. More to the point, despite the assurances of neuroscience that a certain brain state correlates with depression, for example, we need to know more before we are confident that depression simply *is* that type of brain state.

To get from correlation to identity, the identity theorist exploits the notion of *causal role*. Before presenting a formal version of the argument, we can consider two examples.

Imagine bespectacled Ben Franklin, standing out in the open during an electrical storm, kite in hand, with a metal key dangling from the end of the string. Imagine also that the experiment has the desired result—Ben has a shocking experience. Now imagine that Ben decides to call the cause of the shocking experience "electricity." Ben does not know what electricity is; he simply knows that, whatever it is, it causes shocking experiences. Thus, Ben identifies electricity by its causal role. Despite his ignorance of the precise nature—of the "stuff"—of electricity, Ben knows it is made of something. The concept of electricity puts a name on whatever it is that electricity is. More specifically, it picks out whatever it is that accounts for the causal role—the shocking nature—of electricity. Lamentably, it falls to others, not Ben, to discover that electricity is "made of" streams of electrons, which fill the causal role picked out by the concept of electricity. That is what electricity *is*—a stream of electrons.

We need not rely on folklore, for we have another example from science. We possessed the concept of a "gene" long before we knew about DNA molecules. Gregor Mendel (1822–1884) introduced the concept to explain inherited traits. Mendel specified the causal role of genes, without knowing their "matter." He defined a gene as that unique type of thing—whatever it might turn out to be—responsible for the transmission of hereditary traits. Mendel identified genes by their causal role long before—a century later—we discovered that segments of DNA molecules fill this role. The reasoning is now relatively straightforward. If genes are, by definition, whatever it is that is causally responsible for the transmission of hereditary traits, and certain sequences of DNA molecules are the type of thing responsible for such transmission—and nothing else is responsible—then genes just *are* segments of DNA molecules!

Franklin's electricity and Mendel's gene provide us with the form of an argument that can be used for the identity of mental properties and brain processes. We might characterize the concept of a sensation, for example, by its causal role. That is, "pain" is whatever it is that causes us to engage in certain kinds of behavior, such as avoidance or remedy. We then discover, to use the example cited earlier, that the firing of C-fibers fills this causal role. Hence, we identify pain with the firing of C-fibers. The firing C-fibers are not merely *correlated* with pain; according to this argument, they *are* the pain.

The causal role argument for identity was first formulated by D. M. Armstrong (1968, 1981; it is also used to motivate a type of functionalism, as described in Armstrong 1999, chaps. 6–7). The argument goes like this:

1. Some mental type M is defined by its causal role C. That is, M *is* whatever it is that fills C.
2. Some brain state type B fills C.
3. Thus, M is B.

Should we really think that *any* mental type has a distinctive causal role? What, after all, is the causal role of the sensation of red? To distinguish between ripe and unripe tomatoes? To tell a doctor that a person has measles? To tell us what color tie to wear with a blue suit? All of these? None?

The identity theorist might respond as follows. Water may not have a single, unique causal role, but its properties—wet, clear, relieves thirst, extinguishes fires, and so on—distinguish water from other substances. Water thus has a nexus or family of causal roles. Whatever the "stuff" of water turns out to be, that stuff had better fill this nexus of causal roles. Later, once we have a sufficiently sophisticated chemical theory, we will be able to identify the chemical structure, H_2O, possessed by all and only instances of water—that *stuff* that does these things. Since H_2O is uniquely implicated by instances of wet, clear, thirst-relieving, fire-extinguishing stuff, water *is* H_2O. Our commonsense view of water and its properties picks out the substance, and science reveals the real nature of this substance.

How does this help us with extending the causal role argument to every mental type—the sensation of red, say? The sensation "red" plays a variety of causal roles—choosing ripe strawberries or the appropriate tie, noticing someone's embarrassment, or simply admiring the evening sky, to name a few. However, whenever the mental event of "seeing red" occurs, whenever a person has this type of mental property, it turns out that there is a distinctive pattern of activity occurring in the visual cortex. Very roughly, folk psychology says, "We are talking about this type of thing, M, which occurs in these cases." Neuroscience subsequently tells us that whenever M occurs, a certain brain process B occurs. Our best explanation, says identity theory, of the repeated correlation of mental property types with certain brain processes is the identity of the two; M *is* B.

Besides That, It's Simpler!

Identity theorists have another reason for insisting on identity rather than mere correlation. J. J. C. Smart appeals to Occam's razor, a methodological principle which says to prefer the simpler of two explanations. Smart finds it "frankly unbelievable" (1959, 82) that science should one day explain everything, including human behavior, except for this one type of thing—the occurrence of sensations. Insisting on correlation rather than identity leads to this "frankly unbelievable" result. Smart makes three related points on behalf of identity theory: simplicity, the ever-increasing explanatory comprehensiveness of the scientific framework, and the unity of science. Let's take up the last two points first.

Science casts its explanatory net in ever-widening circles. Beginning with the development of modern physics in the sixteenth and seventeenth centuries, science has provided explanations of mechanical, astronomical, and molecular, atomic, and subatomic phenomena. Increasingly since the twentieth century, sciences such as biochemistry, molecular biology, and neuroscience have identified and described the mechanisms underlying not only animal behavior in general but also human behavior. Just as we have scientific explanations for phenomena as diverse as growth and development, science promises eventual explanation of paradigmatically mental states such as thinking, remembering, and visual awareness. Identity theorists find it "unbelievable" that mental properties *alone* should escape the ever-widening net of scientific explanation.

Nor does the identity theorist expect scientific explanations of the mental to be ad hoc. The integration of the various sciences is one of the remarkable features of scientific progress. Neuroscientific findings are compatible with and supported by results in biochemistry, molecular biology, and genetics, to mention but a few, and these in turn find support, for example, in the theories of organic and physical chemistry. Again, the identity theorist finds it incredible and arbitrary that this integrated framework, capable of revealing the nature and behavior of virtually every type of phenomenon, should find itself helpless when confronted with mental phenomena.

Underlying the identity theorist's appeal to explanatory power and unity, however, is the argument from simplicity. Since identity theory requires appeal only to physical kinds and properties, rather than dualism's two distinct categories, identity theory is simpler. Fewer categories seemingly ought to require fewer basic explanatory principles. Here Smart's appeal to Occam's razor is explicit. Once we accept type identity theory, we need only one type of investigation, that of the sciences, to tell us about the nature and operations of the mental. Economy of theory thus leads to economy of investigation. Type identity theory achieves an overall simplicity and is thus preferable to dualism.

A Look Back

Identity theory holds that every mental state type is identical to a brain state type. Discovered through empirical investigation, the type identities are expressed in bridge laws. We thus have two ways of identifying one and the same mental state type, using either folk-psychological terms or neuroscientific terms. While mental and neuroscientific terms differ in meaning, we are describing not two things, but one physical thing. This more comprehensive neuroscientific framework permits us to explain everything we want about the mental without loss of explanatory power.

Identity theorists support their view of the mental with four arguments, two principal arguments and two auxiliary arguments. The two principal arguments are the causal role argument and the simplicity argument, while the explanatory power and the unity of science arguments are auxiliary arguments.

Putting Minds Back to Work: Advantages of Type Identity Theory

The strength of identity theory arises not only from its supporting arguments but also from its consequences. We can conveniently separate these into two categories: a realist view of our folk-psychological categories and mental causation.

Vindication of the Mental

Type identity theory acknowledges the reality of sensations, the propositional attitudes, and other mental states and properties such as moods, feelings, and emotions. Since there is no doubt about the reality of brain activity, and the mental is just a very complicated set of brain states and processes, there is then no doubt about the reality of the mental. Rigorous science not only vindicates the mental but also validates much of our folk psychology. When Sam believes that Chuck can play guitar just like ringing a bell, we know that this mental state of Sam's is a *real* state (the example is from Brueckner 1999).

Type identity theory lets us have our cake and eat it, too. We are guaranteed a continued commitment to physicalism *and* a continued commitment to the reality of the mental. Since identity theory freely admits the reality of our folk-psychological categories, it is a *realist* view of the mental.

Working Minds: Identity and Mental Causation

Dualism and behaviorism stumble on the claim that mental states are often *causes* of our behavior. Whether or not we think that dualism provides an adequate solution to the problem of interaction, there is no doubt that the causal role of mental states is dualism's Achilles' heel. Behaviorism fares even worse on this score, either ignoring or simply rejecting the causal efficacy of the mental.

Discounting mental causation would be a significant retreat from our commonsense view. A view of the mind that leaves us without a means to explain the *causal activity* of the mind challenges some of the most deeply held assumptions of our folk psychology. It will not hurt to remind ourselves of what is at stake. Sam arrives at the restaurant at 4:15 because he *believes* that Sara will be there at 4:30 and he *desires* to be there to greet her. Sara *hopes* that Sam will for once be on time. An appeal to mental states, whether propositional attitudes or feelings and sensations, is our principal mode of explaining the actions of ourselves and others.

Type identity theory assures us that we need not worry about the causal efficacy of the mental. Indeed type identity theory shows us how the mental is frequently at work. We understand how one neuron excites another, and in some cases, we have at least the outline of how one neural structure affects others. Most of us can give a simplified account of raising one's arm, for example. Some part of the brain sends a signal along neural pathways, branching from the spinal column, through pathways along the arm, and these signals cause the contraction of the muscles in the arm, and—voilà!—the arm rises. According to identity theory, mental states—desiring coconut cream pie, believing that just such a food is within arm's reach, deciding to reach for it—are identical with brain states. But now notice: If we know how one set of brain states affects another, and we also know that mental states are brain states, then we know how mental states effect physical changes. *We know how the mental causes behavior!*

Type identity theory clearly has its advantages. It accords well with our scientific understanding of the world, while finding a place for mental properties. And identity theory retains the realism of our commonsense view, including the reality of mental causation.

Reservations about Identity Theory

Despite its initial promise, identity theory quickly met a series of objections that led many to turn to the rival physicalist view of functionalism, which we consider in the following chapter. In this section and the next, we consider the central objections to type identity theory. These objections are of two types: those that arise from considerations of Leibniz's Law and the multiple realizability objection.

Leibniz's Law and Type Identity Theory

"This is not my book," you insist.

Your friend, nonplussed, replies, "Yes, it is; that's An Introduction to Epistemology, just what you said you were looking for."

"No, it isn't; I never use highlighter in my book and just look at all the pink highlights."

This fictional exchange suggests a way of thinking about identity. If we want to know whether two supposedly different things are identical, look at their characteristics. Different characteristics means that there are two things, not one.

You reject this particular book as yours because this mere pretender has *different properties*—it has pink marks in it, while your book has no such marks. This single difference is enough to discount the present book as *your* book. No other book is yours unless it has all the same properties of your book.

This intuitive characterization of a condition for genuine identity is expressed more formally in Leibniz's Law, so named since G. W. von Leibniz (1646–1716) first articulated a version of it. **Leibniz's Law** says that, for any A and B, A and B are identical if and only if they have all the same properties. This principle tells us two things. It tells us that if we find two apparently different things with all the same properties, then we have—in fact—not two things, but only one. Leibniz's Law also tells us that the identity of A and B *requires* that A and B have the same properties.

Leibniz's Law also tells us how we may show that two things are in fact distinct and not identical: Find a property possessed by one but not the other. In our example, you were able to discount a certain book as yours because it has a property—pink highlighting—not possessed by your book.

Critics of type identity theory were quick to exploit Leibniz's Law, suggesting a range of properties sufficient to differentiate mental states and properties from brain states and properties. Some of these objections are easily dismissed; others are less tractable. We begin with an easier target.

Since brains are physical objects, they have fairly common physical characteristics. They have weight, a certain location, a texture, and color. We can even say that a particular brain process takes up space, the space occupied by the neural structures constituting that brain process. The brain process that occurs when having the sensation of red includes the activation of particular structures in the visual cortex, located in the back of the brain. However, although it makes sense to say that a given *brain process* has a certain location or takes up space, it seems at least peculiar to claim that my *sensation* takes up X amount of space or that my belief that an apple is nearby is located a few centimeters in from my left ear (Margolis 1971). It is possible that we

Leibniz's Law: Indiscernibility and Identity

The intuitive sense of Leibniz's Law is twofold. First, if any two objects A and B have all the same properties, then there is in fact only one object. Second, if A and B are identical, then they have all the same properties. These two "if-then" statements, or conditionals, combined give us Leibniz's Law. But each conditional is important enough to deserve its own name.

Consider the first: If any objects A and B have all the same properties, then there is in fact only one object. It expresses a *sufficient* condition for identity. If two things have all the same properties, they are *indiscernible*. This gives us an alternative formulation of this sufficient condition: If A and B are indiscernible, then A and B are identical. This "half" of Leibniz's Law is called the *identity of indiscernibles.*

Consider the second conditional: If any objects A and B are identical, then A and B have all the same properties. This conditional expresses a *necessary* condition for identity. Intuitively it says that whenever you find identity of objects, you must also find exactly the same properties. A logically equivalent formulation would be: You don't have identity unless you find exactly the same properties. As before, we can express this conditional using the concept of indiscernibility: If A and B are identical, then A and B are indiscernible. This condition is known as the *indiscernibility of identicals.*

have a kind of property that distinguishes brain properties from mental properties: Brain states, but not mental states, have physical properties. If so, according to Leibniz's Law, we then have not one type of thing, but two—mental and physical.

The type identity theorist deflects this criticism by pointing out that it presupposes the falsity of identity theory (Smart 1959). Initially it may seem odd that mental states have these types of properties, but identity theory explains how my sensation of red "takes up space." Science often reveals common, ordinary phenomena to have unexpected properties. The hard table before me is actually composed of atoms consisting mostly of empty space; the green I see is actually reflected light of a certain quality. Similarly the identity theorist claims that it is no argument against identity theory that it reveals surprising or unexpected properties of the mental.

A second objection claims—against identity theory—that I can know my own mental states in a way quite different from the way I learn of my brain states. Introspection tells me that my knee hurts, that I am thinking that I left my orange juice on the kitchen counter, or that I doubt it will rain today. But, the objection continues, this is quite different from the manner in which I can know my own brain states. I learn of these perhaps from a neuroscientist or through the use of highly specialized technology, such as magnetic resonance imaging. It would appear then that mental states have a property, "knowable by introspection," whereas my brain states do not have this property.

Notice first that the property "knowable by introspection" is a different type of property from others we have considered. Suppose, for example, that Sara believes that this pair of shoes does not fit. In addition to their more ordinary properties of color, size, weight, or position next to the previous pair tried on by Sara, we might say that these shoes have the property "believed by Sara to be the wrong size." Similarly a piece of cake might be said to have the property "wished by Sara to be saved for later." Objects possess this type of property by virtue of the intentional states of some being.

Two lines of response are open. First, it might be claimed that Leibniz's Law does not apply to properties that do not depend on the particular intentional states of some creature. This is not as arbitrary as it might seem. Again, consider Sara and the shoes. Imagine that the shoes sit for a moment on the floor in front of Sara; nothing changes about the shoes, including their relation to other physical objects. Sara simply engages in a bit of "free association" about the shoes. She wishes they would fit; she fears that they only come in brown; she believes that they would make an excellent gift for Aunt Martha. One might think that it is only in an attenuated sense that the shoes "have" these properties. We would not think our understanding of the shoes particularly diminished or incomplete if we did not know of these Sara-bestowed properties. The identity theorist thus has some reason for restricting the range of Leibniz's Law.

A second, less technical means of defusing the objection claims that an object can be known in different ways or under different descriptions. That an object is known in different ways does not require the admission that there are two objects. Lois Lane (as well as the other benighted souls at the *Daily Planet*) knows that a certain bespectacled, mild-mannered gentleman is Clark Kent; she also knows that a certain cape-and-blue-tights-wearing superhero is Superman. Yet she does not know two different persons. She knows one person in two different ways. More generally, we can use different concepts to think of a single object. But using different concepts to think about an object does not entail that there are two objects.

The identity theorist uses this "one thing, two ways of knowing" in the following manner. You might learn of a certain kind of state by introspection or by some technology. These two different paths lead us not to different places, but to the same place. Introspection and the latest technologies are but two different ways of knowing about a single type of state. Indeed it is open to the identity theorist to claim that although you thought you were introspecting mental states, you were in fact introspecting brain states (Smart 2004).

A third use of Leibniz's Law exploits the qualitative features of some mental states. A headache may be intense or throbbing; a sensation of yellow may be particularly brilliant; an afterimage may be intermittent or fading. We could continue this list indefinitely, but the important point is that such descriptions highlight our experiences' qualitative or *phenomenal* character. It is not obvious, however, that brain processes possess these sorts of phenomenal properties. A brain scan, for example, would not show the intense "throbbingness" of a headache. Qualitative character seems to distinguish mental from brain states. Put simply, some mental states have a qualitative character that brain states do not share; hence, at least some mental states are not identical to brain states.

We will see in later chapters that the qualitative character of the mental proves particularly troublesome for other physicalist theories and for physicalism generally. But type identity theory was among the first to confront the problem directly. And Smart's seminal article (1959) is centrally focused on the qualitative character of sensations.

Smart introduces the notion of *topic-neutral descriptions*, a phrase he borrows from Gilbert Ryle (Smart 1959, 85–86; see also Smart 2004, sec. 3). Topic-neutral descriptions do not commit us to the existence of nonphysical properties. Smart asks us to consider a bright orange afterimage. *Bright-orangish* is a distinctive phenomenal property, not obviously possessed by any brain process. Suppose Sam tells us that he has a bright orange experience. Smart suggests that we can understand Sam's report as a *topic-neutral report*, which claims only, "It's as though I were awake, with my eyes open, in normal lighting conditions, looking at an orange." In Smart's view, Sam is not identifying his experience as either physical or mental; his report is neutral between them. Thus, we need not understand Sam as referring to something distinctively mental. Reports of phenomenal properties are neutral about the *kind* of property, neither claiming it as mental nor physical. And this neutrality, in the identity theorist's view, blunts the move from phenomenal experience to nonphysical properties.

Not everyone is happy with the topic-neutral approach, however. The topic-neutral view may save us from the phenomenal property objection to identity theory, but it does so at a rather high price: It violates our common-sense distinction between mental and physical properties (Rosenthal 1994). Smart's view requires giving up a paradigm case of a mental property. Surely, however, the distinction between mental and physical properties is worth preserving.

Others suggest a different way of handling phenomenal properties, distinguishing between the properties of the *objects* of experience and the properties of the experiences themselves (Heil 1998). The objects that we sense are round and orange, red and octagonal, yet our experiences themselves are not similarly round and orange, or red and octagonal. We experience red things; we don't have red experiences. If we do not confuse the properties of the experiences with the properties of objects, we can begin to think of these experiential properties as the properties of brain states.

This response might explain, say, the qualia a person has as a result of seeing a red rose. But some might suspect that it leaves out certain types of qualitative states. If Danny has a throbbing headache, it does not seem as if there is any "object" that he experiences. Yet there clearly is the "throbbingness" of the headache, and it is this qualitative character that requires explanation.

We leave matters here, unresolved as they are. We will see in later chapters that qualia reappear. That phenomenal properties have yet to go quietly signals a fundamental and difficult issue in philosophy of mind.

The Multiple Realizability Objection

Imagine that as the brain sciences and allied technologies progress, we have prosthetic brain parts and their functioning filling the requisite causal role. Researchers have already implanted small transmitters in brains, permitting a person to move a cursor on a very simple computer, simply by "thinking" the cursor to the appropriate part of the screen. If prosthetic brain events might fill the causal role, do we need brains at all? Couldn't a sufficiently sophisticated computer have mental states without having brain states? Isn't type identity theory chauvinistic in claiming that mental event types are identical to types of brain events? Who needs a brain? This line of thought leads to the most important objection to identity theory; a simple example will get us started.

Golfers are an optimistic lot. They wait patiently for the next advance in golf equipment technology, believing that this new advance will end years of frustration. It is not the golfer's psyche that is of interest here, but his clubs. One in particular; it is called a driver. A driver has a particular causal role or, we might say, a particular function: to advance the golf ball the farthest distance possible—within the rules, of course—toward the hole. Now, drivers are made of many different materials. They were once made of hickory and persimmon; today they may be made of any number of diverse materials, including steel, graphite, aluminum, tungsten, and titanium. As long as the causal role or function is filled, what a driver is made of does not really matter (although golfers have found themselves at times using the oxymoron "metal wood"). More to the point, drivers can be *realized by* many different materials. The function or the causal role of drivers can be filled by steel or graphite, persimmon or titanium.

Multiple realizability is a familiar phenomenon; in general, a type or kind or property is multiply realizable if different instances of the type or property can be brought about by different physical states or configurations.

Hilary Putnam (1975) argues that mental states could be realized by materials other than brains. Imagine a bit of instructive science fiction. We are visited at some future time by extraterrestrial beings. They give every appearance of being extremely intelligent. After all, they found us before we found them. Moreover, they appear on occasion to have feelings or moods, they appear at times to be sad or happy, and they even seem to appreciate a good joke ("A human, a Vulcan, and a Ferengi walk into a space station . . ."). Extensive investigation reveals that their physiology is nothing like ours. Whereas our physiology is carbon based, theirs is, say, silicon based.

Type identity theory would seems to imply that these extraterrestrials do not have mental states. Mental states, according to the identity theorist, are identical to neural types; more precisely, mental states are identical to *human* neural types (or human brain events). Now, one thing is quite clear: if we are even able to identify the extraterrestrials' "brains," they obviously would have radically different types of brain events. And since mental events are identical to brain events, and our intergalactic visitors do not have the requisite brain events, neither do they have mental states!

In an episode of the original *Star Trek*, a rock creature—a *horta*—is discovered. The encountered horta *wants* to protect its "babies," *believes* that miners are threats to its progeny, *plans* for protection, and when injured, *feels* pain. Horta clearly do not have human brains. So, they cannot have human brain events. If type identity theorists are right, then the horta's "mental states" really are science fiction!

The seeming lack of mental states among nonhumans is not restricted to science fiction, either. We attribute mental states of various types to other animals, yet these animals may have very different types of brain states. It might also occur to you that the problem arises even within the human species; very different types of brain events may fill the same causal role in different individuals. If it is true that a creature (or artifact) can have the same type of mental state, but realizes that mental state by means of a very different type of physical state, then something is wrong with type identity theory.

The **multiple realizability objection** claims that identity theory is chauvinistic; it restricts—without good reason—the having of mental states to only those beings that have *human* brain events. Yet it seems plausible that mental states are *multiply realizable*, that a single type of mental state can be realized by many different types of physical events. What matters is the causal role, not what fills the causal role.

Type identity theorists respond by restricting the range of the relevant identities. Instead of pain comprising a single mental type, it actually comprises several types. We have pain-in-humans. But we also have pain-in-eagles, pain-in-Vulcans, and, if it comes to it, pain-in-computers. This move is not unwarranted. We know that eagles, for example, make many of the same visual discriminations as humans, yet the physiology of the eagle's visual system is quite different from ours. An eagle seeing a rabbit is realized differently from a human seeing a rabbit (Nelkin 1996, 63–70). So, we should not be surprised to find that eagle pain is realized differently as well.

One might argue that the type identity theorist is giving away too much. Identity theory, in responding to multiple realizability, points to *restricted* type identity. To critics, this might seem as conceding the point at issue. The restricted type identity theorist concedes that, for example, the belief in the presence of water is realized differently in different species. "Here is some water" has one physical realization in humans, another in dogs, another in chimpanzees, and presumably still different realizations in more exotic species such as Vulcans or computerized robots. Thus, it seems that the *type* of physical state matters less. The greater the physical variability, the more it seems that it's the *function* that matters, not the physical state type. The multiple realizability objection claims that mental state types are realized by different physical types. All that matters is that some physical state or other fills the causal (mental) role. Human brains, monkey brains, Vulcan brains, computer "brains"—we don't care which, so long as the causal role is filled.

Type identity theory initially drew our interest because it promised to tell us something important about the nature of mental states—that they are really brain states. Type identity promised to reveal the *type* of physical realizer—human neural events. In response to the multiple realizability objection, however, type identity theory now makes an apparently weaker promise: Mental state types are identical to perhaps exceedingly diverse physical state types. Restricted type identity seems to promise less in our understanding the *nature* of mental states. So it might be suggested that we learn more about the nature of mental states not by worrying over the physical realizers, but by looking at their function.

Type identity theory has not disappeared (see, for example, Smart 2004 and Kim 1998). But multiple realizability has spurred many to consider a different, functionalist account of the nature of mental states. This is the topic of the next chapter.

Key Concepts

Bridge law

Leibniz's Law

Multiple realizability objection

Reduction

Type identity theory

Type/token

Reading Questions

1. What is the type/token distinction? Why is it important for type identity theory?

2. Briefly explain what is meant by the claim that folk psychology is reducible to neuroscience.

3. Identity theorists claim that mind–brain identities are "empirical identities." What do they mean by this?

4. Briefly explain the causal role argument for identity theory.

5. How does the identity theorist explain mental causation?

6. What is Leibniz's Law? Why is it important for identity theory?

7. Explain one way that identity theorists respond to the objection that mental properties are knowable by introspection.

8. What does it mean to say that a property or state is multiply realized? Why is this important for the critic of type identity theory?

References

Armstrong, David. 1968. *A materialist theory of mind*. London: Routledge and Kegan Paul.

———. 1981. *"The nature of mind" and other essays*. Ithaca, NY: Cornell University Press.

———. 1999. *The mind–body problem: An opinionated introduction*. Boulder, CO: Westview Press.

Borst, C. V., ed. 1970. *The Mind/Brain Identity Theory*. New York: St. Martin's Press.

Brandt, Richard, and Jaegwon Kim. 1967. The logic of identity theory. *Journal of Philosophy* 64:515–37.

Brueckner, Anthony. 1999. Two recent approaches to self-knowledge. In *Philosophical perspectives*, vol. 13, *Epistemology*, ed. James E. Tomberlin, 251–71. Cambridge, MA: Blackwell.

Churchland, Paul. 1988. *Matter and consciousness*. Rev. ed. Cambridge, MA: MIT Press.

Crumley, Jack, ed. 2000. *Problems in mind: readings in contemporary philosophy of mind*. Mountain View, CA: Mayfield.

Damasio, Antonio R., and Hanna Damasio. 1993. Brain and language. In *Scientific American* 1993, 54–65.

Edelman, Gerald. 1992. *Bright air, brilliant fire: On the matter of mind*. New York: Basic Books.

Feigl, Herbert. 1960. Mind–body, not a pseudoproblem. In *Dimensions of mind: A symposium*, ed. Sidney Hook. New York: New York University Press. Reprinted in Borst 1970, 33–41.

Fischbach, Gerald D. 1993. Mind and brain. In *Scientific American* 1993, 1–14.

Flanagan, Owen. 1992. *Consciousness reconsidered*. Cambridge, MA: MIT Press.

Heil, John. 1998. *Philosophy of mind*. London: Routledge.

Kim, Jaegwon. 1998. *Mind in a physical world: An essay on the mind–body problem and mental causation*. Cambridge, MA: MIT Press.

Margolis, Joseph. 1971. Difficulties for mind–body identity theories. In *Identity and individuation*, ed. Milton K. Munitz, 213–31. New York: New York University Press.

Nelkin, Norton. 1996. *Consciousness and the origins of thought*. Cambridge: Cambridge University Press.

Place, U. T. 1956. Is consciousness a brain process? *British Journal of Psychology* 47: 44–50. Reprinted in Borst 1970, 42–51.

Putnam, Hilary. 1975. The nature of mental states. In *Mind, language, and reality: Philosophical papers*. Cambridge: Cambridge University Press, 2:429–40. Reprinted in Crumley 2000, 102–9.

Rosenthal, David M. 1994. Identity theories. In *A companion to the philosophy of mind*, ed. Samuel Guttenplan, 348–55. Oxford: Blackwell.

Scientific American. 1993. *Mind and brain: Readings from* Scientific American. New York: W. H. Freeman.

Smart, J. J. C. 1959. Sensations and brain processes. *Philosophical Review* 68. Reprinted in Crumley 2000, 81–90; page references are to this volume.

———. 2004. The identity theory of mind. In *The Stanford encyclopedia of philosophy*, ed. Edward N. Zalta. Online at http://plato.stanford.edu/archives/fall2004/entries/mind-identity.

Zeki, Semir. 1993. The visual image in mind and brain. In *Scientific American* 1993, 27–39.

Additional Readings

Barker, Roger A. *Neuroscience: An Illustrated Guide.* New York: Ellis Horwood, 1991.

Braddon-Mitchell, David, and Frank Jackson. *Philosophy of Mind and Cognition.* Oxford: Blackwell, 1996.

Kim, Jaegwon. "On the Psycho-Physical Identity Theory." In *Materialism and the Mind–Body Problem*, ed. David M. Rosenthal, 80–95. Englewood Cliffs, NJ: Prentice-Hall, 1971.

Kripke, Saul. "Naming and Necessity" [excerpt]. In Crumley 2000, chap. 9.

MacDonald, Cynthia. *Mind–Body Identity Theories.* London: Routledge, 1989.

Munitz, Milton K., ed. *Identity and Individuation.* New York: New York University Press, 1971.

Rosenthal, David M., ed. *Materialism and the Mind–Body Problem.* Englewood Cliffs, NJ: Prentice-Hall, 1971.

Shaffer, Jerome. "Mental Events and the Brain." *Journal of Philosophy* 60 (1963): 160–66. Reprinted in Crumley 2000, 91–94.

4

Diagramming the Mind: Functionalism

In the middle of the twentieth century, theoretical computer science and cognitive psychology began to take root. In an important way, they form the theoretical background for perhaps the most widely accepted view of the mind: functionalism. Both fields share a common conceptual framework. Cognitive psychology treats the *mind* as an information-processing system, and theoretical computer science treats the *computer* as an information-processing system. Given certain inputs, each system operates on or transforms the information and produces certain outputs, according to the rules that govern the system. Information is *represented* in the system by means of symbols. That is, the internal representational states of the system, whether mind or computer, are symbols that can be variously interpreted. In other words, the symbols have a meaning.

Of course, there are specifically philosophical motivations for functionalism, but there is little doubt that this theoretical background informed functionalism's rise. In a series of papers, Hilary Putnam (1975a, 1975b, 1975c) relies explicitly on the notion of a very simple computing machine to illustrate a functional view of the mental. This same theoretical backdrop informs the multiple realizability objection—already noted in the last chapter and presently revisited—which is perhaps functionalism's most telling motivation. But there are reasons for preferring functionalism, and this chapter and the next will examine functionalism, its comparative advantages, and its shortcomings. We begin with a brief reminder about roles and multiple realizability.

Roles Again—Functionalism

Central to functionalism is the distinction between the functional role and that which fills the role. Every four years, citizens of the United States vote to elect a president, selecting a person to fill a constitutional role. Different persons, some forty-two of them at this point in our history, at different times have occupied the same role. We can put the matter differently: There is a function, a constitutional function, and different individuals at different times fill this function. Indeed we might say that the office of the president is characterized *functionally*, by its role in American government.

Physical objects—spoons, for example—are also functionally characterized. Spoons are roundish, slightly concave instruments used for conveying food or liquid from one place to another, as well as for mixing and stirring. We are often indifferent to the "individual" or particular thing that serves this function. A bit of plastic will often do as well as a bit of stainless steel; a wooden spoon can usually serve the same function as a silver one. The things—the bits of material—fill the function, and so long as they do, we have a spoon.

Now, recall for a moment the multiple realizability objection to type identity theory. Mental state types, the objection claims, need not be identified with neural types. Indeed this is far too restrictive. Instead, it is the *role* of the mental state that matters, and not what fills that role. Human neural events may fill the role, but so can canine neural events, extraterrestrial "brain" events, or even computer states. So, let a thousand flowers bloom! As long as the role is filled, we don't really care what is filling that role—the *functional* role. Thus, types of mental states are understood by types of functional role (Putnam 1975c; Fodor 1968).

Think for a moment about what often happens when a mental state occurs, for example, believing that there is an apple in front of you. First, *sensing* the apple, usually by seeing it, typically causes the belief. If this belief then interacts with other mental states, such as a belief that apples are good for you and a desire to eat something nutritious, such interaction often leads to a typical result—reaching for and eating the apple.

Generalizing the example, we have a schema for identifying the nature of mental states. **Functionalism** defines mental states by their causal role; in particular, it defines them in terms of (1) their connections to their typical causes or inputs; (2) their causal connections to other mental states; and (3) their causal connections to various effects or outputs (Lewis 1980; Lycan 1994). (In this chapter, "functional role" and "causal role" are used interchangeably.)

Varieties of Functionalism

Functionalism is actually a family of theories, with different identifiable members of that family. *Commonsense functionalism* takes our ordinary mental terms—belief, desire, and sensation terms such as pain—and attempts to identify the functional or causal roles identified by these terms. *Machine table functionalism*, a very early version of functionalism, identifies mental states with parts of a computer program that is a very abstract description of psychology of the person. This program specifies how various states are transformed, given certain inputs, to produce certain outputs. Early proponents of functionalism were nonetheless critical of machine table functionalism, noting that it could not distinguish between occurrent states—those we are thinking about at the moment—and dispositional states—beliefs, for example, of which we are not currently conscious (Block and Fodor 1980 [1972]). *Teleological functionalism* suggests that we are to consider the causal roles, but that we should do so by considering the biological purpose of such a state. In identifying the causal role of pain, for example, we need to consider the biological function of pain. *Homuncular functionalism* suggests that we identify our psychological capacities and progressively "decompose" those capacities. That is, we should analyze those capacities into smaller and smaller units until we find the basic functional units. In the next chapter, we consider another version of functionalism, computational functionalism (Lycan 1994; Bechtel 1988).

What sorts of causes lead to mental states? In the preceding example, it was sensory information, seeing an apple. Such sensory information need not be confined to visual information, however. Mental states may result from touch (the bathwater is too cold), taste (this sauce is too salty), hearing (there goes that stereo again), or smell (Sam must be cooking again). Other mental states may also serve as causes: Your remembering that this is an election year may lead to your desire to register to vote.

Typical effects may be either another mental state or some behavior. The belief that Danny is a bachelor may have as its effect the new belief that Danny is unmarried. Or Sam's belief that it is 11:30 (along with the desire not be late) might cause him to grab his keys and rush out the door. Functionalism thus acknowledges the crucial connection between the mental and behavior.

According to functionalism, two individual mental states are the *same type* if they have the *same functional role*. If Sam and Sara both believe that the concert is in November, then, according to functionalism, they each have a mental state that has the same functional role. Similarly, sameness of functional role implies sameness of mental state type.

It is important to be clear that, in the functionalist view, mental states *are* the causal or functional role. Functionalism thus provides a *relational* treatment of mental states. The *essence* or *nature* of Deirdre's belief that some chicken is still left in the refrigerator is to be found in its relation—its causal relation—to various inputs, other mental states, and behavior. The nature of mental states can be discerned only in their relations, a point which critics exploit. A bit metaphorically, mental states come to life only in their connections to their causes, other mental states, and their effects.

Functionalism and Token Identity Theory

In its most widely held form, functionalism is a kind of physicalism. Specifically, it is a **token identity theory**: Every instance or token of a mental state type is identical to an instance or token of some physical state or other, but it is indifferent to the type and nature of these physical states. Something physical occupies the functional role, just as some particular person occupies the role of president, but it doesn't matter what physical thing that is. Of course, the most familiar "occupiers" of the functional role are brain states or properties. Thus, Sam and Sara may have the same type of mental state; they both may believe that there's no place like home. But Sara's brain activity may differ dramatically from Sam's. Token identity theory insists only that there is something physical playing or occupying the role. Different physical tokens—different physical states—may fill one and the same functional role. A more technical way of putting the same point is that different types of physical state may *realize* the same type of mental state. (Remember, tokens are particular examples of, or instances of a type. In what follows, functionalism is to be understood as a token identity theory.)

The Autonomy of the Mental and Irreducibility

Functionalism requires specifying the characteristic connections of mental state types—for example, belief—particularly the connections to typical causes, other mental states, and resultant effects. Similarly specifying the characteristic connections of desire, hope, fear, and the like should enable us, in principle, to say how belief differs from desire and how both differ from fear. We will be able to identify the characteristic features of the type "belief," along with the other mental state types (more technically, we will have *type-identified* belief).

Of course, providing these "functional identity" conditions is no mean feat. Indeed, simply identifying the characteristic functional features of the broad *categories* of belief and desire is a genuine challenge. But functionalism claims that we should expect to find these defining functional features. Once these defining features are in hand, we will have grasped, according to functionalism, the nature of the mental.

The mental types that functionalism identifies are also of interest to psychology. Psychology—the study of the mental—has its own kinds or types, properties, laws, and generalizations independent of whatever occurs at the physical level. The laws that govern the types of interest to psychology (say, memory processes) differ from the laws that govern the types of interest to neuroscience (neuronal activation and the like). In this sense, psychology is an *autonomous* discipline (Fodor 1968). Of course, we are also interested in connections between neuroscience and psychology. Neuropsychology, for example, studies the neural realization of various psychological properties and processes (for instance, it may study the correlation between certain types of reading disabilities and neural damage).

The autonomy of the mental is reflected in functionalism's view that the mental is irreducible. This is a consequence of multiple realizability. Since mental types may have any number of physical realizers, we should not expect that mental concepts could be replaced by neuroscientific concepts (Fodor 1981, chap. 5). It is worth spending a moment to see why.

Since mental states are defined by their functional role, the "stuff"—the physical realizer—that fills the functional role doesn't matter. Functionalists are happy to admit that very different "stuff" can make a mind; it recognizes that in addition to humans, certain animals, Vulcans, or computer-controlled robots might have mental states. All that matters is that *some* physical thing (or property) fills the functional roles. *Mental properties are functional properties.* R2D2 is no less mental than Luke Skywalker.

Now, recall that reducibility requires bridge laws connecting mental concepts to neural concepts; the bridge laws identify mental and neural types. In token identity theory, however, the belief that there is no place like home can be realized by very different physical types. When we ask, "What is the *type* of physical stuff that is identical to this belief?" the answer is "Well, there isn't any one type; there are lots of types, and no one type of physical stuff is any more special than another when it comes to making a mind." The lack of a *unique* connection between a physical type and a mental type entails that we should not expect to find the requisite bridge laws. Hence, the mental is irreducible to the physical.

A rough example illustrates this argument. In the normal case, when a person sees the color red, there is usually a distinctive pattern of activity in area V4 of the visual cortex. Type identity theory claims that having the sensation of red *is* having this pattern of activity in V4. So, some bridge law connects "red sensation" to "V4 pattern of activity," and the way is open to reduction. But once we recognize that any number of different physical types may fill the role of a red sensation—a Vulcan's red sensation may be realized by "P2" brain activity, for example, or "R1" activity in a robot's central computer—we no longer have the required one-to-one connection between mental types and physical types. As we discover still further physical types that yield red sensations, this disjunctive "law" will become increasingly complex. The functionalist claims that we have lost any hope of type identity, and thus there is no reason to talk further about reducibility. Again, simply, for the functionalist, it's the role that matters, not the stuff.

A Brief Comparative Look

How does functionalism compare to previously considered theories of mind? Dualism, whether substance or property, holds to the nonphysical character of the mental. But functionalism (in its token identity version) clearly rejects this view. Nonetheless, functionalism recognizes the reality of the mental. Like behaviorism, functionalism sees a connection between environmental inputs and behavioral outputs, but functionalism insists on the reality of mental states, unwilling to dispense with talk of the mental. Mental states are also defined in terms of their connections to other *mental* states—no mere reliance on physical input and output will serve the functionalist.

Functionalism abandons the troublesome restriction imposed by type identity theory. As a token identity theory, functionalism retains a commitment to physicalism, while recognizing that many different types of physical things may have minds. Consequently, functionalism—like dualism, a bit surprisingly—rejects the idea that the mental is reducible to purely physical types.

Functionalism thus provides a realist and physicalist view of the mind and its properties. Mental states are inner states, relational in nature and token identical to physical states. But this token identity is not strong enough to yield reducibility. If you want to describe fully and explain the mental, you must rely on references to the mental. In the functionalist view, the mental is special enough to require its own, autonomous domain.

Something Left Out? Objections to Functionalism

Functionalism is at its best when it characterizes the propositional attitudes. Intentional states, whether beliefs, desires, or wishes, are important for what we *do*—in our reactions to the environment, in our thinking, and in the behaviors we undertake. Defining mental states by their causal roles, however, locks on to their *extrinsic* features. We don't, as it were, see a mental state in itself; we see it only as it is connected to other things, in its relational connection to other aspects of our mental life.

Yet at least *some* mental states seem to have a distinctive intrinsic aspect: There is a way that they *feel*. Some mental states have a qualitative, nonrelational character. These qualitative features are **qualia** (sometimes called "raw feels"). It would be nice to provide a definition of qualia (or a single quale). Unfortunately this is not easy to do. Instead we have to be content with illustrating the nature of qualia by example. There is a way that an orange tastes, which differs from the taste of a banana. *There is a way that it is like* to have the sensation of an orange, and *there is a way that it is like* to have that of a banana. Similarly, seeing a bright, shocking chartreuse just seems different from seeing a rather ordinary, drab olive. Biting your tongue *feels different* from burning it with hot coffee. Each of these qualia has a characteristic, qualitative character—a feel.

Notice that the *feel* appears to be something *intrinsic* to that state. Qualia are not characterized by their *relations*, but by their feel. Without its characteristic feel, the quale that comes from biting your tongue simply would not be that particular mental state. To put it simply—pains hurt; tickles tickle; an itch itches. Take away the tickle or the itch, and you have taken away the distinctive character of such mental states.

Two of the principal objections to functionalism target the characterization of mental states as *relational states*. These objections claim that functionalism seems unable to account for qualia, the intrinsic, *nonrelational* mental states. Is there no way that it feels to have a mental life?

Absent Qualia

The **absent qualia objection** claims that *mere functional organization is not sufficient to produce all mental properties*; functionalism, by its very nature, leaves out the qualitative aspect of the mental.

Ned Block, a leading philosopher of mind at MIT, takes functionalism at its word—that it is indifferent to the "stuff" of minds. It does not care about the underlying physical matter, but only about the functional organization of the physical. To illustrate the defect of this functionalist approach, he asks us to imagine the following absent-qualia scenario (Block 1978).

Suppose we have a diagram or a flowchart of the functional organization of your mind. Using this as a guide, take the roughly one billion residents of China and arrange them—hook them together—in such a way that they mirror your functional characteristics. Suppose we do this; suppose we organize a billion-plus people so that the causal-functional network they realize is exactly the same as the causal-functional network definitive of your mind.

Now put the functionalist hypothesis to work. Since you and the China-mind are functionally alike, whatever is true of your mental life is also true of the mental life of the China-mind. If you want a cupcake, the China-mind wants a cupcake. If you believe John McCain would make a good president, then it believes that John McCain would make a good president. Block, however, wishes to push a bit further.

It is self-evident (to you at least) that you are conscious, that you have qualitative states. Yet Block thinks that it is counterintuitive to think that the China-mind "has any mental states at all"—especially whether it has what philosophers have variously called "qualitative states" or "raw feels" (1978, 138). Careful: we are not asking whether the individual people making up the China-mind are conscious or have qualia. We are asking whether the functional whole—that thing produced by organizing the billion or so people—is conscious. Consciousness is an indispensable property of your mind; there is a "way that it is like" to have your thoughts, your sensations, your tickles and itches. But Block suggests that the China-mind might very well not be conscious in this way. If, however, we are not willing to count the China-mind as conscious, then there is something defective about functionalism. If functionalism leaves out consciousness or the qualitative character of some mental states, then functionalism leaves out an important property of the mind.

Block's worry stems in part from his view that our mental life "depends crucially on psychological and/or neural processes and structures" (142). Functionalism's indifference to the underlying physical makeup and its emphasis on functional role opens the door to functionally equivalent systems—with wildly different physical makeups—counting as *mental*. Block doubts this apparent consequence of functionalism. If he is right, then functionalism cannot be the whole story of the mind.

Qualia and Inverted Spectra

Functionalism tells us that if we find two individuals that are functionally identical, then there are no differences in their mental states; whatever is true of the mental life of one is true of the mental life of the other. But there is an intuition that two states may differ in their *qualitative* aspects, while remaining functionally the same. And if the two states differ qualitatively, then they are not the same state—contrary to functionalism. The **inverted spectrum objection** exploits this intuition; it claims that we might find qualitative differences, and hence different states, where functionalism tells us that everything should be the same (Block and Fodor 1972; Shoemaker 1980). This is an unhappy prospect for the functionalist.

We are familiar with differences in "qualia preference." Deirdre finds the lemon meringue pie heavenly, while Danny scoffs and reaches for something more promising. Such differences are routine and undramatic. The inverted spectrum argument asks us imagine a more dramatic qualia difference.

Suppose Danny and Deirdre are looking at a very deep red rose. Imagine now two things: first, both experience a particular type of qualitative state; second, in all relevant respects to their individual qualia, Danny and Deirdre are functionally identical. Deirdre thinks it a beautiful rose and wishes to take it home; similarly, Danny thinks it a beautiful rose and wishes to take it home. If Danny believes that it is perfectly shaped, so does Deirdre. But now imagine one difference. When Deirdre looks at the rose, she has the same type of quale the rest of us have when we look at a red rose. Yet when Danny looks at the rose, he has the type of quale the rest of us have when looking at the deep green of a well-kept lawn. Danny's color qualia are inverted with respect to our normal color qualia. But Danny is *functionally* indistinguishable from the rest of us. Like us, he, too, thinks that the Red Delicious apples look better than the Golden Delicious apples or that red roses are growing in the backyard. But Danny has a sensation *different from ours* in each of these cases; his sensory states are "inverted."

It is plausible to think that since Danny and Deirdre differ in their qualia, they have *different* mental states. Since, however, those states are functionally the same, functionalism apparently counts them as having the *same* type of mental state. Hence, something is wrong in functionalism.

Once again, it is not difficult to see why the problem arises. Functionalism understands mental states relationally, but the inverted spectrum objection focuses on a nonrelational property of mental states, their qualitative character. Looking at the functional role of a mental state thus leaves us blind to its intrinsic, qualitative features. Functionalism can't show us qualia.

Functionalism Responds

Functionalists offer a variety of lines of response to the two qualia objections. One route, envisioned by Jerry Fodor, is to concede that since functionalism does not provide an adequate theory of qualia, functionalism ought to be restricted to intentional states. That is, functionalism only provides a theory of the propositional attitudes. (Fodor 1981, 16–17.) Fodor may be right; it may be true that functionalism offers an understanding of only the representational aspects of mental states. Others, however, seek to defend functionalism

as a more comprehensive theory of mind. So, we will look at responses that
do not cleave the qualitative from the intentional.

Absent Qualia Responses

A first option for the functionalist is to insist that the China-mind *is* conscious. Size, distance, speed of interactions, and numerous other factors may
prevent us from gathering the evidence for consciousness, but this is as it
should be. Since the China-mind is a very different kind of physical realization of a mind, it may be difficult for us to gather evidence that it has qualitative states. But in the functionalist view, consciousness comes about whenever and only when a being has the right functional organization.
Consciousness is thus a necessary by-product of appropriate functional organization. Indeed, the functionalist might add, since we know so little about
what causes consciousness in the first place, the critic is hardly in a position
to claim that the functional hypothesis is mistaken. For all we know, functionalism may be our best hope of explaining the appearance of consciousness.

This reply of course shifts the burden of proof back to the critic. We must
be given some reason for thinking that consciousness does not arise wherever
and whenever the right functional organization is realized. The size of the
China-mind, not to mention the oddness of its physical components, may at
first incline us to think that something is wrong with functionalism. But a
fuller appreciation of functionalism, and our lack of understanding of the
physical causes of the qualitative aspects of the mental, may support the idea
that the right functional organization brings about qualia.

A second line of response questions the possibility of absent qualia. Sydney Shoemaker (1980, 1982) challenges the coherence of the absent qualia
argument. Here we will have to be content with the general outline of his argument.

Suppose for a moment that a creature or system, like the China-mind, is
functionally identical to some human mind. Since Shoemaker considers
"qualia-free" but functionally identical Martians, suppose that Sam is talking to
his functionally identical Martian twin, Martian Sam. Both assert the existence
of their qualitative states, since they are functionally identical. If Sam says that
the water is too icy for swimming, then so does Martian Sam. If Sam claims that
the water is so cold that it hurts, then so does Martian Sam. Shoemaker now
draws the following consequence. There is no way—in principle—to distinguish between Sam's genuine hurting and the Martian's "ersatz" hurting.

According to the absent qualia hypothesis, qualia have no causal or functional relations. In this sense, qualia are causally "isolated." Shoemaker holds
that our knowledge of any mental state depends on our knowledge of its causal

relations—what causes the state and the effects of the state. Yet a chief—if not defining—characteristic of pain is that it hurts. We can feel it. That is, according to Shoemaker, the qualitative character of pain is *introspectively accessible* (1982, 198). But notice that this accessibility is a kind of causal relation.

Now, the absent qualia scenario insists that qualitative character "escapes" the functional or causal relations of a mental state: You can't get to qualia by functional role. The separation of functional role from qualitative character seems to preclude relying on introspective access. This separation cuts off our way of knowing who has the real pain! In principle, we couldn't tell whether it's Sam or Martian Sam with the absent qualia. For all we know, it's Sam who has the ersatz pain. And this would seem to count against the absent qualia scenario.

A related consideration may serve to support Shoemaker's conclusion (we will see a similar line of argument about the inverted spectrum case). Suppose that Sam has introspective beliefs about the pain of swimming in icy water; by hypothesis, Martian Sam has the same "introspective" belief. One of two things seems to be true of Martian Sam. Either his introspective belief is causally connected to a certain hurting feeling or it isn't. If the former, then Martian Sam has qualia after all. If the latter, then there *is* a functional difference between Sam and Martian Sam: The *cause* of Sam's introspective belief differs from that of Martian Sam's. In this second case, Sam is introspecting a "hurt," but Martian Sam is not, since he has no "hurts" to introspect. Again, this seems to count against the supposition of absent qualia.

Shoemaker's argument at the very least suggests a functionalist response. Some might worry that it is too verificationist—roughly, that it makes matters of fact depend on what we can know about them (Fodor 1981, 16–17). Or one might worry about Shoemaker's claim about how we come to know of qualia. Still, these responses show that the functionalism has some resources to respond to absent qualia worries.

Inverted Spectrum Responses
While intuitions may not be so clear about absent qualia, the notion of inverted spectra seems deeply appealing to some. It appears intuitively plausible that two people might be in exactly the same functional state and yet "experience" something different. In this sense, the inverted spectrum presents a more difficult challenge for functionalism. Again, we consider two lines of response, the first from Paul and Patricia Churchland.

While they are not themselves functionalists, the Churchlands (1981) suggest that functionalists can claim that functional role is the essence or "type identity" of a mental state, while insisting that qualia are accidental or nonessential features of such states. Functionalism defines or type-identifies mental states in terms of their characteristic causal relations to other states, inputs, and outputs. So, if Sara and Sam have the same type of belief, then their individual beliefs have the same functional role ("their individual beliefs" refers to their having different tokens of the same type of belief). And the essence or identity of a belief *is* its functional role.

But functionalism is not committed to the idea that *every* property of those beliefs must be the same. Sara's belief is realized by her neurons and Sam's belief is realized by his. Sara's belief has the property "brought about by Sara's brain," but Sam's belief clearly does not have this property. Does this present a problem for functionalism? No, for this property is not relevant to the causal role of the mental state. In the functionalist view, such properties are accidental or contingent—they don't tell you anything essential about the mental state.

The Churchlands suggest that functionalism could maintain that the intrinsic, qualitative feel of a mental state is not essential to the *type* of mental state. Some mental states have qualitative features, but these features do not determine whether individual mental states are the same type. Sensations are simply the internal mechanism used to discriminate the mental state type. To put it very loosely, when Sam and Sara—otherwise functionally identical— experience different sensations upon seeing a deep red rose, Sam's sensation is his brain's way of telling him that there is a red rose in the vicinity, and not a yellow one. And Sara's brain tells her, by means of her sensation, that yonder lies a red, red rose. They get to the same belief type—this object is a red rose—by different routes, different qualia. Analogously, consider two students who receive the same *type* of test score, but do so by answering different questions correctly. The functional features of a mental state—not the qualitative features—determine the mental state type.

The Churchlands respond to the criticism that this defense of functionalism still leaves unanswered the claim that, whatever the sensations do, they are different *types* of sensation because they have different qualitative features (1981, 165–69). There is, however, a slightly different line functionalists might take at this point. They might wonder whether qualitatively different states might really occur without *any* functional difference.

Gilbert Harman (1999, chap. 14; see also Shoemaker 1984, 184–205) claims that in normal cases of seeing—the red rose again, for example—there is no distinction between how things look and how we believe them to be. If something looks or seems red, we believe that it *is* red. In a sense, beliefs *normally* "track" how things seem. Harman further notes that in the inverted spectrum case, the two are supposed to be functioning normally. That is, in our example, we are supposing that Sara and Sam are functionally alike. So, if upon seeing a red rose both Sam and Sara are in the same functional state, then they both believe that there *is* a red rose.

Harman now argues that Sam and Sara must have different beliefs. Remember, in the inverted spectrum, whenever it seems to Sara that she is seeing red, it seems to Sam that he is seeing green. Thus, their functional states, their beliefs, are caused by different "seemings"; it looks one way to Sam, another to Sara. Again, in a sense, their beliefs "track" different seemings or how things look. But this suggests that we have a functional difference after all. So, Harman holds that in the inverted spectrum case, "they must have different beliefs about the color" (259).

Critics of this response might worry that this approach doesn't tell us the nature of the qualitative difference. Still, the functionalist could respond that qualia make a functional difference, and this is enough to show that they don't fall outside functionalist theory.

Is This Physical Enough For You?
Types, Tokens, and Physicalism

As a token identity theory, functionalism accepts that everything that exists is physical or a property of the physical; some things—the mental—are functional properties of the physical. The functionalist departs from type identity in two related and now familiar ways. First, mental state types need not be identical to physical state types. The functionalist insists only that each occurrence of a mental state be identical to *some* physical state or other. Functionalists pride themselves on their liberality—very different physical arrangements can bring about the mental.

But this leads to a second difference. Given that many different physical types may bring about the mental, there should be no thought of reducing the mental to the physical. Because of the diversity of ways in which the mental can be realized, we will not be able to find the requisite bridge laws— the laws connecting mental types to neural types—for reduction. The science of the mental is autonomous, according the functionalist.

The type identity theorist has two related concerns about all this liberality and autonomy (Kim 1998, chap. 4; Braddon-Mitchell and Jackson 1996, chap. 6). In the preceding chapter, we considered *restricted type identity*. Here we focus on the worry manifested in the issue of autonomy.

To see how this concern arises, think about the *liquidity* of water. We know that water is liquid because of the chemical bonds between its constituent molecules. The liquidity of the water depends on its molecular structure.

This dependency of observable properties on underlying physical structure is not confined to water. The rust on the iron fence, the brittleness of the glass, the green of the leaf—all are dependent upon the underlying physical structure. In a sense, reduction captures this dependency.

We can now express the type identity theorist's worry. Insisting on token identity and resisting reduction is a very weak physicalist thesis; indeed it leaves us wondering exactly *how* the mental depends on the physical. If there are dependency relations, mental types would be reducible to physical types, at least in the restricted sense previously noted. But token identity rejects reducibility. And this "reducibility resistance" seems a little odd to the identity theorist.

Understanding the necessary connection, the law-like connection, between some property or event and its physical basis allows us to understand the sense in which that property or event is ultimately physical. We understand, for example, a little better how red color sensations might be physical when we understand that the way to get red sensations is stimulation of a part of the visual cortex. But now the functionalist not only loosens this connection but seems to unravel it altogether. Red sensations aren't tied to particular types of neural states, says the functionalist; indeed they aren't tied to neural states at all. Neither are they tied to camera lenses connected to sophisticated computerized robots. Nor are red sensations tied to complex organizations of beer cans and wires. Red sensations could show up just about anywhere in the world! This is multiple realization in the extreme. And now we seem to have only the most tenuous connection between the physical properties of a thing and its mental properties.

All of this autonomy is a little too much for the type identity theorist. A world in which brain processes do not necessitate mental properties is still a world that is physicalist, but just barely. The type identity theorist thinks we should be able to explain *why* brains produce mental states. Answering the why, however, requires that we see some dependency relation between brain states and mental states.

To put matters very simply, if you can't reduce the mental to the physical, then there is no necessary connection between the mental and the physical. In principle then, we could imagine the world physically just as it is, but without any mental properties whatsoever.

How might the functionalist reply to this physicalist worry? The functionalist, as an antireductionist, would claim that generalizations about our mental life are simply not expressible in the language of neuroscience. The challenge for the functionalist is the following. Functionalism must explain the dependency of the mental on the physical. It shouldn't be just accidental that brains produce mental lives. But functionalism needs to explain this dependency without opening the way to reduction.

The functionalist might argue as follows. There is a *nomological* connection between brain activity and mental states. That is, there are physical laws that govern the physical–mental connection: do this to the V4 area of the brain, and you are going to see red; increase the amount of neurotransmitters in the septal area of the brain, and your thoughts will turn from philosophy of mind to more amorous matters. The functionalist admits that neuroscience helps identify the dependency of minds on brains.

But given this, how should the functionalist resist restricted-type reductions? One possibility is that the irreducibility of the mental lies in the way in which mental states interact. Since every mental state is variously connected to other mental states, these interconnections give rise to properties not expressible in the language of neural types. What sorts of properties? Various ones have been suggested, and of these, rationality is especially important. We characterize beliefs as rational because of their logical or probabilistic connections to other beliefs. Similarly we may count a certain fear as irrational. For example, the fear that monsters are hiding under one's bed, if there is no evidence for such a fear, is an unwarranted fear. Here we have certain uniquely mental properties—rational, deducible from, and warranted. These properties manifest certain patterns of connections between mental states. Now, the functionalist need not suggest that such properties commit us to dualism. Rather these kinds of properties and the patterns they exemplify are not reducible to some set of physical, that is, neural types.

The functionalist thus maintains that there is a nonaccidental connection between brain states and mental states—but that this is not enough for reduction. The necessary interaction between mental states gives rise to certain properties or patterns of connections. These patterns preclude reduction to neural types precisely because the patterns would be lost were we to rely solely on talking of neural types. If these suggestions are along the right lines, then the functionalist has a response to the type physicalists' worries.

We have been brief about these issues. Clearly there are some larger issues at stake—such as what sort of commitments are implied by physicalism. In subsequent chapters, we will have occasion to take up these issues again, albeit in somewhat different form. Despite the qualia objections (and other concerns we have not considered), functionalism is still a viable view. According to many, it affords our best hope of retaining some of our most deeply held and familiar views of the mind, while embracing a generally physicalist theory of the world.

We have, however, a bit of unfinished business. It turns out that some functionalists exploit the analogy between mind and computer in quite dramatic ways. And it is to this view of the mind as essentially computational that we now turn.

Key Concepts

Absent qualia argument

Functionalism

Inverted spectrum argument

Qualia

Token Identity

Type-token distinction

Reading Questions

1. Functionalism provides a relational treatment of mental states. What does this mean?

2. Why is functionalism considered a token identity theory? Why does functionalism hold that the mental is not reducible?

3. Why is it thought that qualia create a problem for functionalism?

4. Describe briefly the absent qualia and inverted spectrum arguments.

5. Explain briefly how qualitative states might be given a functional characterization.

References

Bechtel, William. 1988. *Philosophy of mind: An overview for cognitive science*. Hillsdale, NJ: Lawrence Erlbaum.

Block, Ned. 1978. Troubles with functionalism. In *Perception and cognition: Issues in the foundations of psychology*, vol. 9 of *Minnesota Studies in the Philosophy of Science*, ed. C. W. Savage, 261–325. Minneapolis: University of Minnesota Press. Reprinted in Crumley 2000, 130–62; page references are to this volume.

———, ed. 1980. *Readings in the philosophy of psychology*. Vol. 1. Cambridge, MA: Harvard University Press.

Block, Ned, and Jerry Fodor. 1972. What psychological states are not. *Philosophical Review* 81:159–81. Reprinted in Block 1980, chap. 20.

Braddon-Mitchell, David, and Frank Jackson. 1996. *Philosophy of mind and cognition*. Oxford: Blackwell.

Churchland, Patricia, and Paul Churchland. 1981. Functionalism, qualia, and intentionality. *Philosophical Topics* 12, no. 1: 121–45. Reprinted in Crumley 2000, 163–77; page references are to this volume.

Crumley, Jack, ed. 2000. *Problems in mind: Readings in contemporary philosophy of mind*. Mountain View, CA: Mayfield.

Fodor, Jerry. 1968. *Psychological explanation: An introduction to the philosophy of psychology*. New York: Random House.

———. 1981. *RePresentations: Philosophical essays on the foundations of cognitive science*. Cambridge, MA: MIT Press.

Harman, Gilbert. 1999. *Reasoning, meaning, and mind*. Oxford: Clarendon Press.

Kim, Jaegwon. 1998. *Mind in a physical world: An essay on the mind–body problem and mental causation*. Cambridge, MA: MIT Press.

Lewis, David. 1980. Mad pain and Martian pain. In Black, 1980, Chap. 16.

Lycan, William. 1994. Functionalism (1). In *A companion to the philosophy of mind*, ed. Samuel Guttenplan, 317–23. Oxford: Blackwell.

Putnam, Hilary. 1975a. The mental life of some machines. In *Mind, language, and reality: Philosophical papers*. Cambridge: Cambridge University Press, 2:408–28.

———. 1975b. Minds and machines. In *Mind, language, and reality: Philosophical papers*. Cambridge: Cambridge University Press, 2:362–85.

———. 1975c. The nature of mental states. In *Mind, language, and reality: Philosophical papers*. Cambridge: Cambridge University Press, 2:429–40. Reprinted in Crumley 2000, 102–9.

Shoemaker, Sydney. 1980. Functionalism and qualia. In Block 1980, chap. 21.

———. 1981. Absent qualia are impossible—A reply to Block. *Philosophical Review* 90, 581–99. Reprinted in *Consciousness*, ed. Frank Jackson, 183–202 (Aldershot: Ashgate, 1998); page references are to this volume.

———. 1982. The inverted spectrum. *Journal of Philosophy* 79, 357–81. Reprinted in *Consciousness*, ed. Frank Jackson, 3–28 (Aldershot: Ashgate, 1998); page references are to this volume.

———. 1984. *Identity, cause and mind*. Cambridge: Cambridge University Press.

Additional Readings

Block, Ned. "Introduction: What Is Functionalism?" In Block 1980, 171–84.

Fodor, Jerry. "The Mind–Body Problem." *Scientific American* 244, no. 1 (1981): 114–23. Reprinted in Crumley 2000, 118–29.

———. "Special Sciences." Chap. 5 of Fodor 1981.

Lycan, William. *Consciousness*. Cambridge, MA: MIT Press, 1987.

Shoemaker, Sydney. "Some Varieties of Functionalism." *Philosophical Topics* 12 (1981): 93–120.

5

Minds, Computers, and Biology: Functionalism II

In 1950 Alan Turing, a British mathematician and logician, proposed a game—"the imitation game," as Turing called it—in which a player tries to guess the gender of two other players, but one of these other two players might be a computer. A more recent version of this game is called the Turing Test. Connected only by keyboards and a computer screens, the player must guess, after a series of exchanges, whether the other player is a person or a computer (Moody 1993, chap. 4; Turing 1950). Presumably a computer "passes" the test if the player thinks that a person, not a computer, is the hidden interlocutor. The implication is that if a person (in the role of the hidden interlocutor) counts as intelligent, and if a computer performs as well as a person, then the computer should also count as intelligent.

That a machine might *think* has been controversial at least since the time of Descartes. Turing himself notes in his 1950 article the objection that no computer should be counted as equivalent to the human brain until a computer writes a concerto or sonnet because of "thoughts and emotions felt." More recently, a related claim—that we might understand aspects of our mental life by comparing it to a computer—has become similarly controversial. This chapter examines both these ideas. After a brief account of artificial intelligence, we will turn to an examination of computational functionalism, whose chief architect is Jerry Fodor. In the second half of the chapter, we will examine John Searle's famous argument that no computer, no matter how sophisticated, can think.

Artificial Intelligence

The science of artificial intelligence (AI) is roughly a half-century old. Even its staunchest defenders admit that the endeavor has promised more than it has delivered. Margaret Boden (1990)—a philosophical ally of the discipline—provides two definitions of AI. The first suggests that AI studies how computers may be built or programmed to function similarly to minds. It's clear that some computers already perform some of the same tasks as human minds, such as proving theorems, playing chess, answering phones, analyzing geological data and deciding whether a certain location is a good place to drill for oil, and even providing medical diagnoses and "suggesting" treatments. Of course, machines might perform such tasks without showing us anything about the mental, much less demonstrating that the machines have a mental life. Many, if not most, seriously doubt that a simple calculator is intelligent or thinking—even if it knows how much of our 172nd mortgage payment will be going toward the loan principal and we don't.

More important for our purpose is Boden's second definition—that AI is the study of intelligence in general. The aim of AI is to tell us what comprises intelligence, regardless of whether it is the intelligence of cows or chickens, humans or chimpanzees, or computers or extraterrestrials. To do so, AI must provide an understanding of the nature of intentionality, the "aboutness" of mental states, and the related capacities necessary for an intelligent system.

Fundamental to this endeavor is the notion of *representation*; functionalists and AI advocates alike urge that intelligent behavior—thinking—requires both a representational ability and a system of representation. For example, it is claimed that a physical symbol system is both necessary and sufficient for intelligent behavior (Newell and Simon 1976). We can think of a physical symbol system as a system of representation that is physically realized. So, if we think of a computer as a physical symbol system, then it would seem to have the elements necessary for thinking. Further, since humans think, then we must have a physical symbol system also. This leads to an intriguing proposal. Since human thought proceeds by a way of a system of representation, and since computers might be built with a system of representation, it might be possible to draw insights about the nature of human thinking by looking at computers.

Philosophy of mind and AI thus tend to converge at certain points. The philosophy of mind wants to understand the nature of intentionality, and so does AI. The two also seem to converge on the notion of symbolic processing. Or to put it differently, they seem to converge on the notion that the content of a mental state derives from the encoding of a sentence in the "hardware" of the system. We should not overlook the potential significance of understanding the mind as a computer or of considering computers as being capable of thinking. The issue is not about whether AI "dehumanizes" us; rather, it is part of a serious attempt to explain how something like meaning could arise in a purely physical universe. Many of our most prized human characteristics—thinking, communicating, deciding—are tied to this simple but fundamental fact: *Thoughts have meaning.* Descartes dismissed any such mechanical explanation, but advocates of a computational view of the mind are less pessimistic. Indeed they think that the computational view gives us a framework for explaining the semantic character of our mental life.

Computational Functionalism

Functionalism comes in various guises; it is more a family of theories than a single theory of mind. But all members of the family bear a striking familial resemblance to one another—they characterize mental states in terms of their place in a causal network. Computational functionalism views the mind, like the computer, as a symbol-processing system. Fodor characterizes this view as a merging of functionalism about the propositional attitudes and a computational theory of the content of these attitudes. That is, functionalism tells us the nature of beliefs, desires, and the like, while the computational or representational theory provides an account of the *contents* of beliefs and other propositional attitudes.

Three ideas are central to **computational functionalism**. The first is the claim that we have an internal system of representation—a set of mental symbols—on which computations or operations are performed. This representational system is the backbone of our thinking. Fodor calls this representational system the "**language of thought**." Second, this internal symbol system is described syntactically (to be explained shortly). It is worth noting that this is an *empirical* claim. One task for cognitive psychologists, according to Fodor, is discovering the elements of the internal symbol system. Third, Fodor claims that the content of our propositional attitudes derives from this language of thought (Fodor 1979; Sterelny 1990; Rey 1997). The content of our thoughts (for example, our belief that today is a crisp autumn day) comes from the internal representational system. For this reason, computational functionalism is also known as the "representational theory of mind."

Fodor thinks that the nature of thinking itself requires accepting the idea of a language of thought. The general argument is not unique to Fodor, as the preceding section noted. But he deploys the argument to support the existence of a language of thought (Fodor 1979, 1981, 1987). First, he contends, any thinking requires a system of representation. Thoughts need some vehicle, as it were. But thinking might occur without there being a speaker; that is, one can have the ability to think without having mastered a natural language (such as English or French or Lithuanian). Since thinking might still occur, and since thinking requires a system of representation, Fodor identifies this system as the language of thought. The language of thought is prior to any natural language; indeed natural languages derive their content from the language of thought.

Fodor also argues that we are continually making hypotheses about the world and testing them. We make hypotheses about the best course of action to take, in perception, and in acquiring new concepts. Framing these hypotheses, which often occurs unconsciously, requires a system of representation. We need a way of representing different possibilities. (In the appendix to Fodor 1987, Fodor considers these and other reasons for holding that there is a language of thought in more detail.)

Cognitive Science

Computational functionalism is partially inspired by cognitive science. This reasonably new interdisciplinary science, growing out of the cognitive psychology movement, views the mind as an information-processing system. Cognitive science sees itself as lying at the intersection of several disciplines—linguistics, philosophy, psychology, computer science, and neuroscience. Cognitive science views the mind as operating on information, storing it, retrieving it, modifying it. These operations are fundamentally *computational processes*, operating on internal symbols.

Cognitive science sees its task as analyzing the various mental processes, such as language acquisition and processing, memory, perception, reasoning, and problem solving. It takes seriously the analogy between the computer and the mind. Both "systems" are information-processing systems, which can be variously physically realized.

Some cognitive scientists see functionalism as a hospitable framework for understanding the relation of mind and body, although this question is not wholly settled. And it should be somewhat clear from the brief description above that the computational functionalist view of the mind has much in common with cognitive science's view (Stillings et al. 1995, chaps. 1, 2, and 8).

Moreover, Fodor characterizes the internal symbol system as a *language* because of its structure—in particular because the basic or simple symbols combine to form new, more complex symbols. Various rules, something like our rules of grammar, govern how the symbols might be combined or transformed. But we are getting a little ahead of ourselves.

Computational functionalism thus takes seriously the idea that cognitive processes and (suitably constructed) computers can be understood in importantly similar ways. Understanding the internal system of representation, the language of thought, is the key to understanding computational functionalism.

Three Levels of Description

We begin with three ways that we might describe the operations of a computer. These three levels of description are the semantic, the syntactic, and the physical.

At the semantic level, the outputs of a computer—the symbols—have a meaning. The symbols are interpreted or refer to something. Suppose, for example, that a group of meteorologists input various data into a hurricane modeling program. The computer subsequently produces a series of symbols. The meteorologists interpret these symbols as referring to various properties—wind speed, for example, or the projected location of a hurricane. **Semantics** then is the meaning or interpretation of the symbols.

We can also consider the symbols themselves, without reference to the interpretation of the symbols. **Syntax** is the set of symbols together with the rules for their combination and transformation. Arithmetic, for example, provides a set of rules for combining and transforming symbols. An addition table tells us that "3 + 7" is a sequence of symbols that allows us to get still another symbol, "10." Some sequences are acceptable, but others are not. "3 + 7 = 10" is acceptable, but "2 ÷≥ =7" is just so many scratches on the page. The important contrast is between interpreted symbols or symbols that have a meaning—this is semantics—and uninterpreted symbols, symbols that may be combined and transformed according to various rules—this is syntax.

Properties such as truth, falsity, and reference (what a symbol picks out or refers to) are semantic properties. Only at the semantic level are combinations of symbols said to be true or false. In order to know whether "100 + 101 = 1001" is true, we first need to know whether the symbols should receive a binary or a decimal interpretation. Given their normal meaning, the sentence is of course false: One hundred plus one hundred and one doesn't equal a thousand and one. Given a binary interpretation, however, the sentence is true: It is a binary representation of our more familiar "4 + 5 = 9." Similarly, the English sentence "William Jefferson Clinton is the forty-second president" is true because of the interpretation of the symbols: a particular property (being the forty-second president) is assigned to a particular person, and that person is picked out by the symbols "William Jefferson Clinton." As already noted, computational functionalism seeks to explain the semantic properties of our thoughts by appeal to a syntactically characterized language—the language of thought.

Back to our computer. Most of us are familiar with the distinction between hardware and software. A computer program, a kind of software, is a set of procedures for operating on various symbols (or data or inputs). The central idea is that the program treats the symbols purely syntactically. That is, the program "reacts" only to the formal properties of the symbols. To get a rough idea of the notion of a formal property, think of computer passwords that are case sensitive (differentiating between upper-case and lower-case letters), or of putting a space in the middle of an e-mail address, or of completing that address with ".com" instead of ".org." Of course, from our perspective, we assign a meaning to the symbols, but the meanings we assign don't affect the operations of the program.

Of course, were we to open up the case of a computer, we would not see any symbols or programming language. The operations of the computer, the transforming of symbols, are realized or implemented in the hardware of the computer, the various chips, processors, and the like.

The significant point for computational functionalists is that a physical system is designed in such a way that the operations on the symbols preserve or mirror the meanings we assign to the symbols. The computer—hardware and software together—provides a model for thinking about how semantics or meaning could be realized in a physical system. The computational model of the mind seems to suggest how a mental property—meaning—could be realized in a purely physical system, *contra* Descartes. It is an idea exploited by Fodor.

The Language of Thought
You may be wondering what all this has to do with minds. Computational functionalists think that these three levels of description—the semantic, the syntactic, and the physical—illuminate our mental operations. We typically describe our thoughts, beliefs, wishes, and the like at the semantic level, since they have meaning or are about something. Think, for example, about our familiar red, red rose. This thought is *about* something, it is *intentional* or directed toward the very red rose. Your thought has a content; it has meaning. (Often in contexts such as this, "aboutness," "intentionality," "mental content" or just plain "content," and "meaning" are used interchangeably; we will do so here, as well.)

Intentionality—the aboutness of our thoughts—is a central characteristic of the mental. Physicalists, of course, are reasonably certain that this thought of the red, red rose is instantiated in, realized by, the brain. But how is the thought of a red rose—or more specifically, the belief that there is a red, red rose—realized in the brain? The language of thought enters precisely here.

Between the semantic level of intentionality and the "hardware" level—the physical level—of the brain lies the syntactic level of "mentalese," as it is dubbed. Mentalese—the language of thought—has its own set of basic symbols and rules for combining and transforming those symbols. Now, here is the important point: The meaning or the content of our thoughts comes from, or derives from, these mentalese symbols. More specifically, the content of the thought derives from the causal role of the mentalese sentence. Because of the structure of the language of thought, the mentalese sentences enter into various causal relations, and these causal relations determine the meaning of our more ordinary thoughts. To say that Sara believes that there is a red rose is to say that Sara is in a computational relation to an internal sentence, a mentalese sentence. Or as Fodor sometimes describes, Sara has a mentalese sentence in her belief box.

Our more familiar thoughts—Danny's thought that it's quieter in the bedroom—are translations of mentalese sentences into natural language. And two people have the same thought if they have the same internal formula or mentalese sentence. (A little more precisely, two people have the same thought if they each have a token of the same type of mentalese sentence. Where there is little risk of confusion, we will omit mention of tokens of types.) For instance, Danny may express his thought that a dog is barking by using an English sentence, while his French cousin may express it with a French sentence. They have, however, the same mental content by virtue of having the same internal mentalese sentence. And Danny and his cousin have the same propositional attitude if the same mentalese sentence plays the same functional role in each of them. Danny and his French cousin, for example, both have the belief that the dog is barking if their respective tokens of the same internal formula play the same functional role.

We can illustrate a little more how the computational functionalist thinks of the interplay between the "computational" and the "functional." Consider the content that in Chicago it is illegal to take French poodles to the opera. Danny and Deirdre have this same content if they both have the same internal mentalese sentence (or they each have a token of the same type of mentalese sentence). Suppose that Danny *fears* that Chicago bans canine opera companions, while Deirdre *hopes* that the city does. This difference is captured by the different functional roles played by their respective tokens.

Upon learning of the prohibition, Deirdre may walk to the window and smile, while Danny lets his fingers walk through the *Yellow Pages* in search of a dogsitter. So, succinctly: Same mentalese sentence, same content; different functional role, different attitude. (Remember, functionalism identifies types of propositional attitudes by their functional roles.)

Computational functionalists disagree about the extent or scope of this language. Fodor (1979), at various times, argues for *nativism,* the view that the built-in mentalese symbols must be sufficient to represent any concept we might learn or acquire. This seems to imply that even concepts such as carburetor or cell phone are in some sense innate. Some resist this extreme nativism, though, claiming that the language of thought includes only certain basic symbols, for example, symbols for color or shape (Sterelny 1990).

So far we have been explaining the semantic and syntactic levels of the mental, but we have yet to consider the physical level. How is the language of thought physically realized? Unlike the computer, we don't have dollops of metal in our heads. There may be something just as good, however—neurons. Patterns of neural activity realize the mental symbols. In a sense, the mental symbols of the language of thought capture various patterns of neural activity. We now have a way of taking the thought of the rose and realizing it—*encoding* it—in the brain. At the very least, this suggests a way of understanding how something physical might have or realize a specifically mental property—the aboutness of a thought.

Computational functionalism yields this picture of the mind. The contents of propositional attitudes—the meanings of our ordinary thoughts—are determined by the causal interactions of structured sequences of mentalese symbols. A belief about a rose, a fear of a thorn, a hope for a gift all have the meanings that they do because of sentences in the language of thought. The particular attitudes, such as belief, fear, or hope, are still defined functionally. The language of thought itself is realized in patterns of neural activity. And if Fodor is right, cognitive psychologists can discover the basic symbols of and the rules for the language of thought. These internal formulas, the mental symbols, are realized in particular neural structures.

Worries about the Language of Thought

Computational functionalism is widely influential; it is also widely and extensively criticized. Many of the criticisms are directed against Fodor's elaborations of the view. Here we will consider two related issues.

In "A Cure for the Common Code?" (1977), Daniel Dennett finds it dubious that for any thought or belief we might have, there would be an explicit internal representation. Dennett notes that it will "come as no news to any of you that zebras in the wild do not wear overcoats" (275). We have, Dennett suggests, believed this proposition for some time, even though we have not explicitly thought of it before. He finds it very implausible that nonetheless we have an explicit internal representation of this thought. Dennett asserts that Fodor mistakenly ties the thoughts we have to the existence of mentalese sentences.

Dennett assumes that we have a very large number of "tacit beliefs"—thoughts, never before explicitly considered, that we in some sense believe. But it is an open question as to whether there are any such beliefs (Sterelny 1990, chap. 7; Bogdan 1986, chap. 7). Fodor can concede that we have *some* tacit beliefs, but refuse to admit to the numbers envisioned by Dennett. Moreover, Fodor can insist that as a result of the causal interactions of the mentalese sentences, new mentalese sentences are produced. And these newly produced representations are the internal representations of the tacit beliefs.

A related complaint is that the Fodor misrepresents the "architecture" of the mind. In Fodor's view, the language of thought comprises distinct symbols, which correspond to certain objects or properties. Very simply, there is a symbol for tiger, another for tree, another for running; and Fodor expects that each symbol has its own neural representation. Now, the worry is this: It is unlikely that there are distinct symbols realized in the brain. Rather, representations are *distributed*; different features and different combinations of features are spread out through a network. Different activation patterns—different ways of emphasizing different aspects of the pattern—yield different representations. Representation is in the *connections*, not in discrete symbols (hence, the name of this view—connectionism).

This latter debate about the architecture of the mind is ongoing. Allies of the computational view doubt that connectionist models can explain the richness and structure of our cognitive abilities. They can't explain, for example, how a single thought can generate a number of thoughts. A school psychologist once told me of talking to kindergarten students, trying to explain "being nervous." When he told them it felt as though he had butterflies in his stomach, the five-year-olds caught on quickly, each announcing a new thought: "I have cats in my stomach!" "I have elephants in my stomach!" "I have frogs in my stomach!" From a single thought-structure, we are able to generate an unlimited number of *new* thoughts. Computationalists don't think their critics can explain this feature. Of course, connectionists claim they can. But we must leave this story here (for further discussion, see Sterelny 1990, chap. 8; Fodor and Pylyshyn 1988).

Computational functionalism remains a robust view, but it hints at the topic in the next section. We have noted the analogies between the mental and the computer, and we know that functionalism is indifferent to the physical realization of mental states. It seems that a computer could well have mental states; a computer could think. Couldn't it?

Inside the Chinese Room: What the Computer Doesn't Know

In perhaps one of the more famous philosophical arguments in recent years, John Searle claims that a computer *cannot* think (Searle 1980; 1984, chap. 2). Searle contends that this is not simply a limitation on current technology, either software or hardware. *In principle*, Searle claims, we could not produce a computer that thinks. The nature of thinking and the nature of a computer preclude the possibility of a thinking computer. Fiddle about as much as you wish with the programs or the microprocessors; nonetheless, you will never produce a thinking computer. Moreover, the argument is intended to count against any functionalist or computational account of intentionality.

Searle means for his argument to undermine a view that he dubs the "strong AI thesis." Suppose for a moment that we have developed the appropriate hardware and a suitably sophisticated program. The **strong AI thesis** claims that running the right program is sufficient for thinking. That is, an appropriately designed and programmed computer *thinks*. Searle has no quarrel with a weaker claim, the **weak AI thesis**, which maintains that we can simulate or model thinking on computers. But as Searle points out, simulated thinking is no more genuine thinking than a simulated hurricane is a real hurricane. Meteorologists have no need of raincoats while they study a computer simulation of a hurricane. Searle's real target is the strong AI thesis. And he thinks he can show what is wrong with strong AI by means of a thought experiment, known as the "Chinese room."

The Chinese Room

Imagine yourself placed in a room. You are to carry on a conversation with a native Chinese speaker (the example assumes that you do not understand Chinese). The conversation proceeds by your receiving, through an "in-window," cards with Chinese characters on them. The cards represent the input—what the native Chinese speaker has said. Inside the room, you take the cards, and you compare them to a book of rules or instructions. The book tells you that when you receive a particular sequence of Chinese characters, you are to send through the "out-window" another sequence of cards with Chinese characters. The rule book, written in English, says, for example, "Given Chinese characters *x*, *y*, and *z*, send out Chinese characters *a*, *b*, and *f*." But the rule book does not provide an English translation of the Chinese characters; it only correlates Chinese characters with others. You simply manipulate symbols, according to the rule book. The rule book is so complete that from the native speaker's point of view, the conversation proceeds quite normally. As far as the person outside the room is concerned, it appears that whoever or whatever is holding up the other end of the conversation understands Chinese (Searle 1984, chap. 2).

Now, let the conversation continue as long you wish, even from your twenty-first birthday until the day you retire. No matter how long the conversation continues, Searle claims that simply by virtue of your receiving and sending out the Chinese symbols, *you do not understand Chinese and will never understand Chinese.* If the only process available to you is receiving and sending out symbols in accordance with the rule book, you will never understand the *meaning* of the Chinese symbols.

Searle of course has a much larger aim in mind. Searle claims that you are functioning in the same way a computer functions. You and the rule book are analogous to the program and the central processor. You process characters—you take in symbols, check the rule book, and send out symbols. Similarly the computer processes tokens—it takes in symbols, "checks" its rule book (the program), and sends out symbols. Searle now claims the following: *If you could not understand Chinese, then the computer could never understand its symbols.* That is, the computer does not and *cannot* possess semantics; it does not and *cannot* have the *meaning* of the symbols it processes. And if the computer does not have semantics, then it does not think.

Searle claims that the argument illustrated by the Chinese room is simple and straightforward (1984, chap. 2). Thinking minds have semantics. You think that the rain will never end. The concepts that you have or the words you use to express your thoughts have meaning. "Rain" refers to the wet stuff that falls from the sky. No matter what else occurs in thinking, thoughts are about something; that is, they have meaning. Searle's first premise then is: *Thinking requires semantics.*

We are reminded, however, of some aspects of computers. Computers operate the way they do by virtue of their having a program, which operates purely formally. The program guides the operations of the computer solely in terms of the syntactical, or the formal properties of the symbols, not by virtue of the meaning of the symbols. Thus, we have a second premise: *Computer programs are entirely defined by their formal or syntactical structure.*

The Chinese room argument might be viewed as supporting especially Searle's third premise. Symbols by themselves don't wear their meanings on their sleeve; the symbols themselves don't tell us how they are to be interpreted. Standing in the Chinese room, seeing only that certain symbols are connected to others, you will never learn the meaning of the symbols. And the same is true of a computer. Let it run a program for as long as you please, shuffling symbols about, and it will never "know" whether some symbol refers to your account balance, overdue books, pieces on a chessboard, or college football teams in a poll ranking. According to Searle, the Chinese room is designed to illustrate a simple truth (he calls it a conceptual truth), his third premise: *From syntax, you can't get semantics.*

Now, put these three pieces together. Computer programs are purely formal; they are just syntactic machines. If that is so, then—by the Chinese room argument—we know something else. Computers will never have semantics. But this is not good news for the computer. You cannot have thinking without semantics. You cannot have thinking unless you are thinking *about* something. So, the conclusion is clear. Since the computer will never have semantics, *the computer will never think.* Because Searle considers the Chinese room to model functional or computational accounts of intentionality, Searle believes those accounts are similarly misguided, as well.

Two Responses to the Chinese Room Argument

Since Searle's argument first appeared in 1980, it has been the target of frequent and unflagging criticism. Two of these criticisms Searle conveniently dubs the *systems reply* and the *robot reply*. Common to both these counterarguments is the opinion that Searle is misidentifying the locus of understanding or meaning. Critics claim that Searle's insistence that the person inside the room does not and could not understand Chinese takes too narrow view of the matter.

The "systems reply" maintains that understanding is not to be found in the person inside the room, but in the whole system comprising inputs and outputs, the rule book, and the person. When we look at a formal symbol-processing system, we cannot focus on just one element of that system. Analogously, it is a mistake to think that a single place inside the person's brain is the locus of understanding. Understanding is the complicated array of sensory information, memories, information processing, and responses. The computer's understanding consists in the several aspects of the system, not just one aspect. The person inside the Chinese room is one part of a *system* that understands Chinese.

Searle is unmoved by this response. He suggests that we let the person inside the Chinese room "internalize" the system, the rule book, the symbol cards, and any other aspect of the system. We can even do away with the room, Searle suggests. The person is now the entire system. Searle claims the person would not understand Chinese, under even these "person-system" conditions. Hence, Searle claims the systems reply cannot be correct.

Why does the person-system not understand Chinese, in Searle's view? After all, by hypothesis the outputs of this person-system are indistinguishable from a native Chinese speaker. So, if we are willing to count the native speaker as understanding, why not the person-system? Searle's response is that the person-system still does not know the *meaning* of the Chinese symbols. More precisely, the person-system does not know whether the Chinese symbols are *about* restaurants or raccoons. It is as though there are two subsystems inside the person, one Chinese and one English. But nowhere in the person-system do we find a "translation" of Chinese symbols into English, which would enable the person to know that a certain symbol refers to a restaurant. Failing this sort of translation, the person-system does not know what the Chinese symbols mean, and hence does not understand Chinese.

The "robot reply" claims that meaning is found in the system's causal interactions with the environment. Imagine that we shrink the Chinese room to a very small size, putting it inside a robot, and where it is appropriately connected to the robot's systems. The robot now seems to engage in the same behavior patterns as you or me; it walks, talks, sees, picks up things, passes things at the breakfast table.

Let us vary the story a little. Forget about the Chinese room for a moment. Simply imagine that a robot, with a computer for a "brain," accompanies you for a day. It rides with you in the car, and says things like, "Watch out for that bus." It walks along the sidewalk with you, and when asked whether it will rain, responds, "I hope not; water is not good for my resistors and capacitors." Your robot companion is indiscernible in its verbal and nonverbal behavior patterns from a normal person. Now ask yourself: Does the robot know what "bus" means? What "rain" means? If your answer is no, then you agree with Searle.

What does Searle think is missing from the Chinese room–robot and from the robot we just imagined? He claims that the robot does not understand the symbols' meaning because there is no representation in the system that connects cause to symbol. For example, nowhere in the system is the Chinese symbol for "flower" connected to a flower. The causal interactions with the world would not lead to your understanding the *meaning* of these symbols unless "those causal interactions are represented in some mind or other" (Searle 1984, 35). Knowing the meaning of the symbol, according to Searle, requires having a representation that a particular sequence of symbols is the *effect* of a particular interaction with the world. You know, for example, that a particular character refers to rain, not simply because it is caused by rain but because there is a representation that links rain with the appropriate symbol. Meaning consists of an awareness of the connection between symbols and their causes.

In a moment we will consider a response to Searle's diagnosis, but for the moment we might wonder how Searle thinks meaning in fact arises. He claims that the intentionality of thought is an effect of the causal properties of the brain. One of the many effects of the biochemistry of our brains is intentionality. Somewhat loosely, brain stuff causes intentionality. But Searle is no chauvinist. He does not insist that only *human* brains produce intentionality; he allows that even an artifact might think. But nonhuman brains or artifacts would not think by virtue of implementing the formal properties of a program. They would instead possess *the same causal powers as our brains.* If it thinks, Searle insists, then it has the right stuff; its "brain stuff" can do the same things as our brains.

Searle is not alone in thinking that minds must be realized in the "right stuff." Gerald Edelman (1992), a Nobel laureate and neuroscientist, agrees with Searle that no purely formal program is sufficient for intentionality. Although we can't describe here Edelman's account of the nature and origin of consciousness, we can note that he argues that intentionality arises from our very complicated neurobiological processes. Central to his view is the idea that the neurobiological process of *categorization*—identifying an object or property as a certain type—is the beginning of intentionality. Like Searle, Edelman argues that the physical realizer of a system matters. Roughly, the nervous system changes in response to various encounters with the environment. And the patterns of response selected—the patterns that the brain identifies as important—depend on the previous changes and variation in the system. Edelman claims that computers or a purely functional system cannot duplicate this complexity and this variation. For Edelman, like Searle, intentionality is fundamentally a neurobiological notion.

The Right Stuff: Searle's Critics Respond

Searle counts the Chinese room argument as showing that both strong AI and a generally functionalist account of intentionality are mistaken. He assumes that the Chinese room accurately portrays the functionalist view, but there is doubt about the accuracy of the portrayal.

Andy Clark suggests that an accurate functionalist picture must describe what happens at a much smaller or lower level than that described by the Chinese room. In this *microfunctional* approach, the program or the description looks at the behavior of smaller constituent parts (Clark 1989, 30–34). One way to see the gist of Clark's argument is to ask where in the computationalist's programs there is room for the Chinese room. The computationalist imagines that we know the functioning of the relevant portions of the brains of native Chinese speakers. We map or duplicate the formal properties of such functioning; that is, we write a program that captures the relevant activity of a brain. We then run the program on an appropriate machine. Such a machine would possess intentionality if we do. But where in this program, asks the computationalist, are we to imagine you inside a Chinese room? Certainly not in activity between particular neurons. Although it might make some sense to speak of inputs and outputs here, it would be a mistake to think that these inputs and outputs are something like "central processing" or in any way correspond to the Chinese room.

Notice also the complexity of a functional description of an intentional system. Inputs carrying information about the environment need to be coordinated, not only with each other but also with stored representations and behavioral responses. Such complexity is absent from the Chinese room, and thus it is open to claims that the absence of intentionality in the Chinese room shows nothing about functional or computational accounts of intentionality (Rey 1997, chap. 10). As Kim Sterelny points out, not every functionally specified system is an intentional system (1990, 221).

These responses point to another, somewhat informal objection to thinking computers. It is sometimes argued that human cognition involves a flexibility not found in any computer. Since computers are constrained by the limits of their program, they do not have the requisite flexibility of response, and hence, cannot have semantics. Clark points out that a sufficiently sophisticated *microfunctional* program might very well exhibit the relevant flexibility and variability of response. It is no doubt worth noting that human cognizers are not wholly unlimited in their responses. Interestingly Edelman notes that human beings have "a degree of free will" and that their freedom is constrained by a number of internal and external events (1992, 170). Flexibility of response is thus not a principled reason for rejecting the idea of intentional computer states.

Sterelny points out another way in which the Chinese room has the *wrong* sort of functional organization. Computational accounts of understanding or intentionality do not suppose that there is an "understanding center," where meaning arises. Notice also that in the Chinese room only one working component—the person—is described. But it is unlikely that a computational description of the mind would be remotely similar (Sterelny 1990, 222–23).

More recently, Searle has declared that the Chinese room concedes too much to computationalism, since the notion of syntax is an observer-relative property. Unlike "molecule" and "mass," which describe objective features of the world, "syntax" describes only observer-relative properties, like "picnic" or "bathtub." Identifying something as syntax, Searle claims, requires someone who already has intentionality. The suggestion then that semantics might arise from a purely formal system merely pushes the question further back. The identification of a formal system itself requires that something somewhere already possesses intentionality (Searle 1992, 207–12).

It might be open to functionalists to claim that syntax is a way of describing objective patterns no less than "molecule" or "mass" describes objective patterns. Information processing occurs naturally in the world, and computational descriptions capture this aspect.

In an exchange between Searle and Dennett (Searle 1997, chap. 5), both note the extensive, continuing, and at times pointed debate over the Chinese room argument, and computationalism more generally. The assertion by Searle and Edelman perhaps suggests that we take a different line to understand the nature of the mental; maybe we should listen more closely to neuroscience.

Key Concepts

Chinese room argument

Computational functionalism

Language of thought

Strong AI thesis

Syntax/semantics

Reading Questions

1. Explain the distinction between syntax and semantics.

2. What is the role of the language of thought in computational functionalism?

3. How does computational functionalism distinguish between types of propositional attitudes, for example, between beliefs and desires?

4. What is the strong AI thesis?

5. Briefly describe the Chinese room argument. Why is it important for Searle's argument against the strong AI thesis?

6. How might a functionalist respond to the Chinese room argument?

References

Boden, Margaret, ed. 1990. *The philosophy of artificial intelligence*. Oxford: Oxford University Press.

Bogdan, Radu, ed. 1986. *Belief: Form, content, and function*. Oxford: Oxford University Press.

Clark, Andy. 1989. *Microcognition: Philosophy, cognitive science and parallel distributed processing*. Cambridge, MA: MIT Press.

Crumley, Jack, ed. 2000. *Problems in mind: Readings in contemporary philosophy of mind*. Mountain View, CA: Mayfield.

Dennett, Daniel. 1977. A cure for the common code? (originally published as "Critical Notice: *The Language of Thought* by Jerry Fodor"), *Mind* 86:265–80. Reprinted in Crumley 2000, 267–78; page references are to this volume.

Edelman, Gerald. 1992. *Bright air, brilliant fire: On the matter of mind*. New York: Basic Books.

Fodor, Jerry. 1979. *Language of thought*. Cambridge, MA: Harvard University Press.

———. 1981. Introduction: Something on the state of the art. In *RePresentations: Philosophical essays on the foundations of cognitive science*, 1–31. Cambridge, MA: MIT Press.

———. 1987. *Psychosemantics: The problem of meaning in the philosophy of mind*. Cambridge, MA: MIT Press.

Fodor, Jerry, and Zenon W. Pylyshyn. 1988. Connectionism and cognitive architecture: A critical analysis. *Cognition* 28:3–71.

Moody, Todd C. 1993. *Philosophy and artificial intelligence*. Englewood Cliffs, NJ: Prentice-Hall.

Newell, Allen, and Herbert Simon. 1976. Computer science as empirical enquiry: Symbols and search. *Communications of the Association for Computing Machinery* 19. Reprinted in Boden 1990, 105–32.

Rey, Georges. 1997. *Contemporary philosophy of mind: A contentiously classical approach*. Oxford: Blackwell.

Searle, John. 1980. Minds, brains and programs. *Behavioral and Brain Sciences* 3:417–57.

———. 1984. *Minds, brains, and science*. Cambridge, MA: Harvard University Press.

———. 1992. *The rediscovery of the mind*. Cambridge, MA: MIT Press.

———. 1997. *The mystery of consciousness*. New York: New York Review.

Sterelny, Kim. 1990. *The representational theory of mind*. Oxford: Blackwell.

Stillings, Neil, et al. 1995. *Cognitive science: An introduction*. 2nd ed. Cambridge, MA: MIT Press.

Turing, Alan. 1950. Computing machinery and intelligence. *Mind* 59:433–60. Reprinted in Boden 1990, 41–66.

Additional Readings

Boden, Margaret. *Artificial Intelligence in Psychology: Interdisciplinary Essays.* Cambridge, MA: MIT Press, 1989.

Crane, Tim. *Mechanical Mind: A Philosophical Introduction to Minds, Machines and Mental Representation.* 2nd ed. London: Routledge, 2003.

Fodor, Jerry. 2000. "The Persistence of the Attitudes." Chap. 1 of Fodor 1987, reprinted in Crumley 2000, 251–66.

Haugeland, John. *Artificial Intelligence: The Very Idea.* Cambridge, MA: MIT Press, 1989.

Loewer, Barry, and Georges Rey, eds. *Meaning in Mind: Fodor and His Critics.* Oxford: Blackwell, 1991.

6

Does the Mental Matter?
Eliminativism and Instrumentalism

On more than one occasion, folk theories have run up against the progress of science. "Folk physics" gave way to the likes of Copernicus, Galileo, Kepler, Newton, and Einstein; consequently, our "real" explanation of the sun disappearing below the horizon changes, as does our understanding of falling bodies and of the movement of heavenly bodies. Sometimes our folk theories require experts to reconcile our commonsense view, say, of the solidity of a table, with the seemingly contradictory explanation of science—smaller-than-microscopic particles moving about in largely empty space. Sometimes our folk theories are just wrong; no findings of the biologist will underwrite the belief in witches, for example.

Folk psychology is no less a "folk theory," some claim. Common sense explains behavior by appeal to beliefs and desires, to hopes and fears. In so doing, we are guided by the perhaps uncritical assumption that science will tell us of the "stuff" of mental states. As chemistry tells us of the "stuff" of water or the "stuff" of table salt, so we expect that some science will tell us of the "stuff" of belief. And whatever the ultimate explanation, we expect—again, perhaps uncritically—that the scientific explanation will retain the outlines of our commonsense view of the mind. Beliefs and desires are real, we think, even if we don't yet know their ultimate constitution. Our explanation of Danny wanting to go the party because he believes Deirdre will be there awaits only elaboration, not refutation. But should we be so optimistic?

A less optimistic view of folk psychology suggests that it is more likely to go the way of witches or phlogiston. Indeed some suggest that our common-sense view is dramatically mistaken:

> Our common-sense conception of psychological phenomena constitutes a radically false theory, a theory *so fundamentally defective* that both the principles and the ontology of that theory will eventually be displaced, rather than smoothly reduced, by completed neuroscience. (Paul Churchland 1981, 184; emphasis added)

Dualism

Eliminative materialism is the view that the principles and categories of folk psychology will be discarded by a sufficiently complete neuroscience; our propositional attitude concepts, such as belief and desire, correspond to nothing real, and consequently our normal explanations of behavior don't tell us about the real causes of behavior. In short, beliefs, desires, and the like will go the way of witches and spells.

The first half of this chapter will explore the eliminative materialist position. Versions of eliminative materialism are defended by Richard Rorty (1981) and more recently Alexander Rosenberg (1991). Interestingly, there is a suggestion that the world of the movie *The Matrix* represents, if unwittingly, a kind of eliminativism (Barwick 2002, 80–82). But the two persons most associated with the view are Paul and Patricia Churchland; consequently, it is their views that will concern us most.

The second half of the chapter considers Daniel Dennett's version of **instrumentalism, the idea that our folk-psychological notions are only devices for explaining and predicting behavior.** Dennett's theory is known as the "intentional strategy" or the "intentional stance" view. Although some of his hypotheses about phenomenal states are eliminativist, his intentional stance view is instrumentalist, and as we will see, Dennett makes some overtures to realism about beliefs and desires.

Amateur Science: Folk Psychology

Folk psychology is our common vehicle for navigating the mental landscape. We talk about a sibling wanting to buy a CD, a friend hoping to visit this summer, a father who believes that taxes are too high, a mother who fears that her children are not eating right. Such talk is our familiar propositional attitudes at work: desires, beliefs, hopes, fears. Of course, folk psychology is more than just talk; it holds that there "really are" mental states. Somehow, some way, when Deirdre thinks that the CD costs too much and refuses to buy it, the folk are committed to the idea that Deirdre's belief is an existent mental state. Whatever mental states turn out to be, Deirdre's got one, and it's about the high cost of CDs. This much is common sense and quite familiar.

Eliminative materialism holds that a good bit of our commonsense psychology is dramatically mistaken, however. There is no good reason to think that beliefs or hopes, desires or fears, are anything more than fictions that have seen their best day. A sufficiently mature neuroscience will eventually show that folk psychology has failed us and that we should cease thinking that beliefs and desires populate the mind.

A cautionary note: Eliminativists do not doubt that we represent the world around us or that we have representations of others and ourselves. They do not deny that we engage in thinking. Rather they deny that folk psychology is an acceptable way to characterize the nature of our representational and cognitive capacities. Eliminativists think that folk psychology is a bad *theory*.

Eliminative materialists think that folk psychology is a kind of empirical theory about the mind and behavior. We expect at least two things of such a theory. First, it will tell us the kinds of things that exist (the theory's ontology). Second, it will tell us how to explain various phenomena by appeal to these kinds of things. Folk psychology claims that its *categories*—types of mental states such as beliefs, desires, and fears—provide the materials for explaining behavior. If we know, for example, that Danny wants to see Deirdre and that he believes she will be at the party, then we have a pretty good idea what Danny is about to do. And since folk psychology is an empirical theory, we expect that further investigation or further experiment will either support or undermine the theory. In light of this evidence, we conclude about the theory's likely truth or falsity.

Folk psychology is a "radically false theory," say the eliminativists, for the same kinds of reasons that led to the rejection of other empirical theories, for example, the theory of caloric. You won't find the concept of caloric in an introductory physics textbook. But in the eighteenth century, caloric was invoked to explain heating and cooling. An iron bar placed in the fire becomes hotter because "caloric," a weightless, fluid-like substance, moves from the fire to the iron bar. Water cools because caloric leaves the water for the surroundings. Here we have an empirical theory—a plausible working hypothesis that explains heat transfer. We also have a *false* empirical theory—caloric can be identified with no physical state or property and therefore does not exist. We now explain heating and cooling by appeal to increases or decreases in the energy of constituent particles. Temperature measures the mean kinetic energy of a substance, not the amount of caloric. Physics stu-

Is Folk Psychology a Theory?

Not everyone agrees that folk psychology is an empirical theory of the sort that eliminativists suggest. But what would it be, if not a theory? Some suggest that characterizing folk psychology as a *craft* yields better insights into the nature of our commonsense view of the mind. Thought of this way, folk psychology is a practice identified by a set of skills that we acquire (or have developed over a long evolutionary period). The aims of this craft are making sense of our own and others' behavior and using the beliefs and desires of others to reveal information about the environment.

How do we use folk psychology to learn about our environment? Consider Deirdre noticing that Danny is walking hurriedly about the house, opening closet doors, looking behind loveseats, and muttering, "Where is it?" Puzzled, she asks him about the object of his search, and he tells her that he cannot find his umbrella. Ascribing to Danny the belief that it is raining (or will be) tells Deirdre something about her environment—it's wet outside.

Advocates of the "nontheory" view of folk psychology think it is unsurprising that folk psychology fails to measure up as a good scientific theory. Indeed, they say, it is a mistake to think that folk psychology *should* exhibit the characteristics of good scientific theories. (Dennett 1987a; Bogdan 1988, 1991)

dents learn no laws about caloric because caloric doesn't exist. And if caloric doesn't exist, then "caloric explanations" are no explanations at all. Hence, the theory of caloric is a *false* theory.

Calling folk psychology a false theory has similar implications. First, the folk psychological categories—beliefs, desires, and the like—don't exist. Like caloric, there is nothing in the world that corresponds to the commonsense concept of belief. Whatever it is that's causing Danny to put on those spiffy shoes, it isn't his "belief" that Deirdre will be impressed by his keen fashion sense or his "desire" to impress her. And it isn't that we've identified the *wrong* beliefs or desires; it's that *there are no such things as beliefs and desires* to begin with. Any explanation appealing to beliefs and desires is worse than useless, it's misleading. The eliminativist tells us that we are no better off with this sort of explanation than if we explained Danny's behavior by appeal to potions and spells.

Why Is Folk Psychology So Bad?

Of course, it's one thing to be told that our folk theory of the mind is radically mistaken. But we want to know *why* we should accept that. For convenience, we can sort the eliminativists' critique of folk psychology under three headings, and briefly consider each in its turn.

Folk psychology, as an empirical theory, has made no progress. Folk psychology, as an instrument of explanation and prediction, has been around now for a couple thousand years. In Plato's dialogue *Crito*, Socrates rejects Crito's offer of escape by citing his beliefs and desires. Two millennia later, folk psychology provides us no better understanding of the mind than Socrates had. It provides no greater understanding of the nature of intelligence or learning, emotions, mental illness, or any of a host of other mental phenomena. Patricia Churchland (1986) notes, for example, the case of a patient who cries uncontrollably. Neither happiness nor sorrow causes his tears; he simply cannot control his crying. About such pathologies, folk psychology is silent, just as it is about other mental phenomena.

Folk psychology cannot be integrated with the other sciences. Despite differences in subject matter, we have come to expect integration among the sciences. Chemistry may tell us of the interaction between ions, and biology may tell us of the mechanism of cell division. But molecular biology allows us to see that chemistry and biology can work together to give us a more comprehensive, systematic, and unified picture of the world. Similarly, the progress of evolutionary biology, physiology, and neuroscience provide us with an ever-growing understanding of our mental life and our behavior. Different sciences have different perspectives, *but they work together.* Eliminativists suspect that folk psychology plays no role in this growing understanding; worse, there is no reason to expect that matters will change. Paul Churchland asserts that folk psychology "is no part of this growing synthesis. Its intentional categories stand magnificently alone, without visible prospect of reduction to that larger corpus" (1981, 188).

How would folk psychology be integrated with other sciences? Think, for a moment, of a wooden table. Scientists explain to us that the table has its particular surface properties of solidity and brownness because of its molecular and atomic properties. Tables thus count as real; they can be integrated with our scientific view of the world precisely because we can carry out this reduction. The integration of folk psychology, Churchland claims, likewise depends on the reducibility of its categories to the categories of established sciences. You might recall that functionalists admit that our propositional attitude concepts are irreducible, but they think this is a *virtue* of functionalism. On the surface then, it is a bit puzzling why this counts against folk psychology (Kitcher 1984).

What would it take for beliefs and desires, or any of the other propositional attitudes, to be integrated into the other sciences? According to Paul Churchland, we would need to connect the mental state types of folk psychology to neural types systematically. But this is unlikely to happen. Our understanding of the workings of the brain, as revealed in disciplines such as cognitive neurobiology, don't fit neatly with folk psychology. If folk psychology were reducible to neural states, we might expect that for each distinct belief, say, Danny's belief that today is a holiday and a good day for being lazy, we would find a neural state (or complex of neural states) that "match up" with this belief. Churchland, however, doubts that we will find a convenient way to match beliefs or desires with neural states. Indeed, in his view, our current, most promising understanding of the brain makes no room for the discrete, individual states essential to folk psychology. We find instead "distributed representations," complicated patterns of neural activity that cannot be identified one for one with particular beliefs or desires. Such distributed states are perhaps best understood by reference to the mathematics of vectors, not by reference to Danny's belief about the best way to spend a holiday morning. Thus, Churchland claims, there is no reasonable fit between the way we categorize and talk about neural states and our talk about beliefs and desires. Nor does the future offer much promise for connecting the two.

Reducibility thus is the key to integration. Our inability to integrate folk psychology with the advancing brain and behavioral sciences suggest a bleak future for folk psychology, a future of eventual rejection and displacement.

Some mental state types identified by a scientific psychology—sensations, for example—might be reduced to neural types. Patricia Churchland thus points to a "co-evolution" of neuroscience and psychology (1986, chaps. 7 and 9). Similarly Paul Churchland (1989) suggests that sensation terms might be identified with "state space" terms.

Folk psychology is committed to a sentential view of thought, a view that cannot be made to square with other views about the capacity for thought. Propositional attitudes, which are central to folk psychology, have two components: the attitude and the content. The framework for describing the contents of propositional attitudes relies on sentences or propositions. Folk psychology treats the content of, for example, Danny's desire that Deirdre bring him some rainbow sherbet as a sentence—a sentence somehow stored in the brain. Folk psychology is thus committed to a *sententialist* view of such mental states.

The commitment to the sententialist view leads, among other things, to what Patricia Churchland calls the "infralinguistic catastrophe" (1986,

388–92). She notes that we grant that other nonlinguistic animals engage in intelligent behavior. It is, however, hard to see how our ordinary folk-psychological explanations have any hope of explaining such behavior *if those animals do not possess the requisite linguistic ability.* Churchland is not denying our capacity for mental representation. Rather, she is denying folk psychology's commitment to the sentence-like structure of these representations.

A brief example may illustrate Churchland's point. A clever puppy of mine routinely escaped the backyard. Her only escape route had to be under a large fence along the property line. But to get to the large fence, she first had to by-pass a white picket fence about six feet in front of the larger fence. Now, she was too big to squeeze through the pickets, but too small to jump it. Repeated attempts to catch her in her nefarious ways failed. In desperation, I stood one afternoon on the opposite side of the picket fence, coaxing, cajoling, calling, pleading with her to come over. After some twenty minutes, she ran to a tree with a branching trunk near the side of the yard; she made the small jump to the trunk, then walked about three feet out on the branching trunk, at which point she was able to jump down on the other side of the picket fence!

A simple folk-psychological explanation of this behavior is that she wanted to get past the picket fence and that she believed that walking on the trunk would get her there. In order to explain her behavior, we resort to de-scribing her "mental states" with some rather complicated sentences. What-ever else was true of that clever dog, though, Churchland would disallow thinking of the pup's representations of her environment as sentence-like. Churchland has noted this kind of difficulty with the folk-psychological ex-planation of intelligent behavior of other animals and preverbal infants.

Churchland thinks the sententialist view faces a second problem as well, that of tacit knowledge. We seem to have beliefs that we have never explic-itly considered—tacit beliefs. Without ever having thought about it before, we would readily claim, to use Dennett's example, that we believe that zebras in the wild don't wear tweed coats. We have *tacit beliefs* by "automatically" and unconsciously believing logical consequences of our *explicit beliefs.* It seems unlikely, however, that we tacitly believe *all* logical consequences of our beliefs, since there are an infinite number of such logical consequences, and we don't have an infinite number of beliefs. Thus, the problem: The sen-tentialist view must "decide" between our tacitly believing *all* the logical consequences or our tacitly believing *none* of them, or it must find some prin-cipled middle ground.

Churchland rightly rejects the idea that we might have an infinite num-ber of tacit beliefs, and she finds a second option—the "austere option," which rejects *any* tacit beliefs—unpalatable. Hence, commitment to the sententialist view requires trying to find a principled means of selecting out the logical consequences tacitly believed from those that are not. But this, suggests Churchland, cannot be done. There is no obvious principled reason for saying that I tacitly believe wild zebras don't wear tweed coats, but that I don't tacitly believe hippopotami don't wear cashmere sweaters. (Churchland also considers a third problem, the "frame problem," which is notorious in artificial intelligence research, that we cannot consider here; see 1986, 392–95, and Sterelny's response, 1990, chap. 7.)

Is Folk Psychology Really That Bad?

Defenders claim that folk psychology is not so dramatically defective and that eliminativists mischaracterize the aim of folk psychology and the conditions for scientific credibility. Consider Paul Churchland's claim that folk psychology is unable to account for a range of phenomena, from intelligence to mental illness. Defenders claim that accounting for such phenomena is not the *aim* of our commonsense view (Kitcher 1984, 1996; Sterelny 1990; Horgan and Woodward 1985). Rather, the aim of folk psychology is to explain *intentional* behavior, the purposive behavior of humans as they navigate their environment.

Churchland, of course, acknowledges the restricted range of folk psychology. He insists, however, that even within this restricted "domain," folk psychology holds out little promise of genuine explanation. This brings us to the heart of his criticism: Folk psychology stands "magnificently alone" with no prospect for integration with the rest of the evolving scientific explanation of behavior.

That's Incredible

How can eliminative materialists believe their theory? Wouldn't it be incredible—just incredible—if it were true?

Some critics of eliminative materialism have found it both incredible and self-contradictory. Do eliminative materialists *believe* their own theory? How could they, critics argue, since they don't recognize the existence of

(*continued*)

beliefs? They can't even hope that the theory turns out to be true, since there aren't any hopes, either! And seemingly, it just gets worse: Are they trying to persuade others to *believe* or to *accept* eliminative materialism? Do they *want* others to *doubt* the empirical credentials of folk psychology? Eliminativists are apparently unable to tell us what they are doing without contradicting themselves, without making use of the very notions they want to eliminate, urge some critics.

And it would simply be incredible if eliminativism turned out to be true. Folk psychology may not be the most progressive or respectable of scientific theories, but it has worked countless times for at least two millennia! Every time someone explains or predicts another's behavior by citing some group of beliefs and desires, it looks as though folk psychology has a bit of empirical confirmation. It would thus be simply incredible that a "radically false and defective theory" could get things right so often.

In response to the first criticism, eliminativists can claim that referring to propositional attitude states in such contexts is no more self-contradictory than an astronomer asking someone to come outside and watch the beautiful sunset. Second, eliminativists claim that at some point, a suitably detailed theory of the brain will make no use of talk of propositional attitudes, and that folk psychology will be relegated to the same intellectual storage bin that currently harbors Homeric gods, witches, caloric, and all the other miscellany of failed accounts of natural phenomena.

Still, it might seem incredible that folk psychology could turn out to be so wrong when it has—apparently—worked so often. One response to this criticism is to claim that belief-desire explanations of bits of behavior really aren't saying very much. Attributing a belief to Danny (that he believes there is food in the refrigerator) as an explanation for his getting up and walking into the kitchen is not really saying very much. Such "singular causal judgments" say almost nothing about the underlying states—the brain states—that are the real causes of behavior. We might as well say, "Ah, something's happening in Danny's brain again!" And if we are saying so little, then it would not be terribly surprising that we get it right so often (Rosenberg 1991).

First, folk defenders point out that folk psychology is not as isolated as Churchland alleges. Terence Horgan and James Woodward (1985) point out that research in vision science and cognitive psychology is often guided by folk-psychological categories. Thus, for example, cognitive psychologists researching semantic memory attempt to identify the essential features of memories, such as remembering that the battle of Gettysburg occurred in 1863. These types of memories are most straightforwardly characterized as beliefs or "contentful" mental states.

Second, critics note that reducibility to more basic sciences is not a necessary requirement for an empirical theory. Patricia Kitcher (1984) argues that no one doubts that genetics is a legitimate science or that gene structure depends on molecular structure, but genetics is not reducible to molecular biology. It makes use of concepts that capture certain genetic phenomena (why, for example, certain traits are inherited under certain circumstances), but these genetic categories are not in any straightforward way reducible to molecular phenomena. Similarly, John Marshall and Jennifer Gurd, neuropsychologists at Oxford, point out that certain cognitive impairments are not straightforwardly reducible. The same impairment might be realized in one patient by left hemisphere damage, in another by right hemisphere damage (1996, 184). Thus, irreducibility cannot count against our familiar view of the mind.

Defenders of folk psychology might wish to extend Kitcher's argument. Patricia Churchland (1986) argues that tensor calculus allows us to detect patterns of activity among neurons that are not detectable by simply noting the behavior of individual neurons. Put another way, the concepts of tensor calculus illuminate patterns not visible from the perspective of lower levels. Might not the folk theorist make a similar argument? The concepts of folk psychology isolate patterns of information that are not detectable from the lower, neurological levels (see also Bogdan 1986).

Recent work also seeks to place our commonsense understanding of the mind firmly within this growing synthesis of evolutionary theory and kindred sciences. Steven Mithen's *The Prehistory of Mind* (1996) and Merlin Donald's *Origins of the Modern Mind* (1991) both draw on anthropological and paleontological evidence in an attempt to explain how our current cognitive abilities arose. Of course, theirs is not an attempt to defend folk psychology, but their description of the modern mind and the evolution of its abilities is anything but hostile to our commonsense understanding of the mind.

Similarly, some cognitive development research suggests a role for folk psychology. Since the commonsense view is inextricably tied to the sententialist view, it is caught up in the "infralinguistic catastrophe," apparently unable to explain the intelligent behavior of animals and preverbal children.

But we need not think, as Kitcher and Kim Sterelny have pointed out, that folk psychology can only make sense of the intelligent behavior of linguistic creatures. Recent studies specifically invoke notions of belief in *preverbal* infants. Summarizing a study of the responses of infants to a variety of objects that were either partially or wholly occluded, Renee Baillargeon notes that infants at a very early age seem to possess beliefs about those objects (Baillargeon 1999, 607). This sort of study suggests that infants, though prelinguistic, may nonetheless have concepts that figure as constituents of their beliefs. We can therefore sensibly attribute beliefs to preverbal infants, for example, believing that a ball is still behind the screen.

Now, it may be more difficult to identify the "concepts" animals employ; no one, Kitcher notes, thinks animals talk. Instead the claim is that our best understanding of mental life, whether in animals or humans, is to rely on *internal representations* that share certain features with language (Kitcher, 1996). When my dog detects certain sounds and smells, rouses from his afternoon in the shade, and galoomphs to the kitchen, it is doubtful that he has the concept "cheese," much less "mild cheddar cheese." But defenders of propositional attitude psychology might still insist that appeal to *sentence-like* representations is the best way to explain his—and other animals'—behavior. As a more sophisticated example, recent researchers think that our folk-psychological concepts allow us to describe the meaning of the vervet monkey's alarm call (Cheney and Seyfarth 1990, chap. 5).

Some critics of eliminativism argue that neuroscience and folk psychology are fundamentally about different kinds of things and their "explanatory domains" are quite different. Displacement of one theory by another usually occurs, however, when they have more or less the same explanatory domains. Copernican could replace Ptolemaic astronomy because both are about the movement of heavenly bodies. We should not expect, however, developments in particle physics—string theory, say—to threaten genetics. Critics maintain that the relationship between folk psychology and neuroscience is more like that of string theory and genetics; thus, they doubt that neuroscience will displace folk psychology.

In recognizing these points, the Churchlands claim that this is part of what is in question—whether our folk-psychological and neuroscientific notions pick out very different kinds of phenomena. Both neuroscience and folk psychology are concerned with representation. But they claim that there is an alternate account of representation that looks instead to neural structures and thus threatens our commonsense view (Churchland and Churchland 1996, 225). This also suggests why this debate is still ongoing. It is thus still an open question whether some theory, taking its cue from neuroscience, might eventually render our folk-psychological explanations of behavior as pointless as explaining Danny's behavior by appealing to a witch's spell.

A Different Stance: Instrumentalism

A friend of mine once explained the noticeable bend in the lower trunk of a ficus tree, surrounded by Torrey pines, thus: "It wants to grow toward the light." Few suspect that the ficus *really* has any such desire, but it suggests the usefulness of propositional attitude psychology in explaining the behavior of diverse systems.

Instrumentalism about the mind suggests that attributing beliefs and desires, along with other propositional attitudes, to various systems or creatures allows us to predict and explain their behavior. Daniel Dennett, a philosopher at Tufts University, has for several years elaborated and defended a type of instrumentalism about the mind. In the **intentional stance** or the **intentional strategy**, as Dennett calls it, we explain and predict the behavior of another system by attributing beliefs, desires, and other propositional attitudes to the system. We should not infer, however, that a belief or a want corresponds to some identifiable, internal mental state or some particular brain state. It will help at this point to consider the various stances we might adopt, according to Dennett.

Taking a Stance

Often enough we explain phenomena simply by adopting the *physical stance*. We explain the workings of a remote control by appealing to an infrared signal. Similarly, some very knowledgeable persons can explain the storage of information on a computer's hard drive, and others might explain the movement of a person's arm by talking about electrochemical reactions in the central nervous system. The physical stance also serves to explain the breakdown in the normal functioning of objects or systems: A table is wobbly because one leg is shorter than the others; a printer no longer prints because of a defective connecting cable. Adopting the physical stance permits explanations that appeal to the physical constituents of an object or the arrangement of the physical constituents.

In more complicated systems, such as computers and similarly advanced devices, complicated biological systems, or animal life, using the physical stance may be extraordinarily cumbersome. In such cases we very often resort to the *design stance*; we explain a system's behavior by appeal to what it is supposed—designed—to do. Dennett often resorts to computers to explain the design stance. In principle, the physical stance would suffice for explaining much of the computer's operations. But the extraordinary complexity of such devices makes the design stance more useful. The design stance allows us to "abstract" away from each of the individual physical operations and instead focus on their aim or function. The design stance affords us a grasp of the computer that we might otherwise not have. Deirdre need not possess advanced degrees in computer engineering or computer science to know that the function of pushing a certain key is to launch an e-mail program, while another launches a web browser. She understands and predicts the behavior of the computer by appeal to its design.

If the design stance allows us to abstract away from the physical details, the *intentional stance* provides extraordinary flexibility and a genuine increase in predictive and explanatory power. We adopt the intentional stance when we explain and predict behavior by appealing to beliefs and desires, or propositional attitudes.

Three points should be made at the outset. First, the intentional stance is essentially a third-person perspective; *we attribute* beliefs and desires to another system in order to predict and make sense of its behavior. Upon picking up his leash, I explain my dog's irrationally exuberant behavior by attributing to him the belief that we are going for a walk and the desire that he *really* wants to go. Similarly, Julia explains Jack's buying concert tickets by attributing to him a set of beliefs and desires, among them the belief that the Radiators are playing and the desire to see a genuine New Orleans band.

Second, Dennett believes that applying the intentional strategy requires the assumption of rationality. If we are to attribute beliefs and desires to persons, we must assume that they are rational, that they will have certain beliefs and desires in light of conditions in their environment and the goals that they are likely to have. In his "True Believers" (1981b), the essay that Dennett considers to be the "flagship" statement of the intentional strategy, he notes "the fundamental rule: attribute those beliefs that the system *ought to have*" (1981b, 20). Similarly we are also to attribute *desires* that a system ought to have, especially basic desires, such as survival, absence of pain, and food.

As Dennett recognizes, many of our desires are more sophisticated and more detailed than the simple desires for comfort, food, or sleep; such is the benefit of our linguistic ability. Attributions of more sophisticated, finely detailed desires depend on the other attributed beliefs and desires. Again, suppose Julia thinks that Jack wants to see the Radiators, that he believes that he needs a ticket to see them, and that he believes that a ticket can be purchased at the Customer Service window. These other beliefs and desires—together, of course, with the assumption that Jack is rational—lead Julia to attribute a further desire: that Jack wants to go to the Customer Service window.

The intentional strategy's chief virtue lies in its ability to enable predictions of a system's behaviors—predictions that would be practically impossible from either the physical or design stance. But this leads us to the third point about the intentional stance: Which systems are intentional systems? According to Dennett, adopting the intentional stance is warranted whenever we are able to generate predictions that we would be *unable* to get from either the physical or design stance.

To vary one of Dennett's examples: I could adopt the intentional stance toward the table now in front of me; that is, I could treat it as an intentional system. I could attribute to it the persistent and steadfast desire to "stay put." I gain little by doing so, however, since this representation provides no advantage over the physical stance. My dog, however, is another matter. Viewed from either the physical or the design stance, it is practically impossible for me to predict where he will spend his afternoon nap. But attributing to him the desire for a cool place on a summer afternoon enables my prediction that he can be found on the tile landing in front of the screen door. We use the intentional stance when we can explain and predict more of a creature's (or an artifact's) behavior.

Of course, a consequence of this position is that it makes sense to attribute intentional states not only to members of the animal world but also to members of the silicon class. Suitably complex computers are fit subjects of belief and desire attribution. Since in some cases the behavior of a computer is practically inaccessible from either the physical or design stance, we may reasonably attribute beliefs and desires in predicting the behavior of such artificial systems. Dennett accepts this consequence of his theory, claiming that "computers undeniably *are* intentional systems" since their behavior is "most efficiently predicted, by adopting the intentional stance toward them" (1981a, 238).

But we should not ask whether some system or creature *really* has beliefs. To have beliefs is nothing more than to be a fit candidate for the intentional stance. The appropriately constructed computer is just as much an intentional system as the slumbering canine; and both are no less intentional systems than is the system making his way up the escalator to the Customer Service window to purchase tickets.

Why Instrumentalism?

We have yet to see the key motivation for Dennett's instrumentalism. After all, thinking that the intentional strategy is essentially a third-person perspective, that we must assume the rationality of the system, or that even computers and animals might be said to have beliefs is not definitive of instrumentalism. Why doesn't Dennett think beliefs or desires are real in, say, the way that functionalists or type identity theorists think that they are real? We can see why by comparing Dennett to someone he takes to be a paradigmatic intentional realist, Jerry Fodor (Dennett sometimes characterizes Fodor's view as "industrial strength realism"; see Dennett 1991, sec. 4).

Fodor is an intentional realist, recall, because he thinks that beliefs and desires are realized by internal states. Beliefs are mental representations, couched in the language of thought, that are encoded in brain structures. To have the belief that the Radiators are playing Sunday is have a particular internal representation that causally interacts with various other representations.

Consider now how Fodor and Dennett would each answer the following question: Is Julia correct in attributing to Jack the belief that the Radiators are playing on Sunday? In Fodor's view, if Jack is in a brain state that encodes the appropriate "mentalese" sentence, then Jack has the belief. We answer the question, according to Fodor, by looking inside, by checking Jack's internal states. Alternatively, there is a *fact of the matter* as to whether Jack is in the appropriate internal state.

But Dennett holds that this is wildly optimistic. In his view, there are no internal states that will definitively settle the question of whether Jack has this belief; there are no facts of the matter that enable us to determine the correctness of Julia's attribution. So, what is the source of Dennett's pessimism?

Although Dennett worries about Fodor's language of thought hypothesis, his more relevant worry here is his doubt about our ability to make the requisite neural identifications. Contrary to Fodor's hope that we will be able to pair brain states with intentional states, in the sense required by token identity, Dennett suspects that the neuroscientific facts will turn out rather messy.

For some mental states, such as sensations, the neural facts may be straightforward. We know that stimulation of a part of the visual cortex produces a red sensation and that stimulation of the brain's septal area increases feelings of arousal. But neuroscience might not get so lucky when it comes to beliefs and desires. Since having any given belief may involve several distinct regions of the brain, there may be no principled way of determining the relevant neural activity; we will be unable to say definitively "this neural activity counts; that doesn't." Failing such a principled determination, there are no internal facts of the matter that will settle the question of whether Jack believes that the Radiators used to play Luigi's on Wednesday evenings. Hence, intentional realism, at least of the sort envisioned by Fodor, must be abandoned.

Dennett recognizes that this brings him close to the Churchlands' view (Dennett 1987b, 232–34; 1991, 42–43). They too reject the idea that we will be able to either identify or correlate brain activity with mental states. Dennett, however, doubts that neuroscience is likely to yield an alternative strategy that surpasses the predictive success of folk psychology. Indeed, Dennett thinks talk of beliefs and desires captures *objective* patterns in behavior, patterns indiscernible from other perspectives.

Patterns: A Touch of Realism

Dennett engages in a little science fiction, inspired by Harvard philosopher Robert Nozick, which, with a little literary license, runs as follows. Imagine that Martians possess a complete scientific description of the Earth, including a complete neuroscience. Given any complete specification of the physical state of a person, together with the relevant physical and neuroscientific laws, they are able to predict the subsequent neural and bodily states of the person. Now imagine that Deirdre flips open her cell phone one afternoon, says that she's on her way home, and asks Danny if anything is needed from the store. Danny subsequently believes that in about twenty minutes Deirdre will wheel her car into the driveway, carrying a plastic bag containing sourdough bread, asparagus, and a Boston cream pie.

Since our Martians possess the requisite scientific description of Deirdre and her environment, there is no surprise that they are able to predict her ensuing bodily movements, right up to the moment she steps from the car carrying the groceries. Now for some folk-psychological magic: Our very unscientific Danny has predicted exactly the same thing! Dennett observes that the truth of Danny's prediction, to anyone without the intentional strategy, seems "marvelous and inexplicable" (1981b, 27).

The explanation, according to Dennett, of the seeming miraculous coincidence of Danny's and the Martians' predictions lies in the fact that there are "patterns in human affairs that impose themselves," patterns that abstract away from the physical details. According to Dennett, *these are the patterns that we characterize in terms of the beliefs, desires, and intentions of rational agents* (1981b, 27). Importantly, these patterns are objective phenomena, as real as we might wish; the patterns are *really* there.

Dennett's Martian fable seems to tell us that, in principle, we could rely on the physical stance. But this would require a Herculean intellectual effort—an effort, Dennett says, of Laplacean superphysicists, far surpassing any present or future human cognitive abilities. Instead, we abstract away from the physical detail, focusing on the detectable patterns of behavior. Such patterns are the objects of our attributions of intentional states. Our talk of beliefs and desires is the way we describe these patterns of behavior.

Note that the Martian fable is wholly dispensable. Consider, for example, that on more than one occasion I stand in a particular building in central coastal San Diego. Because of a set of beliefs and desires that I ascribe to some twenty-five or thirty people, I predict they will come to my location at around 11 A.M. For all I know, they have very different physical descriptions, begin from very different locations, and take very different routes to my location. Their biological, psychological, and environmental descriptions vary widely; they have different tastes, likes, dislikes, and political opinions. Some will cover five miles in fifteen minutes, and some will scarcely cover fifteen yards in five minutes. Some will meander; some will brook no distraction. But not only am I confident in my prediction, I am also successful. It is not physics or neuroscience that explains my predictive ability, according to Dennett. It is that I attribute to each of them the belief that class starts at elevenish and the desire (admittedly, of differing intensities) to while away an hour or so talking a little epistemology. Put aside physical and environmental differences; put aside biological, chemical, and neurological differences—there is still a common element to their behavior, an objective pattern, namely, the desire to go to class. And I am able to lock on to this objective pattern precisely because I adopt the intentional stance toward each of them.

An Instrumentalist Realism or a Realist Instrumentalism?

It might seem as though Dennett is able to insist on his realism only at the cost of adopting a view incompatible with his instrumentalism. (Dennett [1991] more recently demurs from identifying his view as either instrumentalist or realist.) He tells us that we shouldn't be Fodor-realists because there are no facts of the matter that will settle questions about what belief an agent has. But it now appears that there *are* determinative facts of the matter; we were simply looking in the wrong place. We were looking inside the head, in the brain, but we should have been looking out—we should have been looking at the patterns in human behavior.

Dennett is unwilling to claim that there are determinative facts, however. Two different, incompatible sets of beliefs and desires might be attributable to an agent, and, according to Dennett, in principle there might be no way to choose between the two. If the incompatible sets of beliefs—in general—rationalized an agent's actions, we would find no further facts that allowed us to say, "This is the right set of beliefs to attribute; that's the wrong one." Julia may attribute to Jack the desire to see the Radiators, while Jessie may attribute to him the desire to avoid working. And there may be no way to choose. Given a description of all Jack's bodily movements during the course of his life, you still might not be able say definitively which of the two is Jack's *real* desire. In Dennett's view, one person's pattern is another's irrelevant detail. Nature is too ambiguous to let us be full-blooded realists.

Gene Machines

Still, one might be worried about whether talk of stances genuinely explains the nature of intentional states or the source of intentionality. Danny has beliefs because Deirdre adopts the intentional stance toward him, Deirdre has beliefs because David adopts the intentional stance toward her, David has beliefs because Dominique adopts the intentional stance toward him . . . and so on ad infinitum. But where does it start? Is there some original "intentional stance adopter"? Is there intrinsic intentionality, something that has intentional states independently of the stance others take?

Imagine, along with Dennett (1987b, 292–95), that you have found a way to hibernate for a prolonged period so that you might be a witness to the future, say, the twenty-fifth century. You set about building a machine—a pod—that will keep you safe during your Rip Van Winklesque sleep. Since unforeseen changes in your environment are highly likely, you design your pod so that it can flexibly respond to the environment, all with the goal of keeping you safe over the next few hundred years. The pod needs to be able to pick up information about the environment—to sense, as it were; to move variously, as the moment dictates; to make needed repairs; to assess threats in the environment and act accordingly. In short, it must adopt and execute a great many subplans, each designed to get the hibernating you to the twenty-fifth century.

This is our situation, with one twist. We are the pods, and our genes are the passengers. Dennett claims that we are gene machines, endowed by Mother Nature to respond flexibly to our environment. Mother Nature endows us— gene machines, that we are—with a special tool. We assess, evaluate, and navigate our environment by treating other creatures as intentional systems. But this is a tool for navigation, and it works. Adopting the intentional stance is a navigational tool, which we adopt toward conspecifics and other members of the animal, biological, and artifactual kingdoms. It is but a way of managing, given to us by Nature. If it is the source of intentionality that we seek, if we want to know how we came to be "stance-adopters," then Dennett tells us to look to evolution. Apart from this interactive navigation, there is no intentionality. And to ask which set of beliefs a person really has is about like asking which color scheme better suits the world: the honeybee's or ours.

Patterns, Behavior, and Concepts

Dennett's story of the propositional attitude is that we adopt the intentional stance toward our fellow creatures because it proves extraordinarily useful. Having already survived for millennia, this stance is likely to continue to survive because of its instrumental value. And we can thank evolution for this.

But we can see why someone might think this can't be the whole story by recalling one of the worries with behaviorism.

Behaviorism claims that we can bypass internal mental states by seeing concepts such as belief and desire as ways of talking about dispositions to behave. But which bodily movements should we count as relevant? Which bodily movements are the behavior, and which movements are irrelevant? We saw earlier that we needed notions like belief and desire to identify, to classify, the relevant bodily movements as behavior in the first place.

A similar worry might arise about Dennett's view (Sterelny 1990, chap. 5; Braddon-Mitchell and Jackson 1996, chap. 9; Nelkin 1996, chap. 8). According to Dennett, we attribute beliefs and desires to others because of the patterns in their behavior. In a sense, the patterns are there first, and then we come by the concepts. But why do we detect the patterns that we do? Why do certain aspects of our neighbor's bodily movements, and not others, suggest a pattern to us? Julia sees Jack reach inside his jacket, pull out a wallet, and remove a rectangular piece of plastic. She also sees him shift his weight from his right to his left, put his elbow on the counter, rearrange his jacket, and remove his tie. Why does she select only *some* of these movements as constitutive of the *pattern* that is his desire to pay for the tickets with a credit card? Dennett's answer is that you can't identify the relevant physical movements one belief at a time; you need to look at the whole set of a person's beliefs and desires and the entire range of movements.

But as with behaviorism, we must already have intentional notions—the concepts of belief and desire—in place before we begin to see patterns in the movements of others. It is through the lens of belief and desire that patterns of behavior come into focus. Dennett seems to want us to think that the patterns elicit the concepts of belief and desire. But one might worry that this puts the cart before the horse. It is because I already have these concepts that I am able to see the movements of others as behaviors. First concept, then pattern.

It is important to be clear about what this line of response to Dennett does and does not claim. Dennett agrees with Fodor (and many others, of course) that folk psychology is very useful. Like eliminative materialism, Dennett doubts that we are likely to find the internal states that legitimize Fodor's realism. But Dennett finds something that blocks the eliminativist option: patterns in behavior. Folk-psychological concepts will remain in our predictive and explanatory repertoire because they "lock on" to these patterns. And Dennett seems to think that the existence of the patterns underwrites the reality of folk psychology.

A more thoroughgoing realist, however, would say that it doesn't make sense to talk about the patterns in human behavior unless you already possess the concepts of belief and desire (and hopes and fears and wishes and so on). You don't explain the reality of the concepts by appeal to the patterns; the concepts enable us to detect the patterns. Dennett does not deny that the patterns are "perspective relative." The critic, however, claims that the notion of perspective is itself an intentional notion, which is as yet unexplained.

Still Waiting

Neither the Churchlands nor Dennett thinks that the realism of our folk psychology is warranted, and for at least one common reason. They doubt whether our best empirical theory will, in the end, be a hospitable place for our familiar beliefs and desires. Whether folk psychology is "here to stay" is not, as critic and defender recognize, a purely empirical matter. Our way of thinking about the mental, our conceptual understanding, while constrained by the empirical findings, is not dictated by those findings. There is now and is likely to be considerable room to move on these conceptual issues. Eliminative materialism expects massive revision in our commonsense view; instrumentalism expects folk psychology's usefulness to continue. And defenders expect that there will be more right than wrong about folk psychology. Unfortunately for our story here, as Patricia Churchland observes, "That said, let us all wait and see what happens" (1996, 299).

Key Concepts

Eliminative materialism

Instrumentalism

Intentional stance

Reading Questions

1. Why does Paul Churchland think folk psychology is a radically false theory? Why does he think that it cannot be integrated with other sciences?

2. What is the "infralinguistic catastrophe"? How might the defender of folk psychology resist this suggestion?

3. What is the difference between the design and intentional stances?

4. Why does Dennett appeal to the notion of patterns of human behavior?

References

Baillargeon, Renee. 1999. The object concept revisited: New directions in the investigation of infants' physical knowledge. In *Concepts: Core readings*, ed. Eric Margolis and Stephen Laurence, 571–612. Cambridge, MA: MIT Press.

Barwick, Daniel. 2002. Neomaterialism and the death of the subject. In *"The Matrix" and philosophy: Welcome to the desert of the real*, ed. William Irwin, 75–86. Chicago: Open Court.

Bogdan, Radu, ed. 1986. *Belief: Form, content, and function*. Oxford: Oxford University Press.

———. 1988. Mental attitudes and common sense psychology: The case against eliminativism. *Nous* 22:369–98.

———. 1991. Common sense naturalized: The practical stance. In *Mind and common sense: Philosophical essays on commonsense psychology*, ed. Radu J. Bogdan, 161–206. Cambridge: Cambridge University Press.

Braddon-Mitchell, David, and Frank Jackson. 1996. *Philosophy of mind and cognition*. Oxford: Blackwell.

Cheney, Dorothy, and Robert Seyfarth. 1990. *How monkeys see the world: Inside the mind of another species*. Chicago: University of Chicago Press.

Churchland, Patricia. 1986. *Neurophilosophy: Toward a unified science of the mind/brain*. Cambridge, MA: MIT Press.

———. 1996. Do we propose to eliminate consciousness? In McCauley 1996, 297–300.

Churchland, Paul M. 1981. Eliminative materialism and the propositional attitudes. *Journal of Philosophy* 78:67–90. Reprinted in Crumley 2000, 184–97; page references are to this volume.

———. 1989. *A neurocomputational perspective: The nature of mind and the structure of science*. Cambridge, MA: MIT Press.

Churchland, Patricia, and Paul Churchland. 1996. McCauley's demand for a co-level competitor. In McCauley 1996, 222–31.

Crumley, Jack, ed. 2000. *Problems in mind: Readings in contemporary philosophy of mind*. Mountain View, CA: Mayfield.

Dennett, Daniel. 1981a. *Brainstorms: Philosophical essays on mind and psychology*. Cambridge, MA: MIT Press.

———. 1981b. True believers: The intentional strategy and why it works. In *Scientific explanation: Papers based on Herbert Spencer Lectures in the University of Oxford*, ed. A. F. Heath, 265–80. Oxford: Oxford University Press. Reprinted in Dennett 1987a, 13–42, and in Crumley 2000, 226–42.

———. 1987a. *The intentional stance*. Cambridge, MA: MIT Press.

———. 1987b. Reflections: The language of thought reconsidered. In Dennett 1987a, 227–35.

———. 1991. Real patterns. *Journal of Philosophy* 88:27–51.

Donald, Merlin. 1991. *Origins of the modern mind: Three stages in the evolution of culture and cognition.* Cambridge, MA: Harvard University Press.

Horgan, Terence, and James Woodward. 1985. Folk psychology is here to stay. *Philosophical Review* 94:197–226. Reprinted in Crumley 2000, 198–214.

Kitcher, Patricia. 1984. In defense of intentional psychology. *Journal of Philosophy* 81:89–106. Reprinted in Crumley 2000, 215–25.

———. 1996. From neurophilosophy to neurocomputation: Searching for the cognitive forest. In McCauley 1996, 48–85.

Marshall, John, and Jennifer Gurd. 1996. The furniture of the mind: A yard of hope, a ton of terror? In McCauley 1996, 176–91.

McCauley, Robert N., ed. 1996. *The Churchlands and their critics.* Oxford: Blackwell.

Mithen, Steven. 1996. *The prehistory of the mind: The cognitive origins of art and science.* London: Thames and Hudson.

Nelkin, Norton. 1996. *Consciousness and the origins of thought.* Cambridge: Cambridge University Press.

Rorty, Richard. 1981. *Philosophy and the mirror of nature.* Princeton, NJ: Princeton University Press.

Rosenberg, Alexander. 1991. How is eliminative materialism possible? In *Mind and common sense: Philosophical essays on commonsense psychology,* ed. Radu Bogdan, 123–43. Cambridge: Cambridge University Press.

Sterelny, Kim. 1990. *The representational theory of mind.* Oxford: Blackwell.

Additional Readings

Churchland, Paul. *A Neurocomputational Perspective: The Nature of Mind and the Structure of Science.* Cambridge, MA: MIT Press, 1989.

———. *The Engine of Reason, the Seat of the Soul.* Cambridge, MA: MIT Press, 1995.

Dennett, Daniel. "Intentional Systems." In Dennett 1981a, 3–22.

———. "Mechanism and Responsibility." In Dennett 1981a, 233–55.

———. "Reflections: The Language of Thought Reconsidered." In Dennett 1981a, 227–35.

Rosenthal, David M, ed. *Materialism and the Mind–Body Problem.* Englewood Cliffs, NJ: Prentice-Hall, 1971.

PART II

THE FUNCTION OF THE MIND

7

Images and Concepts

When behaviorism lost its grip on psychology, and with the subsequent rise of cognitive psychology and artificial intelligence, the last three decades of the twentieth century saw a resurgent and decidedly interdisciplinary interest in long-dormant topics. Cognitive psychologists, artificial intelligence researchers, neuroscientists, and philosophers turned to the nature of mental representation—how information is stored or represented in the mind—and the use of representations in cognition. Thus freed, especially cognitive psychologists took note of a common aspect of reports of some of our mental life—it was often like looking at a picture with the "mind's eye." Spurred most notably by Roger Shepard's work, experiments on mental imagery began.

A second explanatory impulse, noted before, likens the mind to a computer. Understanding the mind means understanding its function, which means understanding its "program." Now, programs look decidedly unpicture-like. If the key to understanding the business of the mind lies in seeing it like a computer, then image-like mental representations get pushed aside. Mental images there may be, but they play no role in the mind's information-processing activities.

Not everyone who views the mind like a computer shuns mental imagery, though. As we will see below, a functional understanding of the brain leads to a functional understanding of mental images. Still, it this crossfire—between those that want to see all mental representation as sentence-like or as linguistic and those that think picture-like properties are part of the mind's information processing—that gives rise to the first part of this chapter.

Disciplinary interplay similarly impacts the study of *concepts*, an essential aspect of mental representation. Despite specifically philosophical worries about the approach, philosophers were long content with a "descriptionalist" view—*concepts are definitions*. Again, the experimental results of cognitive psychologists—such as the work of Eleanor Rosch—raised newer doubts about this "classical" approach. Indeed, the adequacy of a theory of concepts is now in part judged by how well it accounts for the empirical data. The second half of this chapter thus will examine this classical view of concepts and two more recent theories of concepts.

Images

Do frogs have lips? Most people describe how they answer this question as forming a mental image of a frog and inspecting it, checking to see whether you can find something "lip-like" in the image (the example is from Tye 1991). Similarly, if asked how many windows are in their living room, people generally report forming an image of the room—and counting.

The idea that mental images are an essential part of thinking traces back at least to Aristotle (384–322 B.C.), who claims in *On the Soul* that thoughts are always accompanied by images. Despite its storied history, however, mental imagery remained largely exiled during behaviorism's dominance. Renewed interest by philosophers and cognitive psychologists has led to two lines of thought about the nature of mental images and their role in cognitive processing. Some doubt whether mental images are anything more than epiphenomenal aspects of our mental life or whether they exist at all, while others insist that imagery plays an important role in our mental life.

This section traces two rival views, the imagistic and the descriptionalist positions. At issue between these two views is whether or not images play a role in our mental life by virtue of their depictive or picture-like properties (Kosslyn 1980, chap. 1). To borrow an example from Ned Block, consider the sentence "Sam is bald" and a painting of a bald Sam. Both the sentence and the painting represent a feature of Sam, his baldness. Descriptionalists think all of our mental representations are like sentences, while imagists claim that at least some of our mental states, represent, like the painting, pictorial or depictive properties (Block 1981a, 3).

It is easy to be seduced by a certain picture of mental images: Mental images are projections onto a mental screen, somewhere in the theater of the mind, and we observe what is projected onto that screen. There are *pictures* in the head, which we view with the "mind's eye." As I try to locate my keys, it seems as though I form a mental "picture" of the keys and see that they are lying on the desk. It is not hard to see, however, that whatever else is going on, there are no pictures in either the head or mind. Among their many properties, pictures have spatial and perceptible qualities. In the dualist view, since minds are *nonspatial*, there is literally *no space* for images to occur. Matters are no better when we ask whether there might be pictures in the brain. If I form the image of a candle burning inside a red hurricane lamp, there is no corresponding red, cylindrical-shaped space in my brain (Tye 1991). But if there are no pictures in the brain, if mental images are not pictures, then what are they?

Two Ways to Look at Images: Imagism and Descriptionalism

A prominent version of the imagist position understands images *functionally*. We can give not only a neuroscientific description of brain processes but also a functional description. The functional description of certain brain processes reveals that they behave and interact *like* images. And this is what it is to be a mental image, according to the imagist position. In the **imagist** view then, images are functional objects or functional pictures; as such, they are functions of brain states.

Stephen Kosslyn (1980, 1983, 1994) presents perhaps the most fully detailed account of this view. Adopting the functionalist reading of images, he utilizes the computer analogy, specifically the images generated on a CRT (cathode ray tube) screen. Many computer screens are no longer of the CRT model, but the principle remains unchanged. It might help here to think of a slightly different analogy, a digital camera.

Unlike "old-fashioned" cameras, which store pictorial images on film, digital cameras contain no film. Instead, once the light from the photographed scene reaches the digital camera, it is encoded into a kind of computer language. This encoded information is decidedly nonpictorial or nonimagistic. We can think of it as very complicated sequences of ones and zeroes. The sequences in turn determine whether and how a certain space, a pixel, on the camera "screen" gets filled. Digital cameras having more "megapixels" yield more-detailed, fine-grained pictures. When the stored information "tells" the camera how to fill in the screen, images are generated from the nonimage-like information. Similarly, the information in a computer, together with the software, tells the computer how to fill in the computer screen.

Of course, our brains contain neither cathode ray tubes nor megapixel camera screens. So how does this help with our understanding of images? Kosslyn suggests we treat the encoded information as *functional pictures* or *quasi-pictures*. Information about a scene—the jacaranda tree in my front yard, for example—is stored in coded form in memory. When I retrieve the image, when I "image" the jacaranda tree, the stored, coded information activates a pattern of cells in the brain that is functionally described as "active memory," the "workspace" of my conscious thinking. Parts of the pattern stand in for parts of the scene, and the entire pattern is a "functional space," corresponding to the actual spatial properties of the tree. Portions of the representation—the activated cells in the brain—preserve the actual spatial relations of portions of the tree. So, for example, if there is a fork in the branch closest to the ground, then the activated pattern must preserve this spatial relationship. The pattern is then interpreted, depending on the nature of the cognitive task.

To oversimplify greatly, a "1001101" sequence and the subsequently activated part of the neural pattern might stand in for or represent the lower portion of the tree trunk. If we want to know whether a branch is close to the ground, we interpret the relevant part of the activated cells. The activated cells in active memory thus function or behave *like* a picture. Activated cells "can then *function* as if they composed something like a television screen without actually *being* one" (Kosslyn 1983, 25; see also his chaps. 2–3 and Tye 1991, chap. 3).

Now, consider again our initial question: Do frogs have lips? You've seen frogs before, or at least pictures of frogs. This perceptual information gets stored in memory, not as computer code but as "brain code." Sometime later, you are engaged in an unusual conversation, which prompts the question about the frog's anatomy. You retrieve the information stored in (long-term) memory, and that information activates certain patterns of brain cells. A complicated brain process then interprets the activated pattern. In the case at hand—frog lips—this interpreting process checks to see whether there is information corresponding to frog lips.

This is a very simplified account of a complicated story, but it helps to give a sense of the imagistic view. Activated brain cells function *like* an image on a computer screen. The functional image—a quasi-picture—is subsequently interpreted by a brain process. Some, however, object to even this updated, functionalist version of imagist theory. Their contrary view is known as descriptionalism.

Descriptionalism holds that there are no mental images, not even functional images; instead we store *structured descriptions*, ordered lists of properties of the relevant scene. Images are thus interpreted on a linguistic model, rather than a pictorial model. To see how this view works, consider again the burning question of whether frogs have lips. In descriptionalism, we have descriptions of the parts of the object. Part of the structured description of a frog might include, among other things, four legs, jumping, bulging eyes, conic-shaped face, and bumpy, speckled, greenish skin. We store—or re-member—these descriptions in an ordered or structured manner. The de-scription "bulging eyes" more immediately activates, or is more immediately connected to, the description "conic-shaped face," whereas the description "four legs" more immediately activates the description "jumping." This im-mediacy of activation or connection provides *structure* in the structured de-scriptions. Our structured description of a frog contains more or less infor-mation—greater or fewer descriptions—depending on how much information we have stored about frogs. When asked, "Do frogs have lips?" you retrieve first the "frog" structure description and then run through the various items in the list to determine the answer.

Let's Look and See: Imagery Experiments

Perhaps more than most issues in philosophy of mind, the interpretation of empirical findings influences our understanding of mental images (Block 1981b, 3). But ordinary introspective reports describing aspects of our men-tal life as something like looking at an internal picture can be misleading or simply wrong. Other psychological findings tell us that people often misrep-resent what is going on inside them—think of rationalization; the same might be true of our picture-like descriptions of facets of our mental life. Cog-nitive psychologists thus design experiments to give us some clue about the existence of images. The evidence for the existence and nature of mental im-agery depends on the plausibility of the theoretical interpretation of the ex-perimental results. We cannot rehearse all the interpretations of the detailed experiments, but we can give something of the flavor of the more notable ex-periments and their relevance to views about imagery.

Much of the impetus for resurrecting images arose from an important ex-periment by Roger Shepard and his colleagues concerning apparent image rotation (Shepard 1978). Subjects were shown pairs of block figures (figures consisting of attached blocks). In each pair, the figures were shown from dif-ferent orientations; for example, one pair might contain a figure and a sec-ond identical figure rotated ninety degrees. Subjects were asked whether each pair displayed congruent figures (some were, some weren't). Not only did the subjects describe themselves as "rotating an image," but the time it took to answer depended on the amount of rotation required. Thus, it took longer to answer for a pair containing a ninety-degree difference in orienta-tion than it did for a pair having only a thirty-degree difference. It is *as though* the subjects were actually rotating images; the more rotation needed, the longer it took to answer.

Scanning tasks are also prominent in the imagery debate. In a series of experiments, Kosslyn showed subjects a drawing of a simple map of a small island, which included markings of various locations, some designated by an "X," some by other symbols or small drawings, say, of a tree. These experiments aimed to show that images employ functional space to represent the actual space of the map drawing (Kosslyn 1980, chap. 2). Subjects were asked, without looking at the map, to scan from a designated point to some other point on the map. Again, the results seem to support imagism: the greater the distance between the two points, the greater the scanning time.

Descriptionalists claim alternative, nonimagistic interpretations equally explain the results. Differences in scanning times, for example, may result from the time it takes to scan a structured list of descriptions. It is also suggested that the task demands—the subject's expectations about the length of time it is supposed to take—or the subject's tacit or background knowledge might influence the results (Pylyshyn 1984, chap. 8). Consider background knowledge first. The subject tacitly knows, based on previous perceptual experience, that visual scanning of greater distances takes longer. Visual scanning of all the houses on my block takes longer than visually scanning the second to the fourth house. This bit of information about perceptual experience is part of my tacit knowledge. Descriptionalists claim subjects drawing on this sort of tacit knowledge would have no need of images.

Similarly, task demands—what the subject *expects* about the outcome of an experiment—could play a role in the results. The subject expects that it should take longer to scan mentally a greater distance, and thus gives that answer. But, descriptionalists claim, it is not because of scanning of a mental image, but simply what the subject expects about the "right answer."

Michael Tye notes, however, that some experimental results do not seem to be explained by adverting to the task demands or a subject's background knowledge. In some experiments, for example, no mention is made of either scanning or images in the instructions to subjects. In still other experimental results, such as the McCullough effect, it is very unlikely that subjects possess the background knowledge that would explain their reported experience (Tye 1991, chap. 4).

Imagists are emboldened by another result. According to descriptionalists, our "image" of a cat is actually a list of its characteristics. If two items or characteristics are closely and more frequently associated, they have a greater association strength. "Cat," for example, is more strongly associated with "mouse" than with "firefighter." Cats rescued from trees are sometimes seen in the company of firefighters, but our folklore links cats more closely to mice. The descriptionalist view thus seems to predict that upon "imaging" a

The McCullough Effect

Interesting results, known as the "McCullough effect," arise from a particular imaging experiment. Subjects are shown two different pictures for ten minutes; one picture is that of black vertical stripes against a red background, while the second is that of black horizontal stripes against a green background. The pictures are switched back and forth during the ten minutes between the red background (vertical black stripes) and the green background (horizontal black stripes). Subjects are then shown black vertical and horizontal stripes against white backgrounds. Surprisingly, the subjects report that the vertical stripes are tinged with green, while the horizontal stripes are tinged with red—the reverse of the images they were shown!

Similar results occur when subjects are shown a red patch and asked to *imagine* black vertical stripes on it, then showed the green patch and asked to imagine black horizontal stripes. Again, upon being shown a white background and asked to imagine black vertical or horizontal stripes, similar color tinges are reported: green with the vertical stripes, red with the horizontal stripes.

How do these results reinforce the imagist view? Neither the instructions—the task demands—nor the subjects' background knowledge are obvious candidates for explaining the results. (Tye 1991, chaps. 3 and 4)

cat, we will more quickly retrieve "mouse" than "firefighter." Kosslyn devised an experiment that asked subjects about the body parts of animals. When asked to rely on images to answer the question, the relative size of the body part mattered more than association strength. Regardless of association strength, subjects gave answers more quickly if asked about a larger body part. This finding seems to run counter to the expected descriptionalist result (Finke 1989, chap. 1).

The debate between imagists and descriptionalists continues. Imagists sometimes protest that descriptionalism is a "moving target," revising its view in order to account for the latest imagery experiment. Indeed the literature notes that it is sometimes difficult to clarify what is really at issue between the two views (Block 1981a; Kosslyn 1980). While imagery effects are robust—supported by a number of different experiments—some imagists have taken a different tack of late. Kosslyn, for example, has set out to identify the brain processes responsible for mental imagery.

Kosslyn, along with others, points to evidence suggesting topographical representations in the brain. Experienced hikers are familiar with topographic maps, which display the relative positions of aspects of the terrain and changes in elevation. Imagine seeing an American Eskimo dog, a white, fluffy creature, looking something like a husky, standing about eighteen inches high. The evidence suggests that a *topographical* representation of the white, fluffy dog occurs in the visual cortex. The topographic representation, while not a photograph-like image, nonetheless encodes or preserves the relative position of various features of the dog.

Now, no topographic image is a *picture* of a mountain or a white dog; a topographic representation of a mountain scarcely takes one's breath away nor does the representation inspire a desire to scratch behind the image's ear. These representations serve as the physical basis, however, for Kosslyn's functional pictures. The representation "resembles" a dark-eyed, snow-white American Eskimo dog *because* the representation's organization preserves the spatial relationships among the parts of the cavorting canine. As Mark Rollins suggests, the rules governing the functional pictures mirror the laws governing objects in the world (1989, 22).

Recent neuroscientific evidence also suggests that when you remember seeing an American Eskimo dog, a similar topographic representation occurs in the visual cortex. That is, imagery shares some of the same cortical mechanisms utilized in perception (Kosslyn 1994; Damasio 1994, chap. 5; Prinz 2002). More importantly for the imagist, it is because of the depictive properties of the topographic representation that it represents an object. Of course, there is a more complicated story to tell about how such "brain images" result in our experience of "visual images," a story that we cannot pursue here. But advocates of imagism argue that as we are able to identify the neural basis of the functional or quasi-pictures, we acquire greater evidence for the imagist view.

Do Images Tell Us What Our Thoughts Are About?

Mental images are part of still another philosophical whirlwind. This particular maelstrom occupies the following chapter, but we might trace in broad outline the role of mental images in this debate. Philosophers of mind ask why it is that a thought is about one object and not another. What is it, for example, that makes my thought about a giraffe and not, say, about a zebra? It is tempting to think that my thought is about a giraffe because the thought *resembles* the giraffe, not the zebra. What do I "do" when I think about a giraffe? A natural and ready answer seems to be that a "giraffe-image" comes to mind.

The view that mental images determine the content of our thoughts has a long, if checkered history, running back at least to Aristotle. The **resemblance theory of content** holds that the content of a thought is determined by what the thought resembles. Now, philosophers such as Aristotle or Aquinas may have thought that there are pictures—photographic pictures—in the head, and we have just seen reason to reject that kind of view of images, but someone might hold the resemblance theory of mental content while rejecting the picture theory of mental images. Functional images may still resemble, in some sense, that which they image. And this resemblance might be enough for the resemblance theory of content.

A cautionary note: Kosslyn explicitly recognizes the possibility that we might have mental images, but says that they do not determine the content of a thought. That is, we might have tiger images, even though the images don't explain why my thought "tiger" is about tigers and not zebras.

Resemblance theory has an initial plausibility. It seems to explain why we are confident that we know what we are thinking. You are sure that you are thinking of giraffes precisely because the image before your mind resembles giraffes and not elephants or meerkats. The view also seems to explain how we might have thoughts of nonexistent or fictional characters and objects. My current thought is about Santa Claus because the mental image—the image in my mind—resembles the look of the fictional character.

Two criticisms of the resemblance view are especially noteworthy. The twentieth-century philosopher Ludwig Wittgenstein (1889–1951) notes that a picture could be variously interpreted. We normally count resemblance as a kind of one-to-one correspondence—a part of a drawing corresponds to an ear, another part to a front leg. The relative arrangement of parts remains the same between the image and the object it resembles. But the resemblance relation might be interpreted differently. While a giraffe image resembles *giraffes*, it also resembles animals with spotted coats, or four-legged mammals, or, under the right circumstances, animals boarding Noah's ark. Hence, the difficulty: any image resembles many different things. And if it resembles many different things, then it is *about* many things. But my thought "Giraffes are on the north side of the zoo," isn't about many things, certainly not about Noah's ark—it's about where the giraffes are located in the zoo. Resemblance relations and "content-determining" relations are apparently different kinds of relation, which is not a happy outcome for resemblance theory.

A further difficulty arises when we consider whether all thoughts have as-sociated images. Thoughts about abstract properties or concepts, such as jus-tice or the German language, are not obviously image related. My thinking that I once knew German very well or that a particular action is unjust are thoughts that have content, but I do not seem to have any associated images for those thoughts.

As a theory of mental content, the resemblance view appears to have some weaknesses. Nonetheless, images might still play a limited role in the information-processing activities of the mind, since they may facilitate or en-hance our thinking. The information-processing view of images may thus be more limited than the historical resemblance theory. A mental image of my keys may facilitate my locating those ornery little things. Still, some people argue that images are much more basic than is allowed in this limited version (Damasio 1994; Rollins 1989; Prinz 2002).

It is too early to predict the outcome of this debate. Yet there is reason to think that some aspects of our commonsense view about mental images will remain, albeit in perhaps more modern guise. It is time to turn, however, from worries about pictures to worries about something more linguistic.

Organizing the World: Concepts

We do not experience the world as a "blooming, buzzing confusion." Our ex-perience is of a world of rivers and rain, of rocks and raccoons, of houses and highways, of tables and chairs. Rain might come as a gentle mist, or it might rain cats and dogs. Our experience of the world is a "classified" experience; we experience a world sorted into categories or classes.

For our purposes, we'll use the terminological convention that concepts pick out or designate the members of categories or classes. Our concept of DOG picks out the category of dogs, and hence, everything that belongs to that category or class—that is, individual dogs. (Here and in the rest of this chapter, words in small capitals indicate concepts.) We will make one other, sometimes controversial, assumption. We will assume that concepts are men-tal representations—thus, they are mental states—and we want to know how concepts are represented.

That concepts classify or organize is perhaps their most obvious and im-portant feature. I can think about the white, fluffy pup asleep by the china cabinet because I possess certain concepts. You can wish upon a star or be-lieve that democracy is the best form of government because you possess cer-tain concepts. Concepts, in a sense, are the building blocks of our thoughts: no concepts, no thoughts.

Five characteristics of concepts are worth noting, and the first two are closely related.

1. Concepts are intentional or have content; they are *about* things. My concept of PUPPY picks out—that is, it's about—very young dogs.
2. Closely associated with the first characteristic is the already noted classificatory (categorization) aspect of concepts. PUPPY identifies those furry, four-legged, playful, barking things, but not those other furry, four-legged, meowing things.
3. Concepts are the components or constituents of our thoughts. I can believe that the puppy is in the dining room or desire that he come in out of the rain.
4. Concepts combine to form new, complex concepts. My concepts WHITE and DOG combine or "compose" to form the new concept WHITE DOG. Similarly, you can believe that Bossy is a brown cow because the concepts BROWN and COW combine to form the new, more complex concept BROWN COW. This feature of concepts—that the content of new complex concepts is some function of the content of the constituent concepts—is known as **compositionality**.
5. Implicit in the preceding characteristics is the assumption that concepts are shared. You and I can *both* think that the rose is red or that the candle is burning. Disagreements may arise about whether a concept picks out some object—Sara and Sam might disagree over whether olives are fruit. In principle, however, concepts are shareable. If Sara can have the concept DIGITAL PIANO, then so may Sam.

These are not the only characteristics of concepts. Jesse Prinz (2002) lists seven desiderata that an adequate theory of concepts should meet, including such things as concept acquisition. Gregory Murphy (2002) identifies still more, including conceptual development in children, the effects of concepts on induction, and the relationship between concepts and word meaning. Our examination of three prominent theories of concepts will necessarily be limited to how they handle some of the key characteristics so far noted.

Before moving on to the three theories, we can briefly note a venerable dispute in philosophy about the acquisition of concepts, that is, whether all concepts are acquired through experience. Rationalists—from Plato through St. Augustine to Descartes and Leibniz—argue that at least some of our concepts are innate or acquired *prior to* experience. Empiricists—beginning with Aristotle, tracing through St. Bonaventure and St. Thomas Aquinas to Locke and Hume—argue that *all* of our concepts derive from experience.

Taking cues from Kant, and reinvigorated by Chomsky and Fodor, the *innateness controversy* continues today and is worthy of exploration in its own right (Block 1981b, part 4).

Our present interest lies, however, with the nature of concepts. Three views offer an answer: the classical view, prototype theory, and the knowledge approach. The latter two are of very recent origin. Developments in psychology, especially cognitive and developmental psychology, and philosophy led to dissatisfaction with the oldest and most venerable theory of concepts—that concepts are definitions. It is here that we begin our survey.

The Classical Theory: Definitions

Socrates, Plato's mentor, annoyed at least a few people (and got into a good bit of trouble) by not only asking for definitions of certain terms but also never being satisfied with the answers. Whether he wanted to know the nature of justice or courage, it's possible to characterize his endeavor as asking for an answer to the questions of the form, "What is love?" In response, he expected something like a definition. He hoped that his interlocutors would provide him with the necessary and sufficient conditions for whether something was an instance of love or courage.

The **classical theory of concepts**, sometimes called *definitionism*, holds that a concept is the set of necessary and sufficient conditions that determines whether an item is a member of the category. Recall that *necessary* conditions are like minimum requirements—a necessary condition of being president is being thirty-five years of age: you can't be president unless you are at least thirty-five years old. But that's not enough to make you president. That's the job of sufficient conditions. *Sufficient* conditions specify what's enough for an item to fall into a category. Receiving a majority of the Electoral College votes and having Congress certify that majority is *enough* to make you president.

Now consider the concept CIRCLE. It classifies every item as either an instance of circle or not. And it does so by specifying the necessary and sufficient conditions for being a circle. You may recall from geometry that a circle is the set of points in a plane equidistant from a given point. There is no "sort of" about it; either something is a circle or it isn't.

The classical theory promises much. It explains the intentionality of concepts. CIRCLE picks out all and only those things that fall into the category of circles. It also tells us what it is to have the concept CIRCLE: Having the concept is having the definition. Furthermore, it looks as though your concepts compose. If you have the concepts CIRCLE and OVERLAPPING (exactly two points in common), you can have the concept OVERLAPPING CIRCLES. And two people may share a concept. Sam and Sara share the concept CIRCLE whenever they both have the definition.

The emphasis on definitions is reminiscent of the emphasis on analytic propositions in the first half of the twentieth century. Analytic propositions specify the necessary and sufficient conditions for membership in a category. Thus, "vixens are female foxes" or "bachelors are unmarried males" are paradigmatic of the definitional approach. Something is a member of the class of vixens only if it is a fox and female. W. V. O. Quine's 1951 article "Two Dogmas of Empiricism" diminished the emphasis on analytic propositions, on unassailable definitions of terms.

The most obvious difficulty with the classical theory is that we seem to possess an extraordinary number of concepts for which we possess nothing like a definition. With a little review, we can remind ourselves of the definitions of circles, squares, triangles, straight lines, and obtuse angles. But how many of our concepts are like the concepts of geometry? Consider the concept MONEY. Although you've probably thought of money recently, do you have a definition of money? "Money is what you exchange for goods and services." If I give you a big hug for mowing my lawn, is the hug an instance of money? "Backed by the full faith and credit of the U.S. government." Something might be money even though it has no connection to the U.S. government or any government. Exceptions may prove the rule, but they make life difficult for the classical theory.

Wittgenstein (1968, secs. 69–86) uses the concept GAME to illustrate the same point. He asks us to recall the very different and various activities we classify as games: board games, card games, athletic games, games that a small child invents. His suggestion is, of course, that no single definition captures all and only games. (Ironically, Quine claims that the project of finding the analytic sentences—which provide the definitions—is hopeless because there is no noncircular account of ANALYTIC. That is, there's no good definition of *analytic*.) Yet the concept GAME, like the concept MONEY, is clearly part of our conceptual repertoire.

Definitions—a specification of necessary and sufficient conditions—have their drawbacks as concepts. And the most telling argument against this theory is that since people can possess a concept X without possessing a definition of X, definitions are not good candidates for understanding concepts.

Reviving the Classical View

Some philosophers have not given up on definitionism. Typical of such views is the distinction between the *core* and *identification procedures*. The core is the definition, a list of necessary and sufficient conditions specifying the properties that any member of the designated category must have. Unlike the classical view, however, revised definitionism does not pretend that we have cognitive access to these definitions. Instead we have something like a rough-and-ready description that functions as an identification procedure. The identification procedure—similar to the prototypes of the second theory—permit the recognition and categorization of objects.

Why rehabilitate the classical view? Defenders are often worried about the publicity requirement. We can be said to share concepts, they claim, only if we possess something in common and invariable from person to person. Definitions are the best candidate for that common feature.

Critics of revised definitionism still worry whether there are such definitions, especially given our inability to provide definitions for all but the most circumscribed of concepts. Another worry is that the core—the definition—plays no obvious role in many of the phenomena that we want a theory of concepts to explain. Since it is the identification procedures that explain such things as typicality effects and categorization, the core appears left out (Rey 1983, 1994; Fodor 1998; Prinz 2002; Murphy 2002).

Prototypes

Is a robin a bird? Is a penguin? Is an apple a fruit? Is an olive? If you're like most people, you think that robins are more typical birds than penguins and an apple is a more typical fruit than an olive. This phenomenon, known as the *typicality effect*, gives rise to a family of views about the nature of concepts. The work of Eleanor Rosch and others in the 1960s and 1970s brought these views to prominence.

Prototype theory holds that concepts are mental representations of collections of features possessed by the best instances—the most typical members—of the category. A concept is thus a kind of summary of the typical fea-

Rosch et al.

A series of studies in the mid-1970s by Eleanor Rosch and various colleagues proved central to the thinking about concepts and the development of theories of concepts. Rosch resisted opting for one theory over another, but handling typicality effects and basic level categorization is virtually indispensable for any theory of concepts. It is worth some mention, especially since typicality effects are well documented.

Rosch found that some members of a category are always more typical than others, and we categorize an object more easily if it is or resembles a more typical member of the category. Importantly, there is no set of necessary and sufficient conditions that characterizes the typical members. Instead, typical members bear a *family resemblance* to one another, a notion first utilized by Wittgenstein in the early 1950s.

Categories divide into three levels: the superordinate, the basic, and the subordinate. For example, consider the category *chair*. *Chair* is the basic level. If *furniture* is the superordinate level, then the basic level comprises such separate categories as *chairs*, *tables*, and *lamps*. At the subordinate level, we find specific types of chairs or tables, for example, *kitchen chairs* and *armchairs*.

According to the studies, an object is judged as typical if it has many attributes in common with other members of the category. Rosch and her colleagues found judgments of typicality remain constant from person to person. Edith and Archie, George and Louise, Lucy and Ricky all count robins as typical birds and penguins as atypical ones. And as pointed out in the text, this is not good news for the classical theory. If there is some set of properties that all and only birds have, and having a concept is having a representation of this set, then penguins should be no less typical than robins.

tures of the most typical members of a category. And this summary is the prototype. (A little more technically, a concept is a *weighted* summary of features. Some features are more important than others.) Think for a moment of the typical features of fruit. Fruits—typically—have a skin, are sweet, are edible, and contain seeds. Since apples and oranges possess all of these features, we more readily categorize them as fruit.

This suggests an apparent advantage of prototype theory over the classical view. A person can possess a concept even though the person has nothing like a complete definition. Sara possesses the concept FRUIT if she has stored the appropriate summary. She stores a list of likely features of fruit, or a rough-and-ready description that is an approximate guide for classifying objects as fruit. Sara's concept is this mental representation, this stored list of likely features. As already indicated, an initial motivation for prototype theory is its ability to explain typicality effects.

Prototype theory recognizes that different objects may be more or less clear instances of a category. We might more readily count a cantaloupe as a kind of fruit than we would a tomato. The cantaloupe is a better example—because it matches better the more important features in the list—than a tomato (which is *legally* a vegetable). The cantaloupe, in a sense, gets a higher grade. Prototype views thus appear to give us grades or degrees of belonging to a category.

This degree of category membership raises a worry, however. Some time ago I was surprised to learn that zucchini is not a vegetable; it is classified as a fruit, along with the rest of the squash family. I had always classified zucchini in the company of green beans, carrots, and broccoli, never in the company of apples, oranges, and bananas. Indeed, no one had *ever* offered me fruit and then handed me a zucchini. Zucchini, it seemed to me, was as much a vegetable as broccoli. (Technically, FRUIT is a botanical concept, while VEGETABLE is a loose classificatory concept. But the example may serve to highlight the problem.)

One of the important characteristics of concept is their intentionality. We expect FRUIT to pick out all and only those things that are fruit. But what should we say about very *atypical* instances of the category? Zucchini may be atypical, but is it any less a member of the category of fruit than is, say, a cantaloupe? If a prototype doesn't clearly identify the members of the category, or if it classifies by degrees, we might wonder whether the prototypes tell us what they are about.

Prinz outlines why some worry that prototype theory may not give us a clear account of the intentionality of concepts (2002, chap. 3). Zucchini may be atypical instances of fruit, but they are no less fruit. Similarly, as Prinz notes, forklifts are not your typical instance of VEHICLE, but they are as much a vehicle as your father's Oldsmobile. It might be suggested that a concept refers to those items that fall above a certain threshold. That is, the concept refers to an object if the object is close enough to the prototype (theorists have developed some complicated formulas for determining "close enough"; the technical details need not concern us here). This suggestion may not work, however. Dolphins are much more similar than eels to the prototype for FISH. Yet FISH refers to eels and not dolphins. Prototype theory seems then to leave us without a clear explanation of the intentionality of concepts.

Two other central properties of concepts seem problematic for prototype views: compositionality and the publicity, or the "shareability," of concepts. We would expect that the typical features of a complex concept would be determined by the typical features of its constituent concepts. But this does not always appear to be the case for certain kinds of concepts. Prinz notes that instances of the concept LARGE SPOON are typically wooden. But being wooden does not seem to be a typical feature of either large things or spoons. (*Phrasal concepts*, like LARGE SPOON, pick out objects that have "emergent" typical features—that large spoons are typically wooden is not something one would expect given typical large things or typical spoons.)

There is, however, an initially optimistic story about the publicity of concepts. A concept is shared by Sam and Sara only if they possess the same prototype. Yet Sam might encounter examples of dogs very different from those encountered by Sara. Since prototypes are summaries of the *typical* features, there is some reason to hope that Sam and Sara's prototypes will eventually converge. Studies suggest, however, that there is only partial agreement over typical features from individual to individual. Differences in typical features yield different prototypes, which of course yield different concepts. It might be suggested that our ordinary concept of CONCEPT permits this discrepancy. This response may be at odds, however, with our expectation that a concept picks out all and only the members of the class. Despite differences in their prototypes, we expect that DOG picks out all and only dogs.

Concepts as Theories: The Knowledge Approach

Before reading the paragraphs that follow, think for a moment about the concept that picks out the category that includes, in no particular order, children, jewelry, photographs, pets, cell phones, checkbooks, toothbrushes. Suggestions for the concept? Don't worry; we'll come back to it below.

The **knowledge approach**, or as it is sometimes called, the "theory theory," claims that our concepts are more than just representations of features or properties. Our concepts are like little theories. My concept DOG is a theory, a theory about dogs to be sure but also a theory about dogs in the world. So, a concept is identified by its role in our overall understanding of the world (Margolis and Laurence 1999, 45).

The knowledge approach is in part motivated by the recognition that a concept is not only a list of features but also an explanation of the links among such features. The classical and prototype views, for example, offer no explanation for which properties are included in the concept and which are excluded; such views are silent about the *constraints* on properties included in a concept (Smith and Medin 1981). My concept DOG includes not only a list of properties or features—four legs, fur, barks, eats meat—but also an understanding of how those features are related. My concept includes the idea that dogs are living creatures in need of sustenance, that dogs are also biological creatures whose characteristic features of having fur or legs are linked to their biological structure. Similarly, the concept BIRD includes not only "has wings" and "flies" but also at least a rudimentary understanding of the connection between having wings and flying: A bird is able to fly *because* it has wings.

Concepts reflect our *background knowledge* about our world. The knowledge view emphasizes that our concepts, like theories, represent aspects of the nature and essence of things, along with causal and explanatory links. One well-known experiment indicates that children's concepts represent natural objects as having an "inner core." Shown a series of pictures of a raccoon transformed—by painting it—into the physical likeness of another animal, children insist that the animal remains a raccoon, that it retains its inner core (Murphy 2002). This leads some to espouse **psychological essentialism,** the view that our concepts represent objects having a hidden, inner essence.

Some proponents of the knowledge approach insist on a rather strict interpretation of the notion of theory (Murphy and Medin 1999; Prinz 2002, chap. 4). They suggest that concepts, like theories, include laws and allow for predictions. Whether or not one accepts this strict interpretation, there are important similarities between concepts and theories, according to the knowledge view. Theories serve to "simplify" reality, and our concepts may represent the world as more organized and structured than it is. More importantly, theories provide explanations. A theory does not simply record our observations but also explains *why* we seem to find certain properties linked. Ecological and evolutionary theories note the whiteness and furriness of polar bears, but importantly they provide some understanding of why polar bears are white and furry. Similarly, concepts, like theories, offer an understanding of why members of a category have certain properties and not others.

We can take some of the theoretical tinge off the preceding by returning to the example that began this section. Remember—children, jewelry, photographs, pets, cell phones, checkbooks, toothbrushes (a slight variation of an example in Murphy and Medin 1999). When you are told "things to take from your home during an evacuation," notice that the items seem to fall into place. Of course you would take members of the family, child and pet alike, but you might also take valuables, money, and keepsakes. As a simple list, the items do not obviously cohere. But the concept THINGS TO TAKE FROM YOUR HOME DURING AN EVACUATION brings a kind of order precisely because it reflects your background knowledge of the world.

Advocates of the knowledge theory also point to its role in explanations of inductive reasoning (Murphy 2002). Although induction is a much vexed topic in epistemology, for our purposes, let us consider induction as taking one of two forms. Induction is either reasoning about already known members in a category to unknown members—since dogs I've already come across barked, I infer that this new, previously unseen dog will bark (a version of Hume's account of inductive inference)—or reasoning about whether a property found in one category will also be true of members another category. We might, for example, infer something about the appearance of a robin from seeing one robin, but would we make a similar inference about a professor's appearance?

Lending support to the knowledge approach is a somewhat striking finding. In performing induction tasks, subjects consider not only similarity relations but also how different properties and categories are related and the relevance of that relation. The concept ROBIN includes a theory or explanation about why robins are red breasted. This particular feature of a robin's appearance is tied to its biology and genetic makeup. But consider that when you observe that some professor is a snappy dresser, you are unlikely to conclude that every professor is a snappy dresser. Why? Because the concept PROFESSOR counts such properties as *inessential* and not tied to genetic or biological makeup. Our concept of professor is linked to the concept HUMAN BEING, which counts certain physical appearance features as more or less essential—a face, torso, limbs—and others, such as clothing style, as inessential. The important point is that concepts, like theories, include our explanatory understanding of the world.

The strengths of the knowledge approach also hint at its weaknesses (Margolis and Laurence 1999). Possessing a concept, in the knowledge view, requires a person to have a theory. You have the concept CAT only if you have a theory about cats. But how much of a theory must a person have? Children apparently have concepts such as DOG or CAT without having much in the way of a theory about their biological makeup. Interestingly, however, some psychologists argue that children have something very much like a theory about various objects. This is supported in part by the raccoon transformation experiments noted earlier (Carey 1999).

The knowledge view might have difficulty with the publicity and the intentionality of concepts. People may vary in their "cat theories"; the knowledge approach, however, doesn't provide a clear indication of how much theory difference is allowed before it counts as a different concept. If Sam, but not Sara, believes that cats don't like to have their whiskers cut, do they have different concepts about everyday furry felines?

This may also suggest worries about intentionality for the knowledge view; do concepts pick out a well-defined category? We would seem to need to know the appropriate theory for CAT, for example, and there may be no principled way to do this. Since the intentionality of a concept is only as well defined as the background knowledge or theory that identifies the concept, the knowledge approach may not yet provide an account of concept intentionality.

Our Concept of "Concept"

"In short, concepts are a mess." In the conclusion of *The Big Book of Concepts* (2002), Gregory Murphy acknowledges that the differing strengths and weaknesses of each account of concepts makes it difficult to say which theory is best. Prototype theory, for example, explains typicality effects, but is less effective in accounting for the role of background knowledge. The classical view explains the intentionality of a concept, but appears inconsistent with typicality effects. Murphy's own solution is to opt for a bit of a mixed view. In this he is probably not alone. Jesse Prinz, as a further example, argues for an empiricist view indebted at least to imagism and prototype theory.

Our point here is not to settle on *the* theory of concepts, but to remind ourselves that an adequate theory must address a range of phenomena. The demise of the classical theory, in large measure due to its inability to account for empirical findings, opens the way to not only more subtle and complex theories, but equally to more controversy and still more research. Still, we expect much from a theory of concepts. Concepts are the building blocks of our thought, the mental file system that reflects the way we categorize and organize the world. It may not be too surprising that things tend to get a little messy.

Key Concepts

Compositionality

Definitionalism

Descriptionalism

Imagism

Knowledge approach

Prototype theory

Reading Questions

1. Kosslyn describes mental images as "functional pictures." What does he mean by this?

2. The descriptionalist counts images as "structured descriptions." Explain this notion.

3. Why is the map-scanning experiment thought to support imagism? What is the descriptionalist's response?

4. What is the principal objection to definitionism, or the classical view?

5. How do prototype theory and the knowledge approach differ?

References

Block, Ned, ed. 1981a. *Imagery*. Cambridge, MA: MIT Press.

———, ed. 1981b. *Readings in the philosophy of psychology*. Vol. 2. Cambridge, MA: Harvard University Press.

Carey, Susan. 1999. Knowledge acquisition: Enrichment or conceptual change? In Margolis and Laurence 1999, chap. 20.

Damasio, Antonio. 1994. *Descartes' error: Emotion, reason, and the human brain*. New York: Putnam.

Finke, Ronald. 1989. *The principles of mental imagery*. Cambridge, MA: MIT Press.

Fodor, Jerry. 1998. *Concepts: Where cognitive science went wrong*. Oxford: Oxford University Press.

Kosslyn, Stephen. 1980. *Image and mind*. Cambridge, MA: Harvard University Press.

——— 1983. *Ghosts in the mind's machine: Creating and using images in the brain*. New York: W. W. Norton.

———. 1994. *Image and brain: The resolution of the imagery debate*. Cambridge, MA: MIT Press.

Margolis, Eric, and Stephen Laurence, eds. 1999. *Concepts: Core readings*. Cambridge, MA: MIT Press.

Murphy, Gregory. 2002. *The big book of concepts*. Cambridge, MA: MIT Press.

Murphy, Gregory, and Douglas Medin. 1999. The role of theories in conceptual coherence. In Margolis and Laurence 1999, chap. 19.

Prinz, Jesse. 2002. *Furnishing the mind: Concepts and their perceptual basis*. Cambridge, MA: MIT Press.

Pylyshyn, Zenon. 1984. *Computation and cognition: Toward a foundation for cognitive science*. Cambridge, MA: MIT Press.

Rey, Georges. 1983. Concepts and stereotypes. *Cognition* 15:237–62.

———. 1994. Concepts. In *A companion to the philosophy of mind*, ed. Samuel Guttenplan, 185–93. Oxford: Blackwell.

Rollins, Mark. 1989. *Mental imagery: On the limits of cognitive science*. New Haven, CT: Yale University Press.

Shepard, Roger. 1978. The mental image. *American Psychologist* 33:125–37.

Smith, Edward E., and Douglas L. Medin. 1981. *Categories and concepts*. Cambridge, MA: Harvard University Press.

Tye, Michael. 1991. *The imagery debate*. Cambridge, MA: MIT Press.

Wittgenstein, Ludwig. 1968. *Philosophical investigations*. 3rd ed., trans. G. E. M. Amscombe. New York: Macmillan.

Additional Readings

Dennett, Daniel. *Content and Consciousness*. London: Routledge and Kegan Paul, 1969.

Fodor, Jerry. *Concepts: Where Cognitive Science Went Wrong*. New York: Oxford University Press, 1998.

Rey, Georges. "Introduction: What Are Mental Images?" In *Readings in the Philosophy of Psychology*, ed. Ned Block, 2:117–27. Cambridge, MA: Harvard University Press, 1981.

Robertson, Ian. *Opening the Mind's Eye*. New York: St. Martin's Press, 2003.

8

What Do You Have in Mind?
Theories of Mental Content

Thoughts have content; they are about something. Whether I am thinking about the morning glories blooming along the fence, where the dog has gotten to, or where the Radiators are playing this weekend, my thoughts are *directed* toward some feature or features of the world. In this sense, a thought is intentional; it is about something. The content of a thought is the object of our thought. It is almost a matter of definition that where there is no content, there is no thought. Indeed, we identify thoughts—we individuate them—by their content. My thought that the keys are under the table is different from the thought that the dog is under the table *because* the two thoughts are about different things—the former about the keys, the latter about the dog.

The problem of mental content, or the problem of intentionality, surfaced especially in the 1970s. Philosophers of mind, and researchers from other disciplines, set out to do two things. First, they wanted to know what makes a thought have the content it does. Why does a particular mental representation, for example, pick out dogs and not morning glories? (The terms "thought," "mental representation," and "concept" are used interchangeably in this chapter.) Is it because I have a picture of a dog in mind, or some other reason? Second, many philosophers of mind think that a theory of content should be naturalistic; that is, they ought to be able to explain content using terms or concepts that are in some sense scientifically respectable, that is, compatible with the rest of natural science.

In a moment we will look at three recent, prominent theories of intentionality. But we begin with a cursory sketch of our commonsense understanding of mental content, after which we will survey a disagreement about the general nature of content.

Common Sense and Content

On the surface it may seem as though common sense doesn't tell us a lot about the nature of mental content. But a little reflection teases out four interesting features. Most obvious perhaps is that—for the most part—each of us knows what we are thinking. Deirdre knows that she is thinking about where she left her calculus book, and Danny knows that he is thinking about nonfat vanilla yogurt. Every person knows the content of their own thoughts. Closely related is the commonsense view that our thought contents are private. Sam knows what he's thinking, but Sara knows what Sam is thinking only if he tells her, generally by saying what he's thinking. Sam has immediate, introspective access to his thought contents. The rest of us must wait for some indication from Sam. Sam has a privileged access to his thoughts. Each of us is the final authority on our thoughts. This immediate access to our own thoughts is variously called "privileged access" or "first-person authority." Thus, we have two features of a commonsense view of mental content: We know what we're thinking, and we have privileged access to what we're thinking.

A third aspect is that—again for the most part—our thoughts are unambiguous, having a definite content. My thought "What's that little devil up to now?" is clearly directed toward the antics of the ill-mannered pup under the table.

The fourth aspect is a little less obvious (and somewhat controversial). Whatever it is that makes my thought about a dog or a duck, a key or a cup, whatever it is that determines the content of my thought, is inside me; it is *internal*. Mental contents are determined by something inside me, some internal condition or state; they are inside the mind or in the head. This intuitively plausible view is **internalism**—the view that what determines the content of a thought is internal (inside the mind or head).

We have then this picture of a commonsense view of mental content: It is an internalist view; we know what we are thinking; we have a privileged access to our thoughts, and our thoughts are specific. But recently the internalist aspect has become extremely controversial, which we now consider.

Externalism and Internalism

Folk psychology and a very long tradition in philosophy consider content to be determined by what occurs inside a person. In principle, determining what any of us are thinking about requires only that we look at internal factors, those factors present or occurring *inside* a person. As it was once picturesquely put, God could look inside a person's head or mind—and look only there—and tell what the person was thinking about. Suppose that I believe that it is against the law in Idaho to fish for trout while sitting on the back of a giraffe. What is it that determines that my thought "giraffe" is about giraffes and not elephants, and that "trout" is about a kind of fish? **Externalism**, which arose in the 1970s, holds that at least some of the factors determining content are *external* to the person.

The crucial challenge in the externalist's argument is persuading us that the referent of a concept—what the concept picks out—is an external factor that at least partly determines content. In other words, the meaning or content cannot be determined solely by considering internal factors. This view is striking, and the argument for it is no less so.

Twin Earth

In what has become a bit of philosophic folklore, Hilary Putnam (1975) asks us to consider Twin Earth, a planet identical to our own Earth in all but one respect, to be explained in a moment. Deirdre, on Earth, wants a glass of water. At precisely the same moment, on Twin Earth, Twin Deirdre—a molecule-for-molecule duplicate of our earthbound Deirdre—also wants a glass of water.

The difference between the planets is that, instead of H_2O, Twin Earth has a substance exactly like water in all its surface properties—it is clear, colorless, falls from the sky, quenches thirst—but its molecular structure is XYZ, not H_2O. When earthlings point to water, they point to a substance composed of H_2O. When twin earthlings point to "twin water," they point to a substance composed of XYZ, which is the sole divergence between Earth and Twin Earth.

Putnam's argument is twofold. First, the meaning of a concept is a function of its referent or what the concept designates. Part of the meaning depends on what the thought is about. Second, what the thought is about—the referent—is (very often, at least) *external* to a person. Taken together, these two points imply that the content of at least some concepts are determined externally. Hence, as Putnam picturesquely puts the matter, "meanings just ain't in the *head*" (1975, 227; emphasis in original).

Deirdre and Twin Deirdre illustrate Putnam's point. Alike in all *internal* respects, if Deirdre thinks, "That glass of water is just what I need," Twin Deirdre thinks, "That glass of water is just what I need." But here's the catch: Deirdre and Twin Deirdre are referring to *two different things*; one refers to H_2O, the other to XYZ. Although Deirdre and her twin are alike in all internal respects, their "water" concepts refer to two different substances. Now, if content depends on the referent, their thoughts have different contents Thus, Putnam claims that meaning or content is not entirely internal. If God wants to know what we are thinking about, then he cannot look only inside our head; he has to look at our environment, as well.

Narrow and Wide Content

We normally explain a person's behavior by appealing to what the person thinks, by what goes on inside the person's head. People act on the basis of what they think, on how they understand a concept. And this is a powerful motivation for internalism. Thus, you and I may know that the department chair is Sara. But if Danny thinks that the department chair is Mike—if Danny thinks "department chair = Mike"—then he will go looking for Mike, not Sara.

Putnam's argument, however, seems to leave us with two "kinds" of content: that which is inside the head—which explains behavior—and that which is outside the head, which explains the *aboutness* of the concept. Some thus distinguish between narrow and wide content, a distinction that is also controversial (see, for example, Fodor 1991 and Stalnaker 1989). **Narrow content** is a function of the internal states of a person. **Wide content** is determined by taking into account a person's environment, both the physical and the social.

Of course, we would like to know the connection between wide and narrow content. Perhaps more important for our present purpose is whether a theory of mental content should be externalist or internalist.

Saving Internalism?

Externalism was not universally welcomed. We can divide the responses into two camps: those who find something wanting in Putnam's argument, and those who attempt to accommodate the externalist argument while preserving a sense of narrow content.

One strategy then is to reject the claim that the meaning of "water" is tied to H_2O in the manner that Putnam thinks. Avrum Stroll (1989), for example, suggests that the identification of water with H_2O is an *additional piece of information* possessed by English speakers; the identification, however, is not part of the *meaning* of "water." The meaning of "water" is given by mentioning the normally associated properties—liquid, wet, colorless, found in lakes and rivers, suitable for drinking, and so on. But is "water = H_2O" part of the meaning of "water" or an additional piece of information? We know a lot of things about water—that water covers 75 percent of the Earth's surface, that humans cannot survive long without it, and so forth—yet we do not think that these facts about water are part of the meaning of the concept. These facts are "collateral information." Similarly, Stroll suggests that the connection to H_2O is a bit of collateral information learned from the progress of science (see also Crane 1991).

The externalist might respond by accepting that we have beliefs about water that are not part of the meaning of "water." Yet when we think of water as having certain properties, we are thinking of "that stuff," whatever it is, out there in our environment. Our thinking of it as "that stuff" exhibits the externalist feature of content. And this is true not only of water but also of many of our other concepts indispensably connected to our environment.

We can leave this dispute for the moment and turn to Jerry Fodor's response to the Twin Earth case. (Fodor's view has changed over the years; here we follow Fodor 1987 and 1992b.) Fodor distinguishes between content and extension by suggesting that extensions are determined by contents *plus* contexts.

The *content* of Deirdre's thought of water is determined by her mental states, according to Fodor. Since Twin Deidre has exactly the same internal states (remember, Twin Deidre and Deirdre are molecular duplicates), then their thoughts have the same content. But how are we to reconcile this sameness of content with the fact that Twin Deidre refers to XYZ and not H_2O? Contents, according to Fodor, are "anchored" to contexts. Deirdre's content is anchored to her Earth context, while Twin Deidre is anchored to her Twin Earth context. And extensions—what a concept picks out—are determined by content *plus* anchoring context. So, if we want to know a concept's content, we look to the internal states of a person. But if we want to know the extension of a thought, we need to look at both content and context. In Fodor's view then, we can insist that Deirdre and her twin *mean the same thing*, while referring to different substances.

What are we to make of the dispute between externalism and internalism? On the one hand, we want to preserve the intuition that mental content depends, in some important way, on the internal states of a person. But we are also aware that no thought is an island. Thoughts, if they are to help us navigate the world around us, must have some connection to the objects and properties in our environment. The difference between internalism and externalism appears to lie in whether they count what a thought is connected to as part of the content. Now, there may be no principled way to settle this difference of opinion. It is clear, however, that any adequate theory of mental content must explain how it is that our thoughts are connected to the familiar world around us. For now, we look at three of the more recent and widely held theories of content.

Cause and Content

Causal or covariance theories of content hold roughly that the cause of a thought determines its content. I am thinking, for example, about American Eskimo dogs and not golden retrievers because an American Eskimo causes the thought. Causal theorists are struck by the fact that our representations carry information about the environment; the information is "contained in" our thoughts. Our representations carry the information because of our causal interaction with the environment. I acquire the information that an American Eskimo dog is nearby because of a causal process, the visual process, linking thoughts to objects in the environment. Thus, we have a reason for identifying thought contents with their causes.

We now have a simplified version of the **causal theory of content**: the content of a thought is what causes it. Thoughts of an American Eskimo puppy are caused by American Eskimo puppies, and thoughts of giraffes are caused by giraffes. The chief proponents of the causal view, also called "informational semantics," are Fred Dretske (1981, 1986) and Jerry Fodor (1987, chap. 4; 1992b).

How to Think about Things You've Never Seen

Many of our thoughts are *general*, referring not to a single object but to all the members of a given group. "Dog" refers to each and every thing that is a dog. But causal theories seem to tie thoughts to specific objects. Suppose you have never seen a dog such as mine before, and I tell you its breed is American Eskimo, a relative of the spitz. Sometime later you think "American Eskimos are white, fluffy things." Causal theory seems to say that your thought is only about the single member of the breed you encountered, and not about American Eskimo dogs *in general*. In the simplified causal view, it looks like we never have truly general thoughts; we have only thoughts that are about the particular objects we have already encountered. How, in the causal theory, can we have general thoughts? Why are we not limited to thinking only of those particular things we have only encountered?

The details of the answer get a bit tricky, but we'll keep matters simple (Fodor 1992b). The key turns on the connection between laws—natural laws—and causation. A natural law governs not only things that have happened but also those that will happen. More importantly, the law governs those things that *would* happen under the right circumstances. These "what would happen" scenarios are called *counterfactuals*, and natural laws support counterfactuals. That is, based on your knowledge of a natural law, you can infer what *would happen* under the right circumstances. (Such circumstances might never occur, but that doesn't invalidate the law.) Causal claims tacitly invoke the relevant law.

Suppose you make the causal claim that striking a match against the side of its box causes the match to light. The relevant law guarantees the truth of the causal claim; even if you never actually strike a match, the law tells us that *were* you to strike a match, it *would* light. Indeed, causal claims about matches would still be true even if no match were ever struck. In a sense, it is your awareness of this connection between laws and causes that prevents you from picking up a large rock and throwing it at your living room window. Although you never actually throw the rock, you know what *would* happen—the thrown rock *would* cause the window to break.

Now, how does this help causal theory? Well, think about seeing a giraffe. The giraffe causes you to have a *giraffe* thought. This causal connection is backed up by a law that says something like the following: Any time you were to detect giraffe features in the environment (that is, you see giraffe-looking objects or have giraffe-like smells), you would think "giraffe." Thus, the claim that giraffes cause you to have a giraffe thought is not only about those already encountered, but also about any giraffe you might encounter. The relevant law governs not only what you now think as you encounter a giraffe, but what you *would* think in any similar giraffe-like situation. The connection between laws and causes guarantees that the thought "giraffes have long necks" is a thought about all giraffes. We now have a slightly modified version of the causal theory: a thought is about what would cause it (under the right circumstances).

Thinking about Santa Claus

The causal theory's solution to the problem of general thoughts also provides a solution to thoughts about things that don't exist. How can something that doesn't exist—a unicorn, Santa Claus—cause anything, much less a thought? Remember the law. It tells us that *were* you to encounter unicorn features or Santa Claus features somewhere in your environment, you *would* think, for example, "Santa seems to have lost a little weight," or "Lo! a unicorn!" In this sense—the sense about what would happen—Santa Claus is the cause of your Santa Claus thoughts. The relevant causal laws governing content cover not only our actual experiences, but counterfactual experiences, as well.

The *modified causal theory* can be summarized as follows: The content of a thought is determined by what properties or features would cause the thought. Don't be dismayed by the reference to "properties" and "features" instead of objects. This is merely a more general way of referring to the relevant objects—after all, it is the *properties* of the giraffe that cause you to have your giraffe thoughts.

Can You Think the Wrong Thought? The Disjunction Problem
A few years ago while walking back to my office, I waved to a young woman, whom I took to be a student worker in our office; call her Sara. My wave and "Hi, Sara!" brought no discernible response. When I returned to the office, there sat Sara. It required only moments for me to realize that somewhere on campus a young lady was wondering why people were calling her "Sara." On all occasions, up to that fateful moment, my Sara thoughts had been caused by Sara. But on this occasion, this Sara thought was caused, not by Sara, but by someone else, say, Sophie.

The causal theory seems to have disconcerting consequences. Since my Sara thoughts are caused sometimes by Sara, sometimes by Sophie, "Sara" apparently means "Sara or Sophie." Of course, it can get worse. More mistakes would lead to my Sara thought being about Sara or Sophie or Sally. One further consequence: Since "Sara" now means Sara or Sophie or Sally, it turns out that *I'm not wrong* when I see Sophie and think "Sara." I've had the "right thought," given that any number of women cause me to have Sara thoughts. Indeed, each time a non-Sara person causes me to think "Sara," the content of my thought appears to change to include this new person. Hence, I can't be wrong! But this is counterintuitive. Our strong intuition is that I made a mistake when I saw Sophie and thought "Sara." I had the wrong thought.

Note how this comes about. Causal theory holds that causes determine content, and apparently wayward causes (such as Sophie) also determine content. Since both Sara and Sophie cause Sara thoughts, then that thought is about Sara or Sophie. Further, if the presence of Sally causes me to think "Sara," I'm not wrong; it's that the content of "Sara" has grown a little. Causal theory seems to yield two odd consequences: (1) that apparently specific thoughts are not really specific, but have a disjunctive meaning (Sara or Sophie or Sally), and (2) that given this disjunctive meaning, my thoughts are not mistaken. This problem is known as the *disjunction problem* (also sometimes known as the problem of misrepresentation).

First Come, First Served: A Solution to the Disjunction Problem
If I did not already know Sara, would I have mistakenly identified Sophie? Undoubtedly not. For me to misidentify Sophie as Sara, *first* I had to know Sara. No Sara, no misidentifying Sophie. What about the other way around? If there were no Sophie, but Sara was still around, could I still have Sara thoughts? Our strong intuition is that, of course, you don't need Sophie to have Sara thoughts. There is a difference then between Sara-caused Sara thoughts (genuine Sara thoughts) and Sophie-caused Sara thoughts (mis-

taken Sara thoughts). Genuine Sara thoughts have a kind of priority over mistaken Sara thoughts.

Fodor calls this difference of priority the *asymmetric dependence* of mistaken Sara thoughts on genuine Sara thoughts. Asymmetric dependence is the key to solving the disjunction problem.

Suppose I have learned, in the presence of cows, to think "cow." But in the presence of a small horse, I think "cow." Fodor claims that I still mean cow, even in the mistaken case. It means cow, Fodor argues, because the mistakenly caused cow thought (the thought caused by a horse) is asymmetrically dependent on the genuinely caused thought (the thought caused by a cow). More precisely, the causal connection between horse and "cow" is asymmetrically dependent on the causal connection between cow and "cow." Without the genuine thought, we wouldn't have the mistaken thought.

Fodor argues that we should identify the content of the thought with the genuine causal connection and not with the asymmetrically dependent causal connection that piggybacks on the genuine one. The genuine causal connection, between cows and "cow," for example, provides our first information about cows. If the genuine connection weren't there in the first place, there wouldn't be any wild connections. Thus, we should count the genuine connection as the content-determining connection, and we have a solution to the disjunction problem.

It is perhaps easy to get lost in the cow-caused "cow" and the Sophie-caused "Sara"; still, we should not lose sight of an intuitive appeal in the asymmetric dependence approach. Consider an informal explanation of mistaking Sophie for Sara. I have a concept of Sara; I associate certain visual properties with her. On this one occasion, Sophie looked sufficiently similar to trigger my Sara thought. But Sophie (or the way she looks) would never have triggered my Sara thought if I didn't have a concept of Sara in the first place. *Mistakes like this depend on the existence of the right connection.* When it comes to content, it's first come, first served.

Worries about Asymmetric Dependence
Rather than survey specific objections to asymmetric dependence, we will try to isolate a common theme. One way to express this is the idea that asymmetric dependence does not *constitute* meaning; it is instead *symptomatic*. In a sense, asymmetric dependence puts the cart before the horse.

Recall the basic idea of Fodor's view—some causal relations between mind and world take priority. These are the causal relations that genuinely determine meaning. The "wild" causal relations, those that yield misrepresentations, depend on the genuine relations. Now, for Fodor's view to work, we need a way of distinguishing genuine from wild causal connections. Yet it looks as though we don't have a good way of doing this; it seems as though we have to already have a sense of the meaning in order to settle on which are the meaning-determining causal relations.

By virtue of what does our cat representation mean those furry, four-legged, feline creatures? Fodor claims that it is the unique causal relation between cats and "cat." Cat thoughts lock onto cats and nothing else. Yet imagine a scenario in which there are counterfeit cats, which for all the world look, sound, and act just like real cats, but there are no real cats. Confronted with the counterfeit, we would still think "cat." Here we have a wild causal connection that does not seem to depend on the genuine causal connection. If we rely on asymmetric dependence, "cat" seemingly means counterfeit cat. Of course, we know that "cat" doesn't mean counterfeit cat because *we already have an established meaning for "cat."* But Fodor can't use this argument because he's trying to explain how we establish those meanings in the first place! Fodor gets to exclude these kinds of scenarios only if he thinks that the content of cat thoughts are already fixed or established. He counts the wild relations as wild because he presupposes that the meaning of "cat" is fixed.

One more example, courtesy of Kim Sterelny (1990). Some concepts, like the concept of "weed," do not pick out a nice, neat class of things. "Weed" refers to a rather heterogeneous mix of plant life, roughly "those things over there that you have to pull this weekend." With such irregular concepts, there is no priority of genuine causal connections over wild connections. Whatever causal connection exists between the real weeds and our representation "weed" also exists between mere weed pretenders and our "weed" thought. No asymmetric dependence relation singles out the real weeds from the pretenders. Thus, asymmetric dependence is unable to explain the meaning of "weed." Fodor could, of course, respond that "weed" is not well defined and is genuinely disjunctive.

We will leave this discussion with this thought. Causal views are initially attractive as accounts of perceptual representations, those arising as a result of perception (Rey 1997). But it may be that as we leave the world of nature's own, as we move to more irregularly defined classes or groups, causal theory—with or without asymmetric dependence—becomes more difficult to sustain.

Conceptual Role Theories

Concepts guide our behavior. The way we think shapes our actions and our thought processes. If Sara wants to buy a coatrack, and she thinks that such a stand is an item of furniture, then she will look in furniture stores. If Sam thinks that college professors are overpaid, and he believes that his neighbor is a college professor, then he will assume his neighbor is overpaid.

These examples illustrate the interconnections between our concepts. For Sara, the concepts of coatrack and furniture are linked; Sam's concept of college professors is tied to his concept of overpaid people. Noticing these connections allows us to say what someone means by a particular concept. For Sam, what does "college professor" mean? It means, in part, "overpaid." If we wanted to know the complete meaning—for Sam—of "college professor," then we have a straightforward, if time-consuming, means of finding out: identify all of the other concepts that are in some way connected *in Sam's mind* to his concept of college professor.

Conceptual role semantics (CRS) holds that the content of a thought or the meaning of a concept is given by its connections to other concepts; mental content is a function of the conceptual role that a thought has for a person. The notion of conceptual role is defined by the inferences that a person is willing to draw among concepts; more generally, these inferences are the causal role of a concept. This view is sometimes known as *holism*, the idea that the meaning of a concept is given by its place in a network of concepts. Gilbert Harman (1982; 1999, esp. chap. 12) and Ned Block (1986) are two of the principal advocates of this view (see also Lormand 1996).

The motivation for conceptual role views is perhaps most clearly evidenced in one of the more famous examples. Oedipus killed Dad and married Mom. How are we to explain such behavior? Was Oedipus without conscience? Hardly. From Oedipus's point of view, there was an obdurate man blocking the road and a recently widowed queen and kingdom for the taking. There was, for Oedipus, no conceptual connection between "mother" and "Jocasta." If we want to know what Oedipus means by a concept, then we will need to look to what *Oedipus* has in mind. We explain the ill-fated marriage and Oedipus's behavior at the end of the play precisely because we know that, in Oedipus's mind, a new conceptual connection has been forged; "Jocasta" now plays a new conceptual role.

Our ability to explain behavior is a principal motivation for conceptual role views. It is worth noting that some see a natural connection between narrow content and conceptual role. This raises the question of the connection between conceptual roles and the objects picked out by our concepts. Danny's concept of butterscotch pudding may be linked to his concept of dessert, but how is that concept linked to the stuff bubbling in the pot?

Some, like Block (1986) and Colin McGinn (1982), argue for a "two-factor" version of CRS: Content has two determinants or contributing factors—the causal role and a referential factor. Harman argues for what has been called a "long-armed" conceptual role theory. Identifying a concept's causal role allows us to identify the referent of the concept. If I know fully the causal role of Danny's concept of butterscotch pudding, I will be led to that stuff bubbling on the stove. The more worrisome aspects of conceptual role theories emerge, however, from tying content to conceptual role. (The following discussion draws from Fodor and LePore 1992, chap. 6.)

First Worry: Changing the Meaning by Changing Belief

CRS claims that the causal role, the inferences a person is prepared to draw, determines the content of a person's thought. Different causal roles lead to different contents. Of course, as one acquires more information and one's concept "grows," the causal role of that concept grows as well. And hence the content of the concept changes.

For example, the content of Danny's concept of ice cream is determined (in part) by his being prepared to infer that there is something sweet and cold in the dish and that it will melt if left at room temperature. Suppose Danny now learns that cold things have a lower mean kinetic energy, and he is willing to draw a new inference about the ice cream in the dish. Given the conceptual role view, Danny now *means something different* by "ice cream" than he did before.

By itself, this consequence of CRS is not disturbing. As we learn more, the meanings of our concepts become richer and more complex. We would expect that an educated adult will be able to tell us more about ice cream than a very young Danny.

Notice, however, that there are further implications. If we think that any concept we possess is connected to every other concept we possess, then *any change in belief results in a change of meaning for every concept.* This result seems more worrisome. If I learn, for example, that France has elected a new prime minister, it might be plausible to think that this will change the meaning of my concept of democracy. But is it plausible to think that it will also change my concept of ice cream? Do I now have a new concept of my dining room table? When we think of all the changes in belief that occur in single day— think of the vast amount of information you acquire just between breakfast and lunch—then it seems the meaning of our concepts is changing so fast that we could scarcely keep up with them!

One line of response is that it is possible to distinguish between the core or the essential content of a concept and collateral information (Block 1986). This distinction might be drawn by identifying those characteristics that a thing *must* have, and counting the rest as collateral. Danny insists, for example, that something is ice cream *only* if it's sweet and cold—but where it is purchased is inessential. Of course, drawing the distinction between collateral and essential information is a daunting task. But the CRS advocate can argue that we are able to do so in practice. We track the essential information, updating the meaning of concepts as we must, and storing the collateral information for later use.

Second Worry: Do You Know What I Mean?

The previous section illustrated the interplay of belief and meaning *intrasubjectively*, the interplay of belief and meaning within a single person. A similar problem arises in the *intersubjective* case: If two people have different beliefs—if the respective conceptual roles of a given concept differ—then their concepts have different meanings. Imagine that Danny says to me, as he sees me headed for the refrigerator, "I would like some ice cream, too, if that's where you're headed." Our normal sense is that Danny and I mean the *same thing* by "ice cream." Yet suppose that Danny and I have quite different beliefs—that I once worked for an ice cream manufacturer and know much more about ice cream than he does. In the CRS view, the greater the difference in our beliefs, the less similar are our concepts. The fifth-century B.C. philosopher Socrates had a concept of water that is very different from that of twenty-first-century chemistry major Sara. The evident problem is to explain our success in communicating, despite our sometimes radical differences in meaning.

Again, the defender of CRS can appeal to the essential meaning or content. No matter that I am familiar with the intricacies of ice cream production and that Danny knows merely that there is ice cream in front of him. As long as the two of us share a common *essential* meaning, he is able to communicate to me his desire that I bring him "ice cream." Similarly, it doesn't matter that Sara is prepared to draw theoretical inferences that the Athenian Socrates could not; so long as they share a common meaning—say, that the clear liquid in the cup quenches thirst—then there is a sense in which they mean the same thing by "water," and hence, Socrates' writings can be understood by Sara.

A Final Worry: Could We Ever Be Wrong?

Intuitively we think that we sometimes get the meaning of a concept wrong. It is not obvious, however, that CRS allows for this commonsense intuition. For example, if Danny is prepared to infer that any quacking thing is also a mammal, then, according to CRS, "duck" means (among other things) "is a mammal." And Danny *is not wrong*; he simply has a different concept of "duck."

It should be apparent that we cannot use the same maneuver we have been using—distinguishing between essential and collateral information—to clarify this anomalous situation. It is easy to imagine that for Danny "is a mammal" is part of the essential meaning of "duck," so the CRS theorist cannot appeal to the notion of essential meanings to explain how we make mistakes. It might be possible, though, to appeal to the referential component of meaning (in a two-factor theory, for example). If you ask Sara and Danny to point to a duck, they will both point to a duck. Ask them whether there are any mammals present in a roomful of ducks, however, and their answers will differ. Danny insists that the room is full of mammals—that brownish, quacking thing over there is a mammal, for example. Sara, knowing that ducks are birds, not mammals, claims that the only mammals in the room are she and Danny.

The CRS theorist then might take the following line. *In principle*, Danny does not make a mistake. Although he changes his beliefs now that he has been enlightened by Sara, the notion of making a mistake has no application here. Nonetheless, we might call this sort of *change of belief* a "mistake," especially when it is brought about by referential differences. Our common-sense view that we often make mistakes about our concepts is thus replaced by the idea of changing our beliefs under a particular set of circumstances.

The CRS theorist may insist on more. Our motivation—our common-sense motivation—for singling out cases of mistakes is precisely to bring about changes in belief. Our interest is not to ridicule Danny because he thinks a duck is a mammal. We are interested in identifying such mistakes so that we may correct them—we want Danny to change his beliefs. Thus, although CRS may not have a rigorous notion of making a mistake, it nonetheless preserves a key feature of our commonsense view.

Conceptual Role and Common Sense
Conceptual role theories begin with the idea that the meaning of a concept depends on its connection to the other concepts. But conceptual role theories have implications that seem to draw them further away from our commonsense view. These differences are not as troubling as they seem initially, according to the CRS advocate. Recognizing that communication is still possible, that we have a way of identifying when a person's concepts differ in meaning from those of others, preserves the fundamental motivations of our commonsense view.

Biology and Content: Teleological Theories

Thoughts aid us in navigating the world around us. They cue us to the presence of food, of danger, or of a quiet place to rest. Looked at in this way, thoughts—contentful mental states—have a function, a biological function. A class of theories, known as teleological theories, seeks to marry the notions of biological purpose and mental content. **Teleological theories of content** identify the content of a mental state with the evolutionary circumstances that are responsible for that mental state. Two principal proponents are Ruth Millikan (1984, 1989, 2000) and David Papineau (1990, 1993).

We can tell a (perhaps overly) simplified evolutionary story. Key characteristics of an organism are selected because they provide an adaptive advantage to the organism. Such advantageous characteristics have a function. For example, it is the function of a heart to pump blood, the function of an eye to provide information about the surroundings. These characteristics are selected because of their function. There is a similar story about thoughts. The function of representations is enhanced environmental navigation—we last longer. The evolutionary circumstances that cause us to have some particular representation determine its content. If we want to know what a representation is about, we should look at what it is *for*.

What is it that makes a thought about a tiger? Under certain circumstances, namely, in the presence of a tiger, it is to our evolutionary advantage to be able to identify a tiger. Those circumstances fix the content of the mental state. Similarly, why have the representation of a banana? Again, it is to our evolutionary advantage to identify bananas. Hence, "tiger" means tiger and "banana" means banana. In principle, according to the teleological view, the content of any representation is fixed by those circumstances selectively responsible for the representation. Alternatively, the biological function of a representation determines its content.

In a recent work articulating a theory of substance concepts, Millikan provides a similar account (2000, chap. 13). Substance concepts allow us to track those substances and to make inferences about them, which she claims is the "first function" of any cognitive representation, and to be able to participate in a variety of propositional attitudes (201–2). Importantly, the content of any "inner sign" or representation depends directly on "how it is designed to be used by the organism that harbors it" (201).

Malfunction and Misrepresentation

Of course, things with a function can *malfunction*. Indeed, we have seen that representations sometimes *misrepresent*. We sometimes think "tiger" when there is no tiger; we sometimes think "cow" when there is only a small horse nearby. Misrepresentation, however, is less problematic for teleological views.

A cell phone may fail to operate, but the malfunction doesn't change the *function* of the cell phone. It is still the function of the cell phone to allow calls without being connected to a land line. We know the function because we know why the cell phone was made.

Similarly, thoughts retain their content despite their occasional "malfunctions." Tiger thoughts are made to pick out tigers, to let us think about tigers. Notice how teleological theory explains this sense of "being for made for." The circumstances that are selectively responsible for the mental state—the representation—tell us the function of the representation and hence its content. Now, suppose I mistake a small antelope rustling in the bushes for a tiger; I think "tiger," yet there is only the benign antelope. Why does the representation still pick out tigers, not antelopes? The circumstances responsible for tiger thoughts were circumstances in which tigers—not antelopes—were present. Thus, tiger thoughts are tied to tigers. Nor does it matter whether I frequently misapply "tiger." If the significant evolutionary function of "tiger" is to pick out tigers, then the content is fixed. Danny may meet a tiger only once in his life; he may subsequently misidentify nontiger-caused rustlings as "tigers." Still, "tiger" means tigers—striped, ferocious felines that threaten Danny's well-being.

Do All Our Concepts Have a Biological Function?

We might wonder whether all of our concepts, all of our mental representations, have a biological function. It is easy to see how the concept of "red" might find its way into our conceptual repertoire—having the concept helps distinguish ripe from unripe berries, and the ability to discriminate healthy from unhealthy food has an obvious evolutionary advantage. It is not so obvious, however, as Jerry Fodor (1992a) suggests, that the belief that seven is a prime number has any evolutionary advantage. Nor is the problem confined to theoretical or abstract concepts. "High definition TV" may have value in guiding marketing strategies or consumer behavior. And Papineau (1993, 96) claims that the teleological view will explain the content of such ordinary desires as wanting to visit a certain place in the park. Questions arise, however, about whether selection pressures might explain the content of such concepts as HDTV, cell phones, or a place in the park.

Sterelny (1990) suggests distinguishing between *modest* teleological theories and *zealous* theories. The modest version holds that only those concepts essential to our continued survival are explained by appeal to biological function. A zealous theory, by contrast, holds that the contents of *all* our representations are explained this way. Adhering to a modest theory avoids the problem of explaining the selectional history of such concepts as cell phones or HDTV.

Sterelny points out that there is some biological basis for preferring the modest theory. Neuroscience identifies concepts that are in a legitimate sense "hardwired" or built into the brain. A particular part of the visual cortex appears built or designed to process information about red rectangles, for example. The difficulty, of course, is identifying which concepts are appropriately explained by a teleological model. The modest theorist must hope that neuroscience and evolutionary psychology can find some principled means of distinguishing the evolutionarily significant concepts from those that are not.

But what of the zealous theorist? Papineau suggests that we think of theoretical, abstract, or culturally based concepts as tied to more biologically basic concepts. Why would natural selection care about the belief that seven is a prime number? Since theoretical concepts are connected to more basic concepts, they enhance our ability to manipulate the more basic concepts. Algebraic concepts, for example, increase our ability to control our environment so that we can more easily secure food or safety. We have a conceptual repertoire that far outruns our need to avoid tigers, find shelter from the storm, or pick out the ripe cantaloupe. According to the zealous theorist, that repertoire is still about biology, since the more sophisticated, theoretical repertoire better serves basic biological needs (Papineau 1990, chap. 4).

Millikan seems to suggest something along these lines—that natural selection endows us with the *ability to acquire* concepts, not the specific concepts themselves. Still, the contents of concepts are identified by why they are selected. Identifying concepts with abilities, she distinguishes innate and learned abilities (2000, 61–63). The contents of innate abilities are determined by what they are selected for, while learned abilities are selected because they allow us to do things in a certain way. The learned abilities allow us to keep track of substances in the world around us by means of making certain kinds of inferences.

Two related thoughts might occur at this point. First, is this really different from the modest teleological view? Skeptics about the zealous theory might argue that all we have is a modest theory with an attached conceptual role theory. Concepts such as salmon croquettes or cell phones are tied to the more obvious evolutionarily advantageous concepts by conceptual role. The *content* of the concepts is fixed by their conceptual role, not their evolutionary function.

A related worry arises when we ask exactly what it is that natural selection acts upon. The zealous theorist asks us to believe that content is fixed by biological function. Natural selection acts upon a certain mental state because of its obvious survival value. But natural selection does not leave us here, according to the zealous view. Theoretical beliefs of various kinds—algebraic, logical, scientific—are also selected since they increase biological "flexibility." We manage better; we last longer.

But we might wonder whether natural selection acts on certain beliefs or certain capacities. Some hold, for example, that the human linguistic capacity results from evolution. It is another matter, however, to insist that natural selection acts upon certain theoretical beliefs (or groups of theoretical beliefs). Evolution might accomplish the same end by selecting a certain ability or capacity and letting the theoretical concept chips fall where they may (although there is some doubt about evolution acting on these capacities, much less on particular beliefs; see Bogdan 1994, 180–81).

Of course, these two worries do not show that the zealous theorist is wrong. But they suggest that it is harder to tell an evolutionary story about those concepts less clearly connected to immediate biological need.

Final Thoughts on Content?

Of the three views in this chapter, conceptual role may come closest to retaining the commonsense assumptions noted at the outset. This is not to say that conceptual role semantics is the best view. It points, however, to the resiliency of our commonsense view and its importance for guiding our reflections. It is worth noting that theories of content are relatively new creatures in the philosophy-of-mind landscape. Debate is ongoing and detailed, and there may be some reason for thinking that aspects of different theories might be combined.

Key Concepts

Causal or covariance theories

Conceptual role theories

Externalism

Internalism

Narrow content

Teleological theories

Wide content

Reading Questions

1. Explain why Putnam thinks the Twin Earth example shows that meaning is external. Briefly explain one way of responding to externalism.

2. Why do some think it is important to distinguish between narrow and wide content?

3. What is the disjunction problem? How does Fodor use asymmetric dependence to respond to this problem?

4. Describe the central features of conceptual role theories. Why does Block think it is important to distinguish between the essential content of a concept and collateral information?

5. Explain the difference between modest and zealous teleological theories.

References

Block, Ned. 1986. Advertisement for a semantics of psychology. In *Studies in the philosophy of mind*, ed. Peter A. French, Theodore E. Uehling, Jr., and Howard K. Wettstein, 615–78. Vol. 10 of *Midwest studies in philosophy*. Minneapolis: University of Minnesota Press.

Bogdan, Radu. 1994. *Grounds for cognition: How goal-guided behavior shapes the mind*. Hillsdale, NJ: Lawrence Erlbaum.

Crane, Tim. 1991. All the difference in the world. *Philosophical Quarterly* 41:1–26.

Crumley, Jack, ed. 2000. *Problems in mind: Readings in contemporary philosophy of mind*. Mountain View, CA: Mayfield.

Dretske, Fred. 1981. *Knowledge and the flow of information*. Cambridge, MA: MIT Press.

———. 1986. Misrepresentation. In *Belief: Form, content and function*, ed. Radu Bogdan. Oxford: Oxford University Press.

Fodor, Jerry. 1987. *Psychosemantics: The problem of meaning in the philosophy of mind*. Cambridge, MA: MIT Press.

———. 1991. A model argument for narrow content. *Journal of Philosophy* 88:5–26.

———. 1992a. A Theory of Content I. In *"A theory of content" and other essays*, 51–87. Cambridge, MA: MIT Press.

———. 1992b. A Theory of Content II. In *"A theory of content" and other essays*, 89–136. Cambridge, MA: MIT Press.

Fodor, Jerry, and Ernest Lepore. 1992. *Holism: A shopper's guide*. Oxford: Blackwell.

Harman, Gilbert. 1982. Conceptual role semantics. *Notre Dame Journal of Formal Logic* 28:242–56.

———. 1999. *Reasoning, meaning, and mind*. Oxford: Clarendon Press.

Lormand, Eric. 1996. How to be a meaning holist. *Journal of Philosophy* 93:51–73.

McGinn, Colin. 1982. The structure of content. In *Thought and Object: Essays on Intentionality*, ed. Andrew Woodfield, 207–58. Oxford: Clarendon Press.

Millikan, Ruth Garrett. 1984. *Language, thought and other biological categories*. Cambridge, MA: MIT Press.

———. 1989. Biosemantics. *Journal of Philosophy* 86:281–97. Reprinted in Crumley 2000, 401–11.

———. 2000. *On clear and confused ideas: An essay about substance concepts.* Cambridge: Cambridge University Press.

Papineau, David. 1990. *Reality and representation.* Oxford: Blackwell.

———. 1993. *Philosophical naturalism.* Oxford: Blackwell.

Putnam, Hilary. 1975. The meaning of "meaning." In *Mind, language, and reality: Philosophical papers*, 2:215–71. Cambridge: Cambridge University Press.

Rey, Georges. 1997. *Contemporary philosophy of mind: A contentiously classical approach.* Oxford: Blackwell.

Stalnaker, Robert. 1989. On what's in the head. *Philosophical Perspectives*, vol. 3, *The Philosophy of Mind and Action Theory*, 287–316. Reprinted in Crumley 2000, 312–28.

Sterelny, Kim. 1990. *The representational theory of mind.* Oxford: Blackwell.

Stroll, Avrum. 1989. What water is; or, Back to Thales. In *Contemporary perspectives in the philosophy of language II*, vol. 14 of *Midwest studies in philosophy*, ed. Peter A. French, Theodore E. Uehling Jr., and Howard K. Wettstein, 258–74. Notre Dame, IN: University of Notre Dame Press. Reprinted in Crumley 2000, 300–311.

Additional Readings

Burge, Tyler. "Individualism and the Mental" In *Studies in Metaphysics*, vol. 4 of *Midwest Studies in Philosophy*, ed. Peter A. French, Theodore E. Uehling Jr., and Howard K. Wettstein, 73–122. Minneapolis: University of Minnesota Press, 1979.

Cummins, Robert. *Meaning and Mental Representation.* Cambridge, MA: MIT Press, 1989.

Fodor, Jerry. *The Elm and the Expert: Mentalese and Its Semantics.* Cambridge, MA: MIT Press, 1995.

———. *Language of Thought.* Cambridge, MA: Harvard University Press, 1979.

———. "Semantics, Wisconsin Style." In *"A Theory of Content" and Other Essays*, 31–49. Cambridge, MA: MIT Press.

McGinn, Colin. *Mental Content.* Oxford: Blackwell, 1989.

9

It's the Law: Mental Causation

In the last couple of decades, philosophy of mind has seen a surprising return to an old and familiar problem—mental causation. And it might surprise you a little to find out that the worry is whether a certain kind of physicalism can explain the causal efficacy, or the causal role, of the mental. This is surely a surprising development. An attraction of physicalism, or so it is thought, is that it promises to escape the problem that most bedevils dualism, that of mental interaction or mental causation. Giving up dualism and adopting physicalism seems to short-circuit the problem. If the mind is itself something physical, then the problem appears to disappear. There is no conceptual problem about something physical bringing about physical changes. Unfortunately, it is not that simple.

The story of this chapter begins with Donald Davidson's seminal 1970 article "Mental Events." Philosophers of mind worry that if we take seriously the idea that there is only the physical and its properties, while holding certain plausible views about the nature of causation, then the mind doesn't matter anymore! Physicalism leaves no genuine causal role for the mind. The mental becomes *epiphenomenal*; the mental is there, but it's just along for the ride. This worry is so pronounced that Jerry Fodor (1989) identifies a new phobia (unique to philosophers of mind, apparently), "epiphobia."

Now that we know how the story of this chapter starts, we can a say a little more about the details of the plot. We'll begin by explaining in an informal manner the conditions for mental causation. Just what do we mean when we say that the mental causes behavior? The real story starts, however, when we turn to Davidson's view, "anomalous monism," and explain how that view is thought to bring us back to the problem of mental causation. After surveying the apparent problems, we will consider recent physicalist responses.

Getting the Mental to Work

I look at my coffee cup and see that it is empty. I want more. Knowing that there is more coffee over on the counter, and seeing no good reason not to have more—it is, after all, decaf—I reach out, grab my cup, push my chair away from the table, and I'm off, anticipating the satisfaction of yet another desire!

A mundane case, to be sure. Yet its general outline is an essential part of the familiar folklore of the mind. For those who take mental causation seriously, it illustrates what we think about the role of the mental in our behavior. It is *because of* my desires and my beliefs that I leave the table in search of coffee. It is because of, or *by virtue of*, the *mental* character of my beliefs and desires that I engage in the coffee-fetching behavior. This is an essential condition of mental causation, and it puts an important constraint on our explanation of causation by the mental. If my behavior occurs because of the *physical* character of my mental states, then we might worry whether the mental plays a genuine causal role. It's there, but it seems to be inessential to my behavior. Perhaps an analogy will help.

Danny and Deirdre start out the door, but notice that it is raining. Preferring to remain dry, they each pick up an umbrella sitting by the door. The umbrellas are identical, except that one is a boring gray and the other is a bright pumpkin color. Suppose Danny takes the pumpkin-colored umbrella, Deirdre the less colorful one. Now suppose we want to explain why the two of them stay dry. Notice that our explanation of the "dry-keeping" properties of Danny's pumpkin-colored umbrella differs in no respect from how we would explain the "dry-keeping" properties of Deirdre's gray one. There is no point at which we would need to say that part of the reason Danny is dry is because he had the good sense to pick up an umbrella that was pumpkin colored. Color is inessential to the umbrellas' role of protecting from the rain.

Ernest Sosa provides a striking example. A gun fires a shot, making a loud noise, and someone is killed. Now, the loud noise is the shot, but it is not the loudness of the shot that kills the person. "The loudness of the shot has no causal relevance to the death of the victim" (1984, 448).

If we want to retain our commonsense notion of mental causation, then mental properties can't be like the pumpkin color of the umbrella. If the explanation of my walking to the counter never mentions the specifically mental aspect of my beliefs and desires—for example, the content of those states—then we haven't succeeded in explaining the causal role of the mental. Explanations mentioning only the complex activity of neural structures cannot guarantee the causal efficacy of the mental. The mental works only if, at some point in our explanation, we advert to either the types of mental states or their content (or, as is more likely, both). We must be able to say that it is, at least in part, by virtue of the content of my desire—to have more coffee—that I behave as I do. This type of causation—of the mental causing the physical *because of its specifically mental character*—is often called "downward causation," the higher-level mental property bringing about some change in the physical. Thus, we want to know: Is all causation "horizontal," physical to physical, or is there room for the mental?

But exactly how did physicalism get in this fix in the first place? How did epiphobia seem to reach epidemic proportions? Many trace this new version of an old worry back to Davidson's account of the mental in "Mental Events."

Anomalous Monism

In "Mental Events" (1970), Davidson presents a short, three-premise argument, which has as its conclusion that all mental events are identical to some physical event or other; the mental is *token identical* to the physical. We've seen a token identity theory before, namely, functionalism. Davidson is no functionalist, but, like functionalists, he argues that any particular mental event is token identical to some particular physical event. It is the premises of the argument that interest us, however. Critic and commentator think they detect a disturbing consequence lurking in the premises: the causal irrelevance of the mental.

Davidson's first premise is an apparent truism, taken for granted by the common folk and many theorists alike: The mental causally interacts with the physical. Mental states—hopes, fears, beliefs, and desires—cause physical states. (Davidson prefers "events" to "states" for reasons that need not worry us here; the occasional reference to "states" is stylistic only and won't affect the development of the argument.) My belief that coffee is on the counter and my desire for coffee, both mental states, cause a certain physical event—the fetching of coffee. Again, causal interaction is a familiar and seemingly obvious feature of the mind.

If the first premise is apparent and easy, the second has a somewhat foreboding name: the **nomological character of causality**, which says that some law governs any causal interaction. Despite the technical-sounding name, a little reflection on the notion of a cause and a simple example will lead us to the heart of the premise.

On a chilly, winter morning Danny decides a little fire (in the fireplace, of course) is the perfect way to start the day. Some crumpled newspaper and a little kindling go underneath a couple of logs. Danny strikes a match and holds the burning match against the paper. Now, you know what happens next—the paper begins to burn. And you know the cause of the paper burning—holding the burning match next to it.

How did you know this? You know that burning matches held next to paper cause the paper to burn. It is not mere coincidence. Neither you nor Danny holds a burning match to paper and *hopes* that the paper begins to burn. Quite the contrary, to say that A causes B is to say that anytime you've got A, B will result. It's no accident; in fact, *it's the law*. It's a *causal law* (thus, the name of the premise: *nomos* is the Greek word for "law"). Causal interactions, according to Davidson, are *law governed*. The interactions are always "backed up" by laws. Very roughly, there is a causal law that says that whenever you hold a lit match to paper, the paper will burn. More technically, any causal interaction *instantiates* some causal law. Causal laws govern any causal interaction.

There is an important qualification, however. Suppose Deirdre, as part of her chemistry project, has invented a new flame-retardant spray, which she surreptitiously sprays on the newspaper. When Danny holds the match next to the paper, nothing happens. He might as well pour water on the match! So, it looks as though the causal law is actually something like: Whenever a lit match is held against paper, and the paper has not been treated with flame retardant, then the paper burns. It's easy to see that there is more than this lone exception. Our law will have to allow for the possibility that the paper isn't wet, or that someone doesn't throw water on the match the moment it touches the paper, or that the oxygen isn't suddenly sucked out of the room, or that . . . . You get the idea. Such exceptions—grouped under the heading of *ceteris paribus* clauses (a Latin phrase for "all other things being equal")—occur only in a special type of law, according to Davidson. Laws containing a ceteris paribus clause, or exceptions, are *nonstrict laws*. We might think of these laws as saying something like "If A happens, and everything goes right, we'll get B." But "if-everything-goes-right" laws—nonstrict laws—are not really causal laws, Davidson claims.

The only genuine causal laws are *strict* or *deterministic* laws, laws that admit of no exceptions. When we think of the cause of some result, we think that the cause is *enough* to bring about the result. *Every time* you have the cause, you will have the result. That's what it is to be a cause. So, we are led to the idea that causal laws are strict laws. Davidson thinks that only physics provides us with strict laws. Indeed, it is perhaps only at the submolecular or subatomic level that we find strict laws. The content of such laws need not worry us; for now, it is important only to see that all causal interactions, according to Davidson, are governed by strict laws.

We may already have reason to worry about the causal efficacy of the mental. Think of the "causal law" that governs my mental states causing my coffee-fetching behavior: "If someone desires to have coffee and believes there is coffee at X, then that person will go to X and get some coffee." But it is very unlikely that such a law is exceptionless. In fact, the potential exceptions are too numerous to count. For example, I may greatly *fear* that Clement will jump in my seat, take command of my computer, and search the Internet for the latest Spiderman paraphernalia, refusing to yield his new place upon my return. So, despite the fact that I desperately desire coffee and believe that there is some on the kitchen counter, here I sit . . . with an empty cup.

Our normal practice is to take for granted the "all other things equal clause." We appeal to a nonstrict law: If someone desires coffee and believes that there is coffee at X—*all other things being equal*—then that person will go to X and get coffee. The exception-laden character of "mental laws" is not unique to filling one's coffee cup, of course. My fear of Z will cause my avoidance of Z only if all other things are equal—I may choose *not* to avoid Z if I do not want someone to realize I am afraid, or if I believe it is my duty to confront Z. Indeed, any law that relates mental events to physical events is inevitably nonstrict.

An immediate consequence of these first two premises is that a strict law governs any occasion of a mental event causing a physical event. It seems then that explaining causal interaction between mental and physical events requires strict laws connecting the mental to the physical. But the third premise of Davidson's argument precludes precisely this.

Where there are no laws, matters can get a bit unruly. One of Davidson's principal claims is that there are no strict laws governing the mental. Or as he says, the mental is *anomalous*. The anomalousness of the mental is simply a way of saying that no strict laws connect the mental and the physical; there are no strict *psychophysical* laws. Consequently, there is, according to Davidson, no hope of reducing the mental to the physical.

We have seen irreducibility claims before. Functionalism resists type identity theory by appealing to multiple realizability—any number of physical types can realize a single type of mental state. Thus, functionalism claims that the mental is irreducible. But Davidson thinks he has another route to irreducibility. An intrinsic and constitutive feature of the mental precludes reducing mental types to brain state types. In the rest of this section, we look at Davidson's argument for the absence of psychophysical laws (laws connecting the mental with the physical).

Davidson thinks we can see the impossibility of psychophysical laws by reflecting on the nature of the mental. Suppose Sam believes that Ronald Reagan is the fortieth president. When we say that Sam has this belief—when we *attribute* this belief to Sam—we must take into account considerations of rationality. We make sense of Sam's having such a belief only if that belief coheres—only if it fits—with the other beliefs we attribute to Sam. We cannot understand Sam as having the belief that Reagan is the fortieth president unless we also understand him as having the belief that Reagan's successor is the forty-first. Similarly, we cannot understand Sara's wanting Sam to bring her the orange juice from the refrigerator unless we also understand her as believing that there is orange juice in the refrigerator and desiring to have some. Rationality is a general and constitutive feature of the propositional attitudes. But the notion of rationality is a normative notion; rationality constraints say what beliefs a person *should have* or *ought to have*.

Now we can see why Davidson thinks we can know a priori that no psychophysical laws—no laws reducing the mental to the physical—are possible. The normative nature of the mental "has no echo" in the precise details of neuroscience (or physics). Newton's famous law tells us that $F = ma$, but it does not tell us what force *should* be. Physics tells us what is, not what ought to be. We cannot, according to Davidson, find anything in our physical theories that adequately replaces the *should* that is the defining characteristic of the mental. We cannot reduce rationality constraints to purely physical constraints. Chart the "geography" of the brain in as fine a detail as we please, and still none of the neural connections, none of the causal laws governing the interaction of different neural structures, can adequately replace the intrinsically normative character of beliefs and desires. If Davidson is right, if there are no adequate physical replacements for rationality, then there are no psychophysical laws.

Nonetheless Davidson thinks his three principles show that the mental is *token identical* to the physical. Strict laws always govern any causal interaction. But the anomalous character of the mental implies that no strict laws are to be found in the mental realm. So, any and all strict laws are about the physical realm. Roughly, you will never find strict laws talking about anything mental; they will always talk about something physical. Now notice—still roughly—what happens if something is involved in a causal interaction. Strict laws apply only to physical things; strict laws govern any causal interaction. So, anything involved in a causal interaction must be physical—in some way or other—and any "causally active" mental event is in some way or other a physical event. Thus, any mental event is *token identical* to some physical event. The mental is anomalous (no strict laws apply) and is token identical to the physical—hence, the name, anomalous monism.

No Room for the Mental?

In the movie 9 *to* 5, the head of a branch office takes credit for the success of his hardworking employees. True, he was there, and his name is on the monthly reports. But no effort of his has gotten the work done. Davidson's critics worry that, in Davidson's hands, the mental turns out a little like the branch boss. The mental—beliefs and desires, for example—gets all the credit, but it's the nameless neurons (or protons and electrons or quarks) that do all the work. Deirdre's desire for orange juice and her belief that juice is just inside the door of the refrigerator get credit for her consequent trip to the refrigerator ("Where did Deirdre go?" "She *wants* some orange juice, and she *thinks* there's still some left in the refrigerator.") But it's hundreds of thousands or hundreds of millions of your favorite microscopic or submicroscopic *physical particles* that send Deirdre gliding across the floor. Davidson's critics worry that the mental is a little like this: It's getting all the credit, but not really doing anything. To see why, think about how, in Davidson's view, the mental and physical causally interact.

Mental events causally interact with physical events. Such causal interaction requires "backing" by a strict law. But strict laws apply only to the physical realm. So, mental events participate in causal interactions only insofar as they are something physical. That is, mental events are involved in causal interaction not because of their *mental* properties, but because of their *physical* properties. It is not, for example, the mental characteristics—being a desire, having a certain content—of my desire for coffee that cause my behavior. It's the *physical* characteristics of my desire for coffee. (The desire has physical characteristics because it is token identical to some physical state.)

Now, the mental event's name might be on the report. But it looks like it's the physical properties doing all the causal work. It is the mental event *as a physical event* that brings about some other physical event. Since physical properties are doing all the causal work, it looks like there's no room for the mental. Mental events begin to look a lot like sleeping dogs: They just lie there. Epiphenomenalism turns out right, after all.

One per Customer: Explanatory Exclusion

Doubts about the causal efficacy of the mental come from still another direction, the explanatory exclusion argument, given by Jaegwon Kim (1989). A simple intuition motivates the argument—there is only one complete causal explanation for an event. This intuition is captured by the **explanatory exclusion principle**: A complete causal explanation of an event excludes an alternative causal explanation. A simple example illustrates the principle.

Imagine for a moment, while visiting your parents, you leave your keys on the kitchen table and later return to find them on the desk. The change in the location of the keys—how the change came about—requires an explanation. But how *many* explanations would you look for? Suppose your father tells you he moved the keys so he could begin working on his new jigsaw puzzle that you bought him for his birthday. A few minutes later your younger sister tells you she moved them as part of a prank. Now, this example is not intended as either a detective story or a test of the maxim that father knows best. It is to get you to see that accepting your father's explanation precludes accepting your sister's explanation. Your father causing the keys to move *excludes* your sister causing the keys to move. Only one cause per event.

And the principle has a dramatic consequence for mental causation. Physicalists hold two claims—that everything is physical and that the physical world is a *closed* system. If you want to explain the occurrence of a physical event, you need appeal only to other physical events. Alternatively, for any physical event, there is always a complete physical explanation of that event. Now, suppose that we have a complete physical explanation for my moving from the table to the counter, pouring coffee into a cup. The mental explanation—that I want more coffee and believe it is on the counter—is superfluous, according to the explanatory exclusion principle. Suppose that we have a neurological account of these mental states, and also some way of reducing the neurological story to some ultimate physical account. Since we have all the explanation we need with this neurological description of the causes of my behavior, the explanatory exclusion principle claims that the mental explanation is excluded—there is nothing for the mental to do!

So, we have a complete physical story detailing the cause of any event, a complete physical story that mentions no mental properties, states, or events. If you have a complete story of the cause of something, there isn't another different causal story. Since the exclusion principle tells us "one is enough," the physical explanation rules out the mental explanation. Therefore, mental properties play no role in the causing of any event; mental properties are epiphenomenal. Or as some philosophers of mind are inclined to say: *minds don't matter.*

Needless to say, this is not welcome news for those who want to retain a commitment to physicalism *and* the causal efficacy of the mental.

Back to Work

We would like mental properties to figure centrally in our causal explanations of behavior. In answer to the question "Why is Sara walking toward the kitchen?" we want to say that it is, at least in part, because she *believes* the orange juice is there. We want this mental property, along with others, to be the star of our causal story. But the argument is that top billing goes not to the mental properties of some particular brain state, but to the *physical* properties of that brain state. The real actors in the causal story are some set of excited neurons and their neural costars. Mental properties may get mentioned in our familiar, commonsense explanations, but they never genuinely appear on the causal stage. Of course, defenders of the causal efficacy of the mental would like to see mental properties back on stage.

Here we consider briefly three recent approaches to restoring the causal efficacy of the mental. These three approaches might be called the supervenience approach, the nonstrict laws approach, and the patterns approach. While it is worth distinguishing the three viewpoints, advocates of one approach may nonetheless have much in common with advocates of another. We will begin with an approach employed by Davidson.

Same Recipe, Same Results: Supervenience

Perhaps the most direct way to restore mental properties to the causal story is to show that they make a difference. If one thing (or event) is at least part of the cause of another, then the first makes a difference to the second. The second would not be what it is unless the first occurred. Since the icing on the cake would not have a pink color unless the red food coloring had been added, the red coloring is a cause of the appearance of the icing. Some philosophers of mind think that the way to show that mental properties make a difference is by claiming a certain relationship between mental and physical properties. That relationship is known as *supervenience*. The concept of supervenience has been much studied over the past thirty years, and it turns out that there is not one concept but many (Kim 1993). Here we will use Davidson's formulation.

Supervenience is a kind of dependence relation between one set of properties and a second set. Physicalists think that mental properties depend on the physical. We would find no mental properties (or mental "things") unless there were physical things and their properties. But this suggests a way of formulating the supervenience relation: If two things differ in some mental property, then there must be some difference in physical properties. Any difference in the mental *requires* a difference in the physical. Why? Well, suppose two persons have exactly the same physical properties—that is, they are alike in all physical respects—but differ in their mental properties. Now, suppose that we arrange two sets of identical physical constituents in exactly the same way, and in one case we get one kind of mental property and in the other we get another kind. It would be as though you used exactly the same ingredients in the icing, and on one occasion it turned out green, on another pink. Recipes would be pointless. Indeed it is precisely because we think "Same recipe, same results" that recipes are used at all. Similarly a difference in mental properties without a difference in physical properties suggests that the physical structure doesn't matter; it suggests that the mental does not depend on the physical, an unwelcome scenario for any physicalist, including token identity theorists.

Imagine Sara and Sam sitting outside in New Orleans on an August afternoon. Sara believes that it is too humid, while Sam believes that it is a perfect August afternoon. Supervenience tells us that since they differ in at least one mental property, they must also differ in at least one physical property.

The preceding gloss of supervenience can be made more precise. Suppose you have two sets of properties, M and P. M **supervenes** on P if and only if whenever there is a difference in M, then there is some difference in P. Any time M differs, there *must* be some difference in P. (Different interpretations of the "whenever" or the "any time" get you different—weaker or stronger—versions of supervenience.) In short, same recipe, same results. So, Davidson insists that if two people have different beliefs or desires, those two people must differ in some physical respect. Indeed, you *know* that if Sara believes it is too humid, and Sam believes it is just right, then they differ in some physical respect. More generally, any mental difference means that there is some physical difference.

(Could you have two different physical arrangements and the same set of mental properties? Yes. Remember that token identity theorists reject the idea that types of mental states can be reduced to types of physical states. Mental states and properties are, recall, *multiply realizable*. And supervenience nicely captures this idea: The mental depends on the physical without being reducible to the physical.)

In Davidson's view, supervenience explains the causal role of the mental. His argument is simple, if very controversial. The supervenience of the mental on the physical means that any difference in mental properties signals a difference in physical properties. In this sense, then, mental properties make a difference; they make a difference to the physical properties. If we come across different mental properties, we know that we have come across different physical properties. Now, the physical properties are clearly causally relevant, and any difference in the mental properties means we have a difference in the causally relevant physical properties. Thus, the mental properties are causally relevant; they make a difference to an object's causal relations (Davidson 1993, 14). This is the promise of supervenience.

Imagine then that Danny has a particular mental property—the desire to learn Spanish. Danny subsequently mails a form, which enrolls him in a

Spanish class. Absent the desire to learn Spanish, Danny would not have mailed the form. He would not have, for example, picked up the envelope and walked to the mailbox. Absent the mental property—the desire to learn Spanish—*Danny's physical properties would have been different*. So, Danny's causal interactions with the world around him are affected by the presence or absence of particular mental properties. But, in Davidson's view, this means that mental properties are—at least sometimes—causally efficacious. The mental brings about changes in the physical world.

Davidson's commentators have not been especially fond of this argument. They are suspicious that, in Davidson's view, mental properties do not make the kind of difference needed to make them causally efficacious. One way to put this counterargument is that changes in mental properties *signaling* a difference in underlying physical properties don't make a *causal* difference. So, according to the critics, supervenience does not restore the causal efficacy of the mental. (Davidson's exchange with his critics is in Heil and Mele 1993, chaps. 1–4.)

Loosen Up: Nonstrict Causal Laws
A *Peanuts* cartoon from some years ago shows Linus attempting to get Snoopy to fetch a ball. Linus explains to Snoopy the nature of the game and throws the ball. The last panel shows Snoopy, still sitting at Linus's feet, thinking "Maybe we should think about this a little more." Evidently seeing the ball fly through the air and Linus's patient instruction were not *enough* to get Snoopy to fetch the ball. Now, Snoopy might want to please Linus; he might want to join in the game. But he might prefer simply sitting, enjoying an afternoon's cool breeze.

Exceptional beagles aside, this is a common and familiar feature of the mental. Sometimes a set of beliefs and desires is enough to bring about a certain behavior; sometimes it isn't. Danny might believe that there is a chocolate truffle torte in the refrigerator, and he may desperately want some. Yet he may resist his craving because he has an overriding desire to lose weight.

These cases illustrate a general feature of the connection between mental states and behavior. Whether a particular group of beliefs and desires is enough to bring about a particular behavior *depends*—it depends on circumstances, including other desires a person might have. In asserting the connection between the mental and behavior, it seems as though we have to hedge our bets. If Danny desires a little chocolate truffle torte, and believes that walking to the kitchen will get him some, then Danny will walk to the kitchen—*all other things being equal*. Circumstances must be right for mental states to cause a behavior.

Some think that we can see the mental as causally efficacious if we give up the idea that only strict laws are causal laws. Notice first that since genuinely strict laws, if there are any, are only found in the most basic of sciences, physics, all kinds of properties are epiphenomenal. For example, the geologic property of being a tectonic plate slipping against another plate is not the cause of the earthquake; the true cause is some vastly more complicated set of properties, which is spelled out in the language of physics. The strict law requirement thus seems to imply that only the most basic constituents of the universe—quarks, perhaps—and a small handful of basic forces possess causal properties. Neurological properties turn out to be epiphenomenal, along with atomic, biological, geological, chemical, botanical . . . pick your favorite special science (sciences other than physics) and none of those properties is truly causal. This may come as a surprise to practitioners of the special sciences. Indeed it would strike any of us as odd were we told that throwing water—H_2O—on the lit match did not cause it to extinguish.

Although the argument is not unique to Fodor, we'll consider his line of response (Fodor 1989; see also McLaughlin 1993). Simply noting that mental properties fall into the same category as so many other special science properties is little comfort to some philosophers of mind. They argue instead that some genuine causal laws are also hedged laws; some causal laws contain ceteris paribus clauses. Alternatively, defenders of mental causation claim that it is false to say that the only causal properties are those mentioned in strict laws. Mental causation advocates thus do not doubt that basic physical properties are causal. They maintain, however, that there are other types of causal properties. Analogously, someone might agree that participating in sports builds character without also agreeing that playing sports is the *only* way to build character.

Of course, we don't want our ceteris paribus laws to be vacuously true. If your employer promises, "You will get a raise at the end of six months . . . unless you don't," you have no idea whether you will get a raise. On the other hand, the promise that you will get a raise unless you fail to complete your project on time specifies the "all other things being equal" condition. This example perhaps provides a clue for seeing why hedged laws may be enough for the causal efficacy of the mental.

If your employer guarantees a raise unless you don't get one, you have no way of checking which circumstances might keep you from getting a raise. Perhaps not dressing appropriately; perhaps your work being less than timely. Or, perhaps your employer will fail to give you a raise because she disapproves of your favorite basketball team. Indeed, there's no limit on what might count as a relevant reason for your failing to get a raise.

Ceteris paribus clauses, however, are not quite like this. While any number of factors may prevent a particular result, we often have a clear sense of
the relevant factors. Recall Danny's desire for chocolate truffle torte. We
have a tolerably clear sense of the relevant intervening factors. Danny may
have some stronger preference, such as desiring to watch his weight, avoid-
ing too much saturated fat, or even that he does not wish to leave his chair
until he sees the end of *Entertainment Tonight*. Of course, we might not be
able to list all the intervening factors, but we can at least tell whether the ceteris paribus clause has been satisfied. Consider a very rough example of an
intentional law: If Danny believes chocolate truffle torte is in the kitchen,
and he desires to eat the torte, and all other things are equal, then Danny
will go to the kitchen. Suppose Danny rises from his chair, heads into the
kitchen, and a few moments later, returns looking quite pleased and carrying
a piece of the torte. Then we know that all other things *were* equal. We know
that the ceteris paribus clause was satisfied.

Why should we think that this approach brings us any closer to making
mental properties causally responsible for certain effects? Recall the essential
feature of a cause: If the cause happens, then the effect *must* occur. More
technically, causes *necessitate* their effects. Notice our ceteris paribus "law"
about Danny. *If* Danny has the relevant beliefs and desires, and *if* all other
things are equal, then Danny *will* set off for the kitchen. And he will do so as
a matter of law—a ceteris paribus law, but a law nonetheless. Since there is
a law governing Danny having certain mental states and Danny's consequent
behavior, then there is reason to think that Danny's mental states are
causally responsible for his behavior. And that, Fodor claims, is enough to
cure our epiphobia.

We've seen the motivation for thinking causal laws must be strict. Fodor's
response, however, challenges this claim. (Davidson may be sympathetic to
this line of thought; see Davidson 1993.) Strict causal laws are *one* way of
guaranteeing the causal responsibility of some event. But they are not the
only way. Causal responsibility is also assured by hedged laws. And it's
enough that a mental property figures in a hedged law—a law containing a
ceteris paribus condition is enough to guarantee that the mental property is
causally responsible.

Patterns

Despite the occasional misfiring of our intentional explanations, the mental,
as we know it, exhibits reasonably predictable patterns. The predictability we
get from mental explanations is not as precise as the predictability we get
from chemistry or physics, but it serves us well enough. We know that Sam

will wince in response to pain, that Deirdre's desire to meet Danny's plane at 4:00 and her belief that it takes twenty minutes to get to the airport will lead her to leave for the airport around 3:30, or that Jessica's fervent wish to see her favorite television show and her belief that it is starting will lead her to end a phone conversation.

The mental thus presents us with certain patterns, and those patterns are no less real than the patterns found by the physicist, the chemist, the biologist, or the neuroscientist. But, it is argued, if the mental patterns are real, then they make a difference; they make a *causal* difference. It is *because* of those patterns that certain physical properties become relevant.

Let us look at why someone might think this. Recall that many abandoned type identity theory because mental types do not neatly correspond to physical (or neural) types. The belief that Jack is a snappy dresser might be token identical to one type of brain state in Jessie and another type of brain state in Kate. Kate's neural activity may very well differ in kind from Jessie's. Still, we can pick out a similarity of pattern or role at the mental level. Such patterns are real enough—they are not tied to any particular physical type, but they remain relatively constant. Jessie's neural activity may change from May to October, but her belief remains constant. Indeed, her belief leads her to insist that the person in the white suit across the way cannot be Jack, because it is, after all, well past Labor Day.

Granting the reality of such patterns still does not tell us why the mental is causally effective. Notice that any physical object has many—in fact, a large number—of causal properties. Which of those properties are active in some situation depends on the context, and this context is given by the pattern. Mental properties are the patterns or the context in which certain physical properties become relevant. As Robert Van Gulick claims, "Higher order properties [e.g., mental properties, such as believing the plane arrives at 4:00] act by the *selective activation* of physical powers not by their *alteration*" (1993, 499; emphasis in original).

Perhaps an informal gloss will help us see what Van Gulick has in mind. It is perhaps easy to be seduced by a certain picture of the mental. A mental "finger"—wholly independently of whatever is going on physically—reaches down and gives a little push to some neuron or group of neurons. Volition then is a kind of mental push; Deirdre decides to wave at Danny, for example, and a mental finger reaches out and touches someone, or in this case, a bunch of neurons.

But Van Gulick asks us to think about matters a bit differently. It is *by virtue of* a pattern that some physical properties, or their causal powers, are "activated" and some are not. As a rough analogy, think for a moment of a classroom. As physical objects, students and teacher alike have many causal powers—Danny can bring it about that there is gum on Sam's seat, or Deirdre can bring it about that a piece of paper is now on Sara's desk, or all four can bring it about that their books are opened to a certain page. When the teacher walks in the classroom, neither Danny nor Deirdre loses any causal powers. It's just that some become especially relevant, for example, opening a book, making ink marks on a piece of paper, or depressing keys on a calculator. More to the point, some causal powers are activated, and some are not. The context or pattern—a class beginning—sets the stage for which causal powers come into play. The activation of some causal powers and not others *depends on* the context, the classroom experience.

Van Gulick asks us to consider beliefs and desires, and other propositional attitudes similarly, as patterns or contexts. We might then think of groups of neurons as having various causal powers. When certain relatively stable patterns occur—beliefs and desires—certain powers of the neural activity are selected. The context—particular beliefs and desires—determines which neurological (or physical) causal powers are relevant, and in this way the mental is viewed as causally efficacious.

Of course, it is open to someone to object that the patterns are themselves nothing more than particular arrangements of physical items, and the only causal powers of the pattern are the causal powers of those physical items. The pattern does not have its own unique set of causal powers. Rather, the causal powers of a belief are to be found in the causal powers of some neural activity. And we still do not have the mental playing a causal role. We might say that the mental is at work, but the mental is at work only because it's at bottom something physical, and that physical thing (or group of things) is doing all the work. A group of horses, say, Clydesdales, are harnessed to a sleigh. The horses become a "team," and we are confronted with a new pattern, a context—the "team." Now we might say that the team pulls the sleigh, as we might say that Jessie's belief that Jack is a snappy dresser makes her ask where he shops. But the "team" possesses no special causal powers; the team is identical to the (perhaps aggregate) causal powers of the individual horses. Similarly, mental states possess only the causal powers of their physical constituents.

Here Van Gulick's central suggestion emerges. Why do we take the lower levels—say, the neurological or the chemical, or ultimately the physical—as more basic? While physical items themselves are patterns, we tend to take those patterns more seriously because we can provide more strict, more deterministic accounts of such patterns. This, however, is not enough to compel our attachment to protons, neutrons, electrons, and quarks as being more real—and hence, more causally efficacious—than beliefs, desires, hopes, and fears. Patterns that are widely distributed despite having very different underlying physical structures (think of the belief that Clinton is the forty-second president of the United States) are no less real than the patterns that we identify as DNA or benzene rings or quarks or electrons.

Van Gulick claims that we should not automatically give causal priority to explanations in physics. He thinks that the patterns identified in physics have no greater ontological status than the patterns typically identified as beliefs or desires. And if he is right about this, then the way is open to seeing mental properties as causally efficacious.

Of the vexing questions in philosophy of mind, this chapter has focused on one of the most vexing. Part of the reason is that how we answer questions about the causal role of the mental depends importantly on how we answer other questions—such as about causal closure, about the nature of causation, and about the nature of causal explanation. This brief account can only provide some of the motivation for the problem and a quick glance at a few of the proposed solutions.

Key Concepts

Anomalous monism

Explanatory exclusion principle

Nomological character of causality

Strict law

Supervenience

Reading Questions

1. What is the principle of the nomological character of causality? What is the difference between strict and nonstrict laws?

2. Why does Davidson think there are no psychophysical laws?

3. What is the explanatory exclusion principle? Why does it seem to preclude the mental playing a causal role?

4. Explain what Davidson means by supervenience and its relevance to mental causation.

5. Does Fodor agree with Davidson about strict laws? Explain.

6. How does Van Gulick use the notion of patterns to explain the causal role of the mental?

References

Crumley, Jack, ed. 2000. *Problems in mind: Readings in contemporary philosophy of mind.* Mountain View, CA: Mayfield.

Davidson, Donald. 1970. Mental events. In *Experience and theory*, ed. Lawrence Foster and J. W. Swanson. Amherst: University of Massachusetts Press. Reprinted in Crumley 2000, 430–42.

———. 1993. Thinking causes. In *Mental causation*, ed. John Heil and Alfred Mele, chap. 1. Oxford: Clarendon Press.

Fodor, Jerry. 1989. Making mind matter more. *Philosophical topics* 17, no. 1: 59–79. Reprinted in *"A theory of content" and other essays* (Cambridge, MA: MIT Press, 1992), 137–59, and in Crumley 2000, 474–88.

Heil, John, and Alfred Mele, eds. 1993. *Mental causation.* Oxford: Clarendon Press.

Kim, Jaegwon. 1989. The myth of nonreductive materialism. *Proceedings and addresses of the APA* 63:31–47. In Crumley 2000, 452–64.

———. 1993. *Supervenience and mind.* Cambridge: Cambridge University Press.

McLaughlin, Brian P. 1993. On Davidson's response to the charge of epiphenomenalism. In Heil and Mele 1993, 27–40.

Sosa, Ernest. 1984. Mind–body interaction and supervenient causation. In *Causation and causal theories*, vol. 14 of *Midwest studies in philosophy*, ed. Peter A. French, Theodore E. Uehling Jr., and Howard K. Wettstein, 258–74. Minneapolis: University of Minnesota Press. Reprinted in Crumley 2000, chap. 37.

Van Gulick, Robert. 1993. Who's in charge here? And who's doing all the work? In Heil and Mele 1993, 233–56. Reprinted in Crumley 2000, 489–503; page references are to this volume.

Additional Readings

Beckermann, Ansgar, Hans Flohr, and Jaegwon Kim, eds. *Emergence or Reduction: Essays on the Prospects of Nonreductive Physicalism.* Berlin: Walter de Gruyter, 1992.

Campbell, Neil, ed. *Mental Causation and the Metaphysics of Mind: A Reader.* Peterborough, Ontario: Broadview Press, 2003.

Kim, Jaegwon. *Mind in a Physical World.* Cambridge, MA: Bradford, 1998.

Walter, Sven, and Heinz-Dieter Heckman, eds. *Physicalism and Mental Causation: The Metaphysics of Mind and Action.* Exeter, United Kingdom: Imprint Academic, 2003.

10

Consciousness from B to Z

Upon typing "zombies" into an Internet search engine, I once had a surprising result. Along with the expected category matches—horror films, rock groups, and so on—there was also a somewhat surprising category, "Philosophy of Mind—Zombie Theory." Now, what in the world could have brought philosophers to worrying about zombies? In a word, *consciousness*. No fact about the mind, no feature of our experience seems less indisputable than that of consciousness. But there is scarcely a more troublesome notion in theories of the mind. Thomas Nagel observes: "Without consciousness the mind–body problem would be much less interesting. With consciousness it seems hopeless" (1974, 534). Perhaps expectedly, there is nothing approaching consensus on the answers to such issues, but there is wide agreement on one matter: consciousness is a hard problem.

We can cover only a small sampling of the issues and arguments relating to consciousness. First, we will look at types of consciousness, followed by a brief description of three theories of consciousness. In the last section, we will examine three arguments about the nature of consciousness, arguments that raise important questions about the mind–body problem.

Three Types of Consciousness

Why is consciousness thought to be such a hard problem? We have encountered before the notion of *qualia*—the qualitative features of our mental life. Sensations, whether they are of pain or of blue or of sweet, have a distinctive "feel" to them. There is "something that it is like" to sense blue, and this sensation is different from the sensation of red. But consider how difficult it is to describe to someone the unique quality of a blue sensation. Indeed, we very often refer to other sensations to explain the nature of a particular sensation: "Remember the shirt that you wore to dinner last week? It's that shade of blue," or the ubiquitous "It tastes like chicken."

According to some, these qualitative aspects of our mental life are *different in kind* from the physical. Suppose we knew everything physical there was to know about a particular quale, say, the scent of vanilla. That is, suppose you knew everything there was to know about the vanilla-scent-experiencing neural structures in the brain and precisely what happens in the brain whenever a person has the experience of the scent of vanilla. The question is, once we know that certain neural processes produce certain qualitative experiences, do we know all we need to know? This issue—whether our physicalist understanding of the mind can explain why qualitative features are correlated with the particular neural processes that they are—is sometimes known as the "**explanatory gap**" (Levine 2001).

Some suggest that it is a mystery why there should be consciousness or subjective experience at all. Thus, David Chalmers (2000) says that while we may have theories that explain phenomena such as introspection or attention, it is not clear why certain functionally organized neural states should give rise to a subjective feeling or a qualitative experience. (Note that the use of "subjective" in this context is not meant to suggest that it is a matter of opinion, a common understanding of the term. Rather, the term refers to the qualitative character of a mental state.) Of course, some agree that explaining consciousness may be a hard problem but hold that it is not an intractable or unsolvable one. Many physicalists, some of whom we will encounter in this chapter, think there is a physical story to tell about consciousness and that what we want to know about qualia or the subjective character of some mental states can be explained by our physical theories.

Consciousness seems to be a very diverse phenomenon. Ned Block distinguishes different types; here we mention three (Block 1994). **Introspective consciousness** or introspection is, roughly, our awareness of our own mental states and the contents of those states. This type of consciousness is reflected in the simple introspective realization that you believe your friend will be on time for a 3:45 appointment or that you wish you had an apple. **Access consciousness** is that type in which the content of a mental state can play a role in your drawing inferences and in the guidance of your behavior. A state is access conscious if the content is available for use in cognition or directing action. This is a kind of functionalist construal of consciousness, which perhaps makes it easier to accommodate access consciousness within a physicalist framework.

Phenomenal consciousness is the subjective feeling or qualitative aspect of various mental states. The experience of the scent of vanilla is an example of phenomenal consciousness, as is the sensation of blue, the tingling feeling when your hand falls asleep, or the throbbing of a headache. A being that experiences—whether it is you, a friend, a Martian, a dog, or a bat—is phenomenally conscious. Certain mental states have a characteristic subjective feeling that is described by Nagel (1974), as "what it is like to be" that type of being. There is something that it is like to have human experiences, something that it is like to have canine experiences, something that it is like to have the experiences of a creature with far different sensory and cognitive apparatus than we possess.

Some believe that the existence of phenomenal consciousness forces us to adopt a type of property dualism and reject physicalism (property dualism, recall, holds that there is only one type of substance—the physical—but that in addition to physical properties, there are irreducibly mental properties). Still others claim that we cannot reconcile our physicalist views with phenomenal consciousness. And some are "eliminativist," suggesting that apparent problems about phenomenal properties arise because of a kind of conceptual confusion.

Three Theories of Consciousness

There are far more theories about the nature, function, and origin of consciousness than can be covered here. To give some flavor of the variety of these theories, this section briefly describes three views of consciousness: the global workspace view, the multiple drafts view, and the higher-order view.

Global Workspace

Bernard Baars, a leading researcher in psycholinguistics and cognitive neuroscience, views consciousness as a kind of cognitive blackboard, in which various unconscious cognitive processes make information available for distribution and dissemination. Baars characterizes his approach as "contrastive phenomenology," a method that attempts to understand consciousness by comparing its absence and presence (Baars 1997).

Global workspace theory is a modern version of the "theater of the mind" metaphor. Consciousness is a kind of focusing that distributes information to various unconscious processes; this distribution of information facilitates coordination among the various cognitive subsystems. In a sense, consciousness is a clearinghouse, making sure that the available information gets to those systems that need it. Some item in our mental life is conscious if it is in this workspace. Consciousness thus plays an important causal role in our mental life.

Baars's work draws heavily on neurophysiological and psychological data; here we give but one example of the type of data. Most of us are familiar with "Aha!" experiences: Working on a complex problem and unable to solve it, we move on to other things; sometime later we "suddenly" become conscious of the solution. This perhaps suggests that while we were no longer conscious of the problem, unconscious processes drew on information, facilitating a solution.

An advantage of global workspace, Baars claims, is that we can learn much about consciousness without having first solved the mind–body problem. Those who think there is an explanatory gap may, however, be suspicious that while we learn about the neural basis and function of consciousness, the global workspace approach may not resolve our worries about qualia.

Multiple Drafts

In *Consciousness Explained* (1991), Daniel Dennett decries "Cartesian materialism," a view that holds that there is a locus, a center in the brain "where it all comes together" (107). Instead, Dennett argues for a "multiple drafts" model of consciousness, where various cognitive subsystems compete with one another for cognitive resources. Central to Dennett's view is the idea that our descriptions of phenomenal experience are very misleading. We think there are facts of the matter to our experience, but Dennett argues that there are none. There are competing interpretations of various mental events, but there is no way to choose which is the right one. Thus, there is no need for some solution to the problem of qualitative experience since the nature of these qualitative experiences is an illusion. Indeed Dennett is thought by some to be eliminativist about phenomenal consciousness.

Perhaps the real target of Dennett's objections is not some center in the brain but rather the idea that consciousness is some editor-in-chief, some central organizer, where the disparate bits of information about a mental event, such as tasting an orange, are brought together in some final, definitive story of that experience. In this "editor-in-chief" perspective, when some event enters the mind, various story lines are written, and these are edited and put together into the final draft. This definitive draft provides the facts of experience; it says what "really happened." And it is this commitment to this idea of a final, definitive story that is perhaps the main feature of Cartesian materialism's view of consciousness.

Instead, Dennett (1991, chaps. 5 and 12) suggests that there is no editor-in-chief; rather there are many different "reporters" at various times, each with their own draft of the story of some experience. The different reporters correspond, roughly, to different functional parts of the brain. At various times, depending on circumstance and need, one of the reporters grabs control of the system, making public its then unique draft. It is, as has been described, a "cognitive pandemonium." The "facts" of experience are continually rewritten by the various subsystems (reporters). Traces of the various drafts remain (in memory), but there is never a finished draft. There is a never a point at which we can identify *the* nature of the mental event.

Dennett uses various examples drawn from the literature and some thought experiments to try to shake our faith in Cartesian materialism and the notion that there is a fact of the matter of the nature of some qualitative state. One thought experiment concerns the taste of coffee to a particular person. Imagine, Dennett suggests, that a person claims that he no longer likes the coffee that he once thought was the best tasting. According to Dennett, we have no way of choosing between two interpretations—that the *way it tastes* has changed or that his *judgments* about the way it tastes have changed. Dennett argues that there are no facts that would settle this matter. Of course, the point of such examples is to persuade us that we have been misled into thinking that there are facts about qualia, and once we give up this idea, the problem of consciousness will be explained.

Needless to say, Dennett's view attracts significant criticism, primarily making two points. First, it might be claimed that Dennett uses a notion of qualia—as unanalyzable and essentially private—that one need not accept. Owen Flanagan (1992, chap. 4) argues that we might have neuroscientific and psychological theories that allow us to analyze qualia. This leads to Flanagan's second point that our best theories might give us good empirical reason to prefer one story to another. We might have reason, for example, to think that the taste of the coffee has remained the same.

Higher-Order Theory

The higher-order theory (HOT) holds that a thought is conscious if it is the object or the content of another thought. This is a relational and representational view of consciousness, since it counts being represented by some other thought as the condition of consciousness (Rosenthal 1991, 1997).

HOT has three important elements. First, of course, I must have a thought of something—of a cup, say. This thought is not yet conscious, however, according to HOT. Second, I must have another thought, a second thought *about* the thought of the cup. And third, this new thought must be caused directly by the first one. My initial thought about the cup becomes conscious when I *think about that thought*, and my so thinking is caused directly by the original thought. This view captures a strong intuition about consciousness—that consciousness is consciousness *of*.

The higher-order view has certain consequences worth noting. First, in order to have a higher-order thought, we must have some concept that allows us to think about the first thought. And from this it follows that the more concepts a person has, the more conscious states a person can have. To illustrate, someone may think about the glass of water. But unless the person possesses certain concepts, such as the concept of glass, that thought cannot be conscious.

Those who think the essential nature of conscious states is intrinsic and nonrelational will clearly not be satisfied by HOT. To say that a state becomes conscious when it is represented in some other thought is yet to explain why a state *feels* some way, why it has its qualitative character.

This perhaps occasions our turning to three arguments about the nature of consciousness, arguments that emphasize the qualitative character of some of our mental states.

Three Arguments about Phenomenal Consciousness

Bats and the Subjective Nature of Experience

In "What Is It Like to Be a Bat?" (1974), Nagel argues that we cannot understand how to reconcile the subjective features of our experience with physicalism. It is important to be clear about this claim. Nagel is not arguing that physicalism and the phenomenal aspects of our experience are in fact irreconcilable; he is arguing for the weaker claim that it is beyond our current ability to see how to do this, given our current understanding of what it is to be physically explicable. And this, Nagel claims, is due to the essential difference between the nature of the subjective and the objective.

We are accustomed to thinking of science as objective. But what do we mean by this? Science, in its drive toward objectivity, abstracts away from the particular point of view; it isn't interested in the unique, particular features of an object or property. This abstracting away from particular features is encapsulated in formulas such as $F = ma$. We don't care what color the car is, how much it costs, whether it is driven only on Sundays. Once we know its mass and its acceleration, we know how much force it will exert. This bit of knowledge is not privileged; in principle, anyone could come to know it. The force exerted by the metallic blue Saturn is something that can be understood by someone in Budapest or Prague, in Stockholm or San Diego. Science not only strives for this sort of objectivity, but it is the distinctive feature of the scientific endeavor.

Nagel contrasts this objectivity with the essentially subjective feature of experience. For any conscious creature, Nagel claims there is something that it is like to be that creature. This "something that it is like" is the subjective feature of experience. This subjectivity is, according to Nagel, "essentially connected with a single point of view" (1974, 535). If we lose that point of view, then we lose what it is that is unique to that subjectivity. This implies that we cannot make that point of view *objective*; we cannot identify the unique features of some subjective experience and make them objectively available. Indeed, Nagel claims, "It seems inevitable that an objective, physical theory will abandon that [subjective] point of view" (535). Nagel illustrates this by asking us to consider how we might understand what it is like to be a bat.

We are familiar with the basics of bat experience; they navigate by sonar. Bouncing their own sounds off surrounding objects, their brains correlate the outgoing sounds with incoming echoes. This allows the bat the ability to navigate its environment and to make some subtle discriminations. Now, any sentient being, including a bat, is conscious. Since it is conscious, there is something that it is like to be a bat; bats have subjective experiences. Nagel generalizes the point: "Whatever may be the status of facts about what it is like to be a human being, or a bat, or a Martian, these appear to be facts that embody a particular point of view" (537).

Nagel now asks us to think about what it would take to make such subjective bat-experience accessible to us. We might, Nagel proposes, try to *imagine* what it is like to be a bat. But any such imagining is necessarily failed or incomplete. To imagine ourselves, for example, as trapped in a bat's body or brain, is only to imagine what it would be like to be us navigating by sonar. We would not have genuinely succeeded in identifying what it is like to be a bat. Alternatively, were we to try to imagine what it would be like to be transformed into a bat, our imagination would fail us. We would necessarily arrive at a point beyond which we could no longer identify with the transformed creature. We would not know what it is like to have a bat brain *and to have no other sensory or cognitive resources* (535–37). From this perspective our understanding of bat subjectivity is necessarily incomplete.

The appeal to bat phenomenology is intended to remind us of this point: the subjectivity of experience is intrinsically tied to a type of point of view. But this means that we cannot make this point of view, this subjectivity, objective.

We can summarize Nagel's argument in the following way. The subjective feature of consciousness, phenomenal consciousness, is essentially tied to a point of view. The explanations of science—physicalism—are from an objective point of view. But an objective explanation of subjectivity will necessarily lose the point of view essential to that subjectivity. So, we cannot see how to reconcile the objective explanations of science with the subjective character of the mental.

Nagel's argument might be formulated as follows:

1. Conscious mental states have a subjective feature.
2. This subjectivity of the mental is tied to a point of view.
3. A physicalist explanation of the mental must make the features of experience objective.
4. We cannot make these features of experience objective without losing their essential feature, their point of view.
5. So, we cannot—at least at present—understand how to explain the "what it is like to be" feature of the mental from a physicalist perspective.

Someone might go on to argue that this shows that we must admit that there are two kinds of property, physical and mental. But Nagel does not draw this conclusion. His aim is to show that given our present understanding, we cannot reconcile the subjective aspects of experience with the mental.

Nagel's argument of course has its critics. In particular, it is argued that physicalism *can* capture the subjective character or the "point-of-view" character of experience. Notice that the physicalist need not say that all there is to the subjective aspect of experience is neural activity; physicalists, as we know, need not be reductionist. The physicalist can allow that there are distinctive non-neural aspects of consciousness, for example, functional aspects. Nagel claims that these functional aspects are not the real aspects of subjective experience, but the physicalist can wonder in what sense this is true. If Nagel means that we cannot have another's experience, then that is certainly true. But as Flanagan (1992, 93–96) points out, the physicalist has a very good *objective* explanation of this fact. We understand why Deirdre is uniquely connected to her experiences and why Danny is uniquely connected to his. But it is not clear that we cannot give an objective explanation of these unique points of view. We can learn, according to the physicalist, how this point of view is tied to the agent's other mental states and behavior.

The physicalist might also claim that as we continue to discover more about the *physical* nature of subjectivity, we come closer to filling the explanatory gap (Van Gulick 1997). Indeed, physicalists can point to the work of researchers such as Francis Crick and Christof Koch who suggest that visual awareness is due to the synchronized and rhythmic firing of particular neural structures. Physicalists are thus unpersuaded that the subjective character of the mental falls outside science's explanatory scope. Of course, as we are about to see, this is not quite the end of the debate.

What Mary Knows: The Knowledge Argument

Appearing first in 1982, Frank Jackson's **knowledge argument** (Jackson 2000) has generated a range of responses and debate. The argument is an explicitly *epistemological* argument for the existence of nonphysical properties. Jackson thus argues for a kind of property dualism. (Jackson [1998] has since dismissed the argument, but it still has many adherents.) Remember that property dualists hold that there is but one kind of substance—physical substance—but that under certain conditions and configurations, physical substance gives rise to nonphysical properties. The properties that interest Jackson are, of course, qualia. These properties, according to him, are *epiphenomenal*; that is, they have no causal properties of their own.

The hurtfulness of pains or the experience of tasting a lemon are designations, of course, for our familiar qualia. Since such qualia properties cannot be physically explained, Jackson claims they are nonphysical properties; hence, he argues, we are forced to property dualism. But before we get too far along, consider one of the examples Jackson uses to illustrate the knowledge argument.

Jackson asks us to imagine Mary, a brilliant scientist, who spends her life investigating the world from the confines of a black-and-white room, with her only access to the outside world coming from a black-and-white television monitor. Mary, we are to suppose, learns everything there is to know about the neurophysiology of vision. She knows, for example, precisely what occurs in our brains when we see ripe tomatoes, yellow bananas, stretches of green grass, or panoramic sunsets. She knows under what conditions we see our familiar colors, whether it be red, indigo, chartreuse, or magenta. Mary has at her disposal all the relevant physical facts for a complete neuroscience of vision.

At some point, Mary leaves the black-and-white room and enters our familiar world of colors. Jackson asks a simple question: Does Mary learn anything new? Jackson claims that she obviously does: she learns what it is like for us, normal people in the world with all its colors, to see red and all the other colors. If the answer is, as Jackson claims, that she learns something new, then he thinks that demonstrates something very telling. Since Mary had all the physical information available, since she knew everything science could tell us, then *there must be something more than just the physical information*, and therefore, *physicalism is false*. Jackson characterizes the argument succinctly:

(1) Mary (before her release) knows everything physical there is to know about other people.

(2) Mary (before her release) does not know everything there is to know about other people (because she *learns* something about them on her release).

Therefore,

(3) There are truths about other people (and herself) which escape the physicalist story. (2000, 579)

It might be worthwhile to notice how we move from an epistemological claim to the metaphysical conclusion that physicalism is false. Suppose I know that Mary is wearing a red sweater. To say that I *know* is to say, among other things, that it's true that Mary's wearing a red sweater. Furthermore, to say that it's true is to say that there is some feature or aspect of the world that fits with or corresponds to my knowledge. Put roughly, my knowledge is about some real aspect or feature of the world. Now we can see how Jackson intends the argument to work. If Mary learns something new, then she learns about some feature of the world that wasn't contained in her "physical knowledge." Since this "physical knowledge" was about all the relevant physical features of the world, then Mary's new knowledge must be about something in the world, but something that is *not* physical. Thus, there is something over and above the physical, and physicalism—understood as the claim that there are only physical objects and properties in the world—is false.

Critics of the argument respond in several ways. The first strategy denies that Mary learns anything new. A second strategy appears when we consider whether Mary knows everything there is to know. It is these two ideas that we pursue in the following.

In what sense is it true that Mary learns something new? We have seen something like this strategy on previous occasions. When our benighted souls at the *Daily Planet* are finally able to see that Clark Kent and Superman are one and the same, what is that they learn? Well, one thing that they learn is that they now have two ways of referring to one person—"Clark" or "Superman" will get the same person's attention. The physicalist can argue that something similar occurs here—Mary doesn't learn a new fact; instead she learns a new way to pick out an old fact, something she already knew (Churchland 1985).

A more radical version of this approach also denies that Mary learns anything new. Dennett, for example, asks us to imagine that when Mary comes out of the room, her "overseers" have decided to trick her. They have left a brightly painted blue banana in the fruit dish. Why, Dennett asks, could we not assume that Mary, upon spying the blue banana, would remark simply that bananas are yellow, not blue? Dennett's suggestion is that we cannot be sure that were we to have a *complete* account of the visual process, we would not also have an understanding of the connection between certain qualia and the associated neurophysical activity (1991, 393–406).

Others suggest that while Mary does not acquire new knowledge, she does acquire a new ability; hence this type of response is known as the *ability response*. Mary acquires a new discriminative ability. Previously Mary was able to pick out sensations only by noticing activity, say, in the visual cortex. She now has a new ability, however; she can discriminate sensations by the type of experience she is having (Nemirow 1990).

What does Jackson say in response to these objections? Consider first the ability response. Jackson doesn't deny that Mary might indeed acquire a new ability. He rejects, however, the claim that this is *all* she acquires. She learns something about the nature of a certain kind of experience. And it is this that Jackson claims cannot be explained by physicalism (Braddon-Mitchell and Jackson 1996, chap. 8).

In response to the claim that she learns only a new way to pick out old facts, Jackson suggests that the two cases are not analogous. Precisely because the Superman case involves some relevant information that is *not* known, Jackson could claim that Mary's situation is different. In the knowledge argument we are assuming that Mary has all the relevant information; she knows all the relevant physical facts. This perhaps opens a way to respond to Dennett, as well. Dennett might be right that there is another way to continue the story. But the determined property dualist might claim that despite Mary's ability to recognize an inappropriately colored item, she still learns something new—it is *like this* to see blue.

This leads us to the second counterargument, that of denying that Mary, inside the room, could know everything there is to know. Jackson's critics argue that the physicalist is not committed to this apparently reductionistic view. They think that Jackson assumes that the terms or the vocabulary of the physical sciences will be sufficient to describe any and every feature of the world. Yet that is not obviously so, they argue. Functionalists hold, for example, that some of the concepts or terms that we use to describe our mental life cannot be straightforwardly exchanged for terms from the physical sciences. It might be that the itchiness of pains cannot be caught by some scientific vocabulary. This need not imply, however, that we have discovered some new feature of the world. One could argue that here—feeling itchy— we have encountered a property of the physical. Yet, for this property we don't have a comprehensive scientific vocabulary. But that doesn't mean we have encountered something nonphysical. We don't have a scientific vocabulary for tables or fountains. We would say things about tables and fountains that have no analogue in a precise scientific vocabulary. This, however, does not imply that tables or fountains are in some way nonphysical.

Again, the property dualist has a line of response, which arises from the physicalist position. Physicalism promises us that everything we find in the world is either a physical object or a physical property. This seems to mean, according to the physicalist, that you can talk about everything in a recognizably physical vocabulary, but such talk need not be couched—expressed—in a precise scientific vocabulary. The "table-ness" of tables still has recognizably physical properties, even if given the wide variety of tables in the world, there is a wide variety of physical properties associated with them. But, the property dualist continues, no purely physicalist vocabulary seems to capture the way an itch feels or the way a toothache throbs or the way blue looks.

We seem to arrive at a place similar to that with Nagel's argument. Critics of both arguments claim that the reaches of our physical explanations—whether drawn from rigorous science or functional characterizations—capture qualitative character. Defenders of the nonphysical character of qualia is suspicious of this line of thought, however, believing that it does not address the essential feature of qualia.

Regardless of the outcome of this dispute, it is clear that Jackson's argument isolates something important that we might characterize in the following way. To be a physicalist is to make certain commitments about the way that real properties can be described. Moreover, physicalists may shun reductivist strategies, but they still owe us an account of the properties that we typically describe in this nonreductivist vocabulary.

Zombies, or the Absence of a Phenomenal Life

The zombie argument sees two interesting features of previously encountered arguments come together, logical possibility and the idea of a molecule-for-molecule duplicate. Although first introduced into the philosophy of mind landscape in the mid-1970s, zombies drew increasing attention in the last decade. In what follows, we are interested in the more recent version of the argument, formulated by David Chalmers (1996, 93ff).

Before we state the argument, we need one bit of terminology, which Chalmers employs to isolate a feature of physicalism. Chalmers assumes that physicalism is committed to the idea that mental properties necessarily depend on the physical. The force of this "necessarily" is that it is not logically possible to have two different types of mental state without some difference in brain states (or some other physical feature). The concept, which we have seen before, is that of supervenience, specifically *logical supervenience*: suppose that property A logically supervenes on property B. Then there are no two logically possible situations in which A differs but B remains the same.

As we have seen before, this claim of necessity opens up a line of attack for the dualist: give an argument that shows that it's logically possible to have differences in mental properties without a difference in physical or functional properties. This is the goal of the zombie argument, to show that it's logically possible to have all the physical properties the same while the mental properties differ. So, let us take a look at the argument.

Chalmers asks us to imagine that we have a *zombie* twin. Your zombie twin is a molecule-for-molecule duplicate of you; moreover, the zombie has the same functional organization as you. In all physical and functional respects, you and your zombie twin are identical. The difference, Chalmers asks us to imagine, is that *there's nothing that it feels like to be a zombie*. You might both express how good some chocolate tastes; you might both reach for more. But while you have a "chocolate quale," the zombie has none. Indeed, your zombie twin never has any qualia.

(Such zombies differ then from the zombies familiar from various Hollywood epics. Those zombies are rather functionally impaired. Your zombie twin is not so impaired; it is functionally identical to you. Thus, the zombies of our argument are actually *phenomenal zombies*.)

Chalmers acknowledges that the zombie scenario is probably not empirically possible. He claims only that it is logically possible. This, he claims, is all that he needs, the logical possibility of zombies. If phenomenal zombies are logically possible, then this is enough to show that mental properties do not logically supervene on physico-functional properties. This last claim, however, entails that physicalism is false, since physicalism asserts a necessary dependency of mental properties on physical properties.

We can summarize the **zombie argument** thus:

1. Physicalism holds that mental properties logically supervene on physical properties. (Alternatively, if physicalism is true, then mental properties supervene on physical properties.)
2. We can imagine a case in which mental properties differ while the physical properties remain the same, namely the phenomenal zombie case.
3. Zombies are logically possible.
4. If zombies are logically possible, then mental properties do not supervene on physical properties.
5. Therefore, mental properties do not supervene on physical properties.
6. Therefore, physicalism is false.

Notice that Chalmers takes advantage of a logical consequence of the physicalist's position. If physicalism claims that there is a necessary dependence of the mental on the physical, then showing that zombies are logically possible is sufficient for showing that physicalism is false.

One entirely predictable line of response is to question whether phenomenal zombies are indeed logically possible. It is of course one thing to claim that something is imaginable or conceivable; it is, as we already know, something else again to show that such imaginings are indeed coherent and not self-contradictory. Chalmers insists that the burden of proof lies with the zombie skeptic, however. Since nothing seems amiss in the description of the zombie case, the skeptic must give us some reason for thinking that the description hides some logical confusion.

Skeptics who claim that zombies are not logically possible argue that when we try to elaborate what it is to be a zombie, we can see that they are not logically possible. (The subsequent discussion follows Cottrell 1999.) Remember that these hypothetical zombies are creatures psychologically and functionally like us. Yet for them it is information only that is registered; there is no qualitative experience of the information. Recall the example of you and your zombie twin eating chocolate. Your zombie twin "registers" or is able to discriminate the different shapes, sizes, textures—it knows the difference between chocolate-covered coconut and chocolate truffles. But we are asked to imagine that all of this is merely information for your zombie twin; its sensory registers are working—just like yours—but for the zombie, there is nothing that it is like to taste chocolate.

Critics of the zombie argument think that the more we add to the story, the richer and more kinds of information a zombie discriminates, the less credible the zombie hypothesis becomes. Dennett adds a further little twist. Imagine the story in the previous paragraph, but now suppose that at the end of the various reports, the zombie says that despite its complex verbal descriptions, its allusion to qualitative experiences, it is only "registering" the information. Both Dennett and Cottrell invite us to consider whether it is genuinely conceivable, whether we could imagine a creature identical to us in all respects, save this one: *it's all dark inside*. Critics of the zombie argument insist that zombies seem logically possible to us only because we haven't thought through the description of the zombie scenario in sufficient detail. The zombie hypothesis gets our attention and casts its spell only because we haven't thought it through in sufficient detail. Once we do this, once we imagine a creature that is like us in all physical, functional, and behavioral respects, it becomes much harder to "conceive" that we can separate the experiential properties of sensing, thinking beings from the physical and functional properties of such beings. Others, such as Joseph Levine (2001), also suggest that we cannot make the move from conceivability to logical possibility.

Chalmers and defenders of the zombie argument suggest, nevertheless, that there are ways to show the connection between conceivability and logical possibility. Although we cannot follow those strategies here, we can make a general observation. We have seen before that physicalists claim that the more we learn, the more we will see the necessary dependence of the mental on the physical. But this requires some effort; it requires not only gathering the results of various scientific investigations but also seeing the way in which two apparently different concepts refer to the same property. Similarly, the zombie argument may require a detailed elaboration of the relationships between various concepts, and the relation between concepts and the properties they pick out. Lamentably, this is not an easy matter, nor a matter that we can follow here. (Of the many places one might start this investigation, two very good ones are Chalmers 1996 and Levine 2001.)

Back to the Beginning

We have, in a sense, come full circle. We began several chapters ago by examining the claims of dualism. And we find the mind–body problem arising again. Hopefully the intervening chapters show that, while we may not have a solution in hand to the mind–body problem, as Bernard Baars suggests, we can at least make significant headway with our understanding of the mind. Doing so may lead in unexpected directions, as we have seen, yet we can continue the attempt to understand those familiar features of the mind.

Key Concepts

access consciousness

"bat" argument

explanatory gap

introspective consciousness

knowledge argument

phenomenal consciousness

Reading Questions

1. Describe the essential features of phenomenal consciousness.

2. Explain why Nagel thinks the notion of subjective point of view is important. How might critics of the argument respond to Nagel's contention that science cannot capture the subjective point of view?

3. Why does Jackson think that the knowledge argument shows the falsity of physicalism? Describe two responses to Jackson, and indicate how he might respond to them.

4. As the text notes, Jackson has since rejected the knowledge argument. Do you think he should have?

5. What is a "phenomenal zombie"? What is the physicalist claim that the zombie argument challenges?

6. What is the importance, for critics of the zombie argument, of the connection between conceivability and logical possibility? How might Chalmers respond to someone like Cottrell?

References

Baars, Bernard. 1997. Contrastive phenomenology: A thoroughly empirical approach to consciousness. In Block, Flanagan, and Güzeldere 1997, 187–201.

Block, Ned. 1994. Consciousness. In *A companion to the philosophy of mind*, ed. Samuel Guttenplan, 210–19. Oxford: Blackwell.

Block, Ned, Owen Flanagan, and Güven Güzeldere, eds. 1997. *The nature of consciousness: Philosophical debates*. Cambridge, MA: MIT Press.

Braddon-Mitchell, David, and Frank Jackson. 1996. *Philosophy of mind and cognition*. Oxford: Blackwell.

Chalmers, David. 1996. *The conscious mind*. Oxford: Oxford University Press.

———. 2000. Facing up to the problem of consciousness. In *Explaining consciousness: The "hard problem,"* ed. Jonathan Shear, 9–30. Cambridge, MA: MIT Press.

Churchland, Paul M. 1985. Reduction, qualia, and the direct introspection of brain states. *Journal of Philosophy* 82 (1): 8–28. Reprinted in Crumley 2000, 564–76.

Cottrell, Allin. 1999. Sniffing the Camembert: On the conceivability of zombies. *Journal of Consciousness Studies* 6:4–12.

Crumley, Jack, ed. 2000. *Problems in mind: Readings in contemporary philosophy of mind*. Mountain View, CA: Mayfield.

Dennett, Daniel. 1991. *Consciousness explained*. Boston: Little, Brown.

Flanagan, Owen. 1992. *Consciousness reconsidered*. Cambridge, MA: MIT Press.

Jackson, Frank. 1998. Postscript on qualia. In *Mind, method, and conditionals: Selected essays*, ed. Frank Jackson, chap. 7. London: Routledge.

———. 2000. Epiphenomenal qualia. In Crumley 2000, chap. 46.

Levine, Joseph. 2001. *Purple haze: The puzzle of consciousness*. Oxford: Oxford University Press.

Nagel, Thomas. 1974. What is it like to be a bat? *Philosophical Review* 83:435–50. Reprinted in Crumley 2000, 534–42; page references are to this volume.

Nemirow, Laurence. 1990. Physicalism and the cognitive role of acquaintance. In *Mind and cognition: A reader*, ed. William G. Lycan, 490–99. Cambridge, MA: Blackwell. Reprinted in Crumley 2000, 581–87.

Rosenthal, David. 1991. Two concepts of consciousness. In *The nature of mind*, ed. David Rosenthal, chap. 52. Oxford: Oxford University Press.

———. 1997. A theory of consciousness. In Block, Flanagan, and Güzeldere 1997, chap. 46.

Van Gulick, Robert. 1997. Understanding the phenomenal mind: Are we all just armadillos? Part 1: Phenomenal knowledge and explanatory gaps. In Block, Flanagan, and Güzeldere 1997, 559–65. Cambridge, MA: MIT Press.

Additional Readings

Baars, Bernard. *In the Theater of Consciousness: The Workspace of the Mind*. Oxford: Oxford University Press, 1997.

Dennett, Daniel. "The Unimagined Preposterousness of Zombies." *Journal of Consciousness Studies* 2 (1995): 322–26.

Jackson, Frank. "What Mary Didn't Know." *Journal of Philosophy* 83 (1986): 291–95. Reprinted in Crumley 2000, 577–80.

Metzinger, Thomas, ed. *Conscious Experience*. Paderborn, Germany: Schöningh/ Imprint Academic (Lawrence, KS: Allen Press), 1995.

Seager, William. *Theories of Consciousness: An Introduction and Assessment*. London: Routledge, 1999.

Smith, Quentin, and Aleksander Jokic, eds. *Consciousness: New Philosophical Perspectives*. Oxford, England: Clarendon, 2003.

Glossary

absent qualia objection. An objection to functionalism which claims that mere functional organization is not sufficient to produce all mental properties, that functionalism by its very nature leaves out the qualitative aspect of the mental.

access consciousness. A type of consciousness in which the content of a mental state can play a role in the drawing of inferences and in the guidance of one's behavior. A state is *access conscious* if the content is available for use in cognition or directing action.

anomalous monism. A type of token identity theory. This view holds that there are no strict psychophysical laws governing the mental. The mental is thus irreducible to the physical, while every token of a mental state is identical to some physical state.

bridge law. Bridge laws connect the terms of one theory with the terms of another. Such laws are important for the reduction of one theory to another; using them, the terms of a theory can be reduced to the terms of a second theory.

classical theory of concepts. Sometimes called *definitionism*, this theory of concepts holds that a concept is the set of necessary and sufficient conditions that determines whether an item is a member of the category.

compositionality. An important feature of concepts—specifically, that concepts combine to form new concepts.

computational functionalism. A type of functionalism that holds that we have an internal system of representation, a set of mental symbols, called the "language of thought." This language is described syntactically. Moreover, the content of the propositional attitudes derives from the language of thought.

conceivability argument. An argument for dualism. The argument claims that since it is conceivable that minds and bodies are separable, it is logically possible that they are separable. And since it is logically possible that a mind might exist independently of any physical body, physicalism is false.

conceptual role semantics. A theory of mental content which holds that the content of a thought or the meaning of a concept is given by its connections to other concepts and that mental content is a function of the conceptual role that a thought has for a person.

descriptionalism. A theory of mental images which holds that there are no mental images having pictorial properties; instead, we store *structured descriptions*, ordered lists of properties of the relevant scene.

dualism. The view that certain things—minds, in particular, or mental properties such as the contents of our thoughts, sensations, or consciousness—are not physical in nature. Dualism holds that a complete physical inventory of the world would leave something out—the mental. The nature of the mental, the *essence* of the mental, cannot be explained by appealing only to physical entities and their properties, no matter how physically complex those entities and properties might be.

eliminative materialism. The view that the principles and categories of folk psychology will ultimately be discarded by a sufficiently complete neuroscience; our propositional attitude concepts, such as belief and desire, correspond to nothing real, and consequently our normal explanations of behavior don't tell us about the real causes of behavior.

epiphenomenalism. A type of property dualism which holds that physical events may cause mental properties, but denies that mental properties have any causal powers.

epistemology. The philosophical discipline that explores the conditions and sources of our knowledge and justified beliefs.

explanatory exclusion principle. The principle that a complete causal explanation of an event excludes an alternative causal explanation. This is thought by some to rule out mental events being causes, due to their specifically mental properties.

explanatory gap. A gap in our understanding of the mind, according to some; we cannot explain why qualitative features of the mind are correlated with the particular neural processes that they are.

functionalism. A view of the mind that defines mental states by their causal role; in particular, it defines them in terms of (1) their connections to their typical causes, or inputs, (2) their causal connections to other mental states, and (3) their causal connections to various effects, or outputs. Most functionalists are token identity theorists.

idealism. A version of monism which holds that everything that exists is either a mind or a property of a mind.

imagism. A theory of mental images. In Stephen Kosslyn's view, images are functional objects or functional pictures; as such, they are functions of brain states.

instrumentalism. The view that our folk-psychological notions are only devices for explaining and predicting behavior, that concepts such as belief and desire do not correspond to real internal states. The view is opposed to intentional realism.

intentional stance or **intentional strategy.** In Daniel Dennett's view, we explain and predict the behavior of another system because we attribute beliefs, desires, and other propositional attitudes to the system (*see also* **instrumentalism**).

interactionist property dualism. A type of property dualism which claims that mental properties have "causal powers." One thought may cause another, or a mental state may bring about physical changes.

introspection or **introspective consciousness.** Our awareness of our own mental states and the contents of those states.

inverted spectrum objection. An objection to functionalism which claims two people might have mental states that are functionally the same but qualitatively different. The objection claims that functionalism must view such mental states as being of the same type, but that intuition suggests that such mental states differ in type, since they differ qualitatively. Functionalism, according to the objection, cannot account for the qualitative aspects of the mental.

knowledge approach. Sometimes called the "theory theory." This view claims that our concepts are more than just representations of features or properties, that our concepts are, in some sense, theories, containing not only representations of properties but also explanatory and causal principles.

knowledge argument. An explicitly *epistemological* argument for the existence of nonphysical properties or qualia. Many supporters of the knowledge argument, which claims that physicalism is false, are property dualists.

language of thought. An internal system of representation; a set of mental symbols described syntactically (*see also* **computational functionalism**).

Leibniz's Law. A principle, credited to Leibniz, which says that for any A and B, A and B are identical if and only if they have all the same properties.

logical behaviorism. A theory (sometimes called *philosophical behaviorism*) about the *meaning* of mental or psychological terms. According to logical behaviorism, any sentence containing mental or psychological terms can be "translated into" or reduced to a sentence containing only behavioral terms.

logical positivism. An early twentieth-century view of the nature of philosophy, claiming that the principal task of philosophy is linguistic analysis, or clarifying and analyzing legitimate concepts.

mental representation. A characterization of (at least some) mental states; the function of such mental states is to carry information about or represent aspects of the world around us.

metaphysics. The attempt to understand and explain the nature and structure of the most general features of our world. It is especially relevant to philosophy of mind in that some claim that there is only one type of thing—the physical—while others claim that both physical and mental states exist.

methodological behaviorism. A type of behaviorism that holds that as a matter of scientific practice we should focus only on the observable characteristics of an individual. Since inner mental states are not observable, we should restrict our attention to environmental stimuli and behavioral responses. Interpreted in this way, methodological behaviorism is agnostic about the existence and nature of inner mental states.

monism. A metaphysical view which holds that there is only one kind (or type or category) of thing, that everything that exists is either an instance of that kind of thing or some modification of that type.

multiple realizability. A type or kind is multiply realizable if different instances, or tokens, of the type can be realized by different types of physical states. The multiple realizability objection is an important objection to type identity theory.

nomological character of causality. A principle which says that any causal interaction is governed by laws. The principle is important for discussions of mental causation.

occasionalism. A type of substance dualism. Occasionalism concedes the absence of interaction between mental and physical substance, declaring that apparent cases of interaction are really *occasions* for God to intervene and bring about the appropriate event.

ontological behaviorism. A type of behaviorism that rejects the existence of inner mental states; mental states such as beliefs and desires (and perhaps sensations) are claimed to be mere fictions. In this sense, it is the most radical of the types of behaviorism.

ontology. A part of metaphysics specifically focused on identifying the kinds of things that exist.

parallelism. A type of substance dualism which holds that mental and physical substances do not interact but are coordinated in such a way as to give the *appearance* of interaction.

phenomenal consciousness. Our awareness of the subjective feeling or qualitative aspect of various mental states, such as tastes, smells, and other sensations. Such qualitative aspects are sometimes known as qualia or raw feels. The existence and nature of qualia are one of the major disputes in philosophy of mind.

physicalism. A version of monism which claims that only physical things and their properties exist. Physicalism, sometimes called *materialism*, takes a variety of different forms.

property. A characteristic or feature of some object or substance.

property dualism. Property dualism, unlike substance dualism, accepts that there is only one type of substance—physical substance—but claims that there are distinctively mental properties that are not physical in nature.

propositional attitudes. A characterization of mental states, such as beliefs, desires, and hopes, comprising the content of a thought and the attitude toward that content. The content of such attitudes are typically characterized by a proposition.

prototype theory. A view of concepts which holds that concepts are mental representations of collections of features or properties possessed by the best instances—the most typical members—of the category.

qualia. See **phenomenal consciousness**.

reduction. Reduction is a relation between theories; bridge laws connect the concepts of the reducing theory with that of the reduced theory. The issue in philosophy of mind is whether our commonsense view of the mind might be reduced to some more basic science, such as neuroscience.

resemblance theory of content. A theory of mental content which holds that the content of a thought is determined by what the thought resembles.

strict law. Causal laws, governing the behavior of physical objects, that are exceptionless.

strong AI thesis. A view about the aim of artificial intelligence (AI). The thesis claims that running the right program is sufficient for thinking; thus, appropriately designed computers could have mental states. This thesis is the target of John Searle's Chinese room argument.

substance dualism. A type of dualism holding that minds are a unique category of thing or substance (historically, the notion of *substance* referred to an entity that could exist by itself), distinct from the category of physical substance.

supervenience. A kind of dependence relation between two sets of properties; some physicalists hold that this relation best characterizes the relation between mental and physical properties. One version of the relations says that if two things differ in some mental property, then there must be some difference in physical properties; any difference in the mental *requires* a difference in the physical. More formally, given two sets of properties, M and P, M **supervenes** on P if and only if whenever there is a difference in M, then there is also some difference in P.

teleological theories of content. Theories of mental content that identify the content of a mental state with the evolutionary circumstances responsible for that mental state.

token identity theory. A view of the mind which holds that every instance or token of a mental state type is identical to an instance or token of some physical state or other (but this view is indifferent to the type and nature of these physical states). Functionalists are generally token identity theorists.

type identity theory. According to type identity theory, every kind of mental phenomenon, whether a kind of thought, feeling, mood, or sensation, is a kind of brain process. Thus, any *kind* of mental property is identical to a *kind* of brain property. Roughly, identity theory claims that we have two ways of talking about minds (*see also* **type/token**).

type/token. A type is specified by citing a characteristic or property or a group of properties. For example, "coffee cup" picks out a type. A **token** of this type is any particular thing that has the specified properties.

verification criterion of meaning. A view about the nature of meaning, held by many logical positivists. The criterion claims that a contingent sentence is cognitively meaningful if and only if it is verifiable or falsifiable by some set of experiences.

weak AI thesis. A view about the aim of artificial intelligence that by developing the right computer programs, we can simulate or model thinking on computers (*see also* **strong AI thesis**).

zombie argument. An argument against physicalism. The argument claims that since phenomenal zombies—creatures that in all physical and functional respects are like humans, but have no qualia—are logically possible, physicalism is false.

Index

About the Author

Jack Crumley is a professor of philosophy at the University of San Diego; he has served as chair of the department since 1998. He regularly teaches classes in epistemology, philosophy of mind and philosophy of human nature. He is the author of *An Introduction to Epistemology* and the editor of *Problems in Mind: Readings in Contemporary Philosophy of Mind* and *Readings in Epistemology*. He is also the author of articles in metaphysics, epistemology and philosophy of mind.